OUR RURAL COMMUNITIES

OUR
RURAL COMMUNITIES

A GUIDEBOOK TO
PUBLISHED MATERIALS ON
RURAL PROBLEMS

BY LAVERNE BURCHFIELD

The University of Chicago

PUBLIC ADMINISTRATION SERVICE

CHICAGO · 1947

FOREWORD

THE PURPOSE of this book is, first, to present a brief picture of the major problems that challenge our rural communities today, and, second, to provide a guide to the very considerable body of literature that has grown up around these problems. Its aim is to open up and make more readily usable the extensive materials upon which a program of action may be based. This book does not attempt to present a definite program of action. It does, however, contain material that will be of great assistance to those who are engaged in planning action programs.

For a number of decades the economy of the United States has been predominantly industrial. Yet until far into the nineteenth century the nation's economy was primarily agricultural, and, indeed, developments during and since the second World War have served to underline anew the vital role of agriculture—and of the millions engaged in all rural occupations—in the balance sheet of the nation's activities.

When the significance of this role has been recognized, however, it must be admitted that each national census, with but a single exception, has disclosed a steady increase in the flow of population from rural areas to urban centers. Between 1790 and 1940 the percentage of the population classified as rural declined from 94.9 to 43.5, and there is no sign that this trend will change in any substantial manner in the predictable future. Higher wages and more congenial living and working conditions have in the main been the lodestones that have drawn people from the rural communities, but, in addition to these attractions, the urban centers offer facilities for education, recreation, and a fuller cultural life not generally available in smaller communities.

While these cultural and recreational opportunities have been constantly broadened and expanded in most cities, limited financial resources and facilities have prevented rural communities from improving in anything like a comparable manner the services they can offer. The federal government has furnished a measure of assistance and guidance, and state and county agencies have in many instances contributed to the extent of their abilities. But in a democracy such as ours, with its emphasis on local responsibility and initiative, the task of improving and enriching the life of the people of a community rests ultimately with the community itself. Even though it may receive aid from the federal government or from its state government, no community is likely to get better services or be provided with more adequate facilities than its more progressive citizens demand or its public and private agencies see fit to supply.

Rural communities face a challenge that they themselves must meet. With the body politic as with the human anatomy, the diagnosis of an ailment is the first step toward its cure. True, the simple identification and cataloging of its problems will not solve them. Moreover, no community can lift itself up by its own bootstraps. Nevertheless, a community which has identified and squarely faced its most pressing problems is in a fair way to getting something done about them.

The problems of rural communities in such fields as education, recreation, welfare, and health have been the object of much thought and research, and a very considerable literature has developed around each of these aspects of rural life. This literature is very diverse in character, ranging from large volumes to small pamphlets and leaflets, produced variously by individual writers, private agencies and organizations, and governmental units at all levels. The present volume, compiled principally from printed sources but supplemented with information secured through interviews and correspondence, provides rural leaders and others interested in the problems of rural America with a valuable guide to the materials available in the various fields. Action in the solution of local problems must be taken by the leaders, officials, and agencies of the community itself, but such action is likely to be more effective if based on the experience, research, and thought of many other communities, investigators, and agencies.

The idea for this book originated in the work of a committee of the American Country Life Association. In 1944 the conference of the Association met to discuss "Farm and Rural Life after the War," and as an aid to the work of the conference, the President of the Association appointed a committee to prepare a brief digest which would describe current activities of agencies interested in country life and present short abstracts of published materials relating to postwar planning for farm and rural life. The members of this committee were Nat T. Frame, formerly of the Division of Farm Population of Rural Welfare, Region III, Bureau of Agricultural Economics, U. S.

Department of Agriculture, (Chairman); Julia Wright Merrill, formerly Chief of the Department of Information and Advisory Services, American Library Association; and Floyd W. Reeves, Professor of Administration and Director of the Rural Education Project, the University of Chicago, a project financed in part with a grant from the Farm Foundation. The initial brief draft of this digest was largely the work of Miss Merrill and of Laverne Burchfield, Research Associate on the staff of the Rural Education Project.

At its meeting in April, 1944, the Board of Directors of the American Country Life Association expressed the opinion that the digest should be greatly expanded and prepared for publication in the form of a book. It requested that Miss Burchfield do this work. Because of the interest of the Rural Education Project in assembling background materials for use in connection with research, instructional, and service activities, Miss Burchfield undertook this revision, and the present monograph is the result.

FLOYD W. REEVES

PREFACE

THIS BOOK is directed to furnishing rural leaders and others interested in the problems of rural America with brief factual statements about major areas of rural life and annotated bibliographies where they may gather additional information. Specialists will find somewhat elementary the statements in sections concerned with their own specialties. It is hoped that they will find in other sections materials and references that will be new and useful to them. It is hoped, also, that the monograph may prove helpful to many leaders and groups desirous of gaining an over-all view of rural life and of pursuing major problems with a view to helping in their solution.

The reader may find a certain unevenness in the materials presented in the various chapters. This unevenness results, in part, from differences in the amount of attention paid to these problems by governmental and private agencies and by individuals concerned with inquiries into rural problems.

In a digest as broad in its coverage and at the same time as brief as this one is, attention has had to be centered largely upon the programs and activities of national agencies and organizations, public and private. This is not to minimize the importance of the activities and publications of state and local groups and agencies. In a democracy decisions must be made and action taken by the people at the grass roots. The user of this book is urged to investigate the resources of his own community—What groups are interesting themselves in local problems? What are the county, town, township, and village governments doing and what can they do? He should also find out what is being done by the land-grant college in his state with reference to problems in which he is especially interested. State government departments and state organizations of rural people may also have programs. Public school officials and the office of the county agent are among his most immediate sources of information on local and state, as well as national, programs and activities.

Persons interested in following current happenings relating to rural problems will do so through their local papers and through farm magazines and journals. In each chapter of this book there are also listed some of the periodicals that describe current activities and thinking relative to the subject matter of the chapter and carry reviews of current books, pamphlets, and legislative action in the particular field.

The author wishes to acknowledge the substantial assistance given by a number of individuals and agencies. The entire first draft of the manuscript was reviewed by Carl C. Taylor, Head, Division of Farm Population and Rural Welfare, Bureau of Agricultural Economics, U. S. Department of Agriculture; Nat T. Frame, formerly of the Division of Farm Population and Rural Welfare, Region III, Bureau of Agricultural Economics, U. S. Department of Agriculture; and Julia Wright Merrill, formerly Chief of the Department of Information and Advisory Services, American Library Association. All offered helpful suggestions. Floyd W. Reeves, Professor of Administration and Director of the Rural Education Project, the University of Chicago, has given considerable assistance throughout the preparation of the manuscript. Individual chapters were reviewed by Dr. Milton I. Roemer, Associate in Medical Care Administration, States Relations Division, U. S. Public Health Service; Leonard D. White, Professor of Public Administration, the University of Chicago; Louis E. Hosch, Administrative Consultant, American Public Welfare Association; and Mrs. Dorothy Gazzolo, Assistant Director, National Association of Housing Officials. Victor Obenhaus, Associate Professor of Social Ethics, Federated Theological Faculty, University of Chicago, and Rockwell Smith, Professor of Rural Sociology, Garrett Theological Seminary, gave major assistance in providing materials for Chapter 4. Members of various bureaus and offices of the U. S. Department of Agriculture advised on content and materials for a number of chapters. The regional offices of U. S. Soil Conservation Service and U. S. Forest Service, Milwaukee, Wisconsin, were helpful in providing materials for Chapter 13. The author made extensive use of the Joint Reference Library of Public Administration Clearing House; the regional library of the U. S. Department of Agriculture, Milwaukee; the University of Chicago libraries; and the John Crerar Library, Chicago, in all of which she received excellent assistance.

LAVERNE BURCHFIELD

CONTENTS

Contents

1 SCHOOLS

IN THE PERIOD from 1910 to 1914, farm families constituted 34 per cent of the population of the United States and received 17 per cent of the national income. Twenty years later, the farm population was about one-fourth of the total, but received only about 9 per cent of the national income. These facts explain in large part the quality of service given by the rural schools. In general, teachers in rural areas have less preparation and experience than teachers in cities. Supervisory services are less adequate. The school year is shorter; the curriculum is more restricted; guidance services are slight; instructional materials are less satisfactory. The school plant and equipment compare unfavorably with the plant and equipment in cities. While there are notable exceptions to these generalizations and many individual examples can be found in rural communities of superior teaching, satisfactory curricular offerings, and fine school plants, rural schools generally are less satisfactory than the schools in urban communities.

School district organization is a major factor contributing to the unsatisfactory school situation in rural areas. In many areas poor organization results in the wasteful spending of limited resources. There are some 110,000 local school administrative districts in the United States, the number of units per state varying from fewer than 200 in each of thirteen states to over 5,000 in each of ten states. Frequently in rural farm areas each school is set up as a separate administrative unit with its own board of education and its own local taxes. Many of these units have very limited tax resources and small enrollments. Over one-third of the rural school pupils in the United States attend schools having only one or two teachers—two and one-quarter million children in one-teacher schools and about one and one-third million in two-teacher schools. A small school can be a superior school, but if it is its costs will be excessively high. It will have to attract and pay a well-qualified teacher, and it will need, among other things, circuit teachers of special subjects, bookmobile services, and specially supplied health and guidance services. Some small administrative units can afford these services, but most cannot.

There are great differences in the ability of districts within states to support schools. There are also great differences in financial ability among the states. Most of these inequalities result from differences in income in rural and urban communities and in rural and urban states. Poor school systems do not result primarily from lack of effort; almost always they are the result of low income. With few exceptions the states that have low financial ability rank high in the percentage of their income that they devote to schools, though they rank low with respect to the quality of schooling provided.

The quality of education provided in rural areas is a matter of state and national interest. Each decade several hundred thousand young persons educated in rural schools migrate to cities in their own and other states to find work opportunities. State and federal aid for the support of schools is essential if the children in rural and urban areas are to have comparable educational opportunities.

GOVERNMENTAL INTEREST IN EDUCATION

The United States Office of Education, located in the Federal Security Agency, is the federal agency with primary responsibility for educational leadership, although many other agencies of the federal government carry on educational activities. The Office collects statistics and facts to show the condition and progress of education in the states and territories; makes studies needed as guides to educational practice and publishes reports thereon; disseminates information respecting the organization and management of schools and methods of teaching to aid in the provision of efficient school systems; serves in an advisory and consultative capacity to state and local school officials; administers federal funds appropriated as aids to education; operates certain specified educational programs; publishes documents pertaining to education; and furnishes special booklets to schools throughout the United States. The Office administers the acts for the promotion of vocational education. Its work is described in its *Annual Report.* The *Biennial Survey of Education in the United States,* compiled and published by the Office, provides a wealth of source material on the educational situation.

The federally reimbursed program for vocational education provides support for occupational training programs in home economics, agriculture, trades and industries, and business in schools of less than college grade and for the preparation of teachers of these subjects. The program is conducted cooperatively by the United States Office of Education and state departments of education. Enrollments in vocational agricultural classes in 1944 numbered 470,000 and in home economics more than 800,000. The Future Farmers of America, a national organization of pupils and former pupils in vocational agriculture, is an integral part of the vocational agricultural program, as is a like organization for Negro youth, the New Farmers of America. The history of federal cooperation in vocational education is presented in Lloyd E. Blauch's *Federal Cooperation in Agricultural Extension Work, Vocational Education, and Vocational Rehabilitation.* A description and an evaluation of the federally aided program are given in *Vocational Education,* by John Dale Russell.

The whole subject of the relationship of the federal government to education was canvassed in 1937 by the Advisory Committee on Education which published a *Report* and a series of nineteen studies. The Committee concluded that "although schools in all areas need improvement, the outstanding fact emerging from this study is the great need for the improvement of the public schools in a number of broad geographical regions and in the rural areas generally. Most of the new grants to the States here recommended derive their importance from the improvement they will make possible in the educational opportunities in rural areas." It continued: "The proposals set forth in this report have been carefully related to each other to form a unified and coherent pattern of recommended Federal policy. The objective throughout has been to preserve the strength achieved through local control of the educational system and at the same time to give that system down through its local units the financial aid that is needed."

In addition to the study *Vocational Education* referred to above, three of the studies prepared by the research staff of the Advisory Committee on Education include materials especially pertinent to problems of rural education. *Education in the Forty-Eight States,* by Payson Smith, Frank W. Wright, and Associates, describes the educational programs of the various states with special reference to variations in their quality. Besides references to rural education throughout the study, one chapter is concerned exclusively with education for children in rural areas. *Organization and Administration of Public Education,* by Walter D. Cocking and Charles H. Gilmore, describes the organization and evaluates the effectiveness of the administration of public education in the United States. Rural-urban differences are indicated at a number of points. *The Land-Grant Colleges,* by George A. Works and Barton Morgan, presents the programs and activities of these institutions whose "influence has been felt in the conservation of natural resources; the preservation and improvement of rural life; the strengthening of the farm home; and the training of a force of workers in fields largely neglected by other institutions of higher learning."

It is pointed out in the study *Organization and Administration of Public Education* that education is a vital concern of each level of government and that all levels are participating in its administration. In most states at the present time educational activities are under the direction of numerous agencies, and in no state have all the functions relating to education been placed in a single state board or department of education. Boards have been created in most states which control the general school system in varying degrees, but these boards differ greatly in authority. All states have established the position of chief state educational officer. State departments make numerous studies of educational problems and issue reports and information. Their staffs are available to local school officers for consultation and advice. In the local units, control of education is almost always vested in a board. The administrative officer or superintendent of schools may or may not be selected by the board. As federal and state governments have assumed more responsibility for the financing of educational programs, they have tended to issue regulations governing various phases of these programs. Joint planning has also assumed increased importance.

Information relating to the work of state departments of education is contained in a series of sixteen monographs issued by the United States Office of Education in 1941 (based on a survey made in 1939) entitled *Studies of State Departments of Education*. The topics covered include problems of administrative organization and relationships, financial control and assistance, legislation and regulatory standards, and various types of supervisory services. The monographs aim to point out common elements, analyze differences, and present significant factors in state educational structure.

To a large extent education has been set up as a fourth branch of state and local government comparable with the executive, legislative, and judicial branches. This is especially the situation at the local level, where educational boards and administrators are largely independent of general governmental administration. The results of an inquiry into the relation of the governmental organization for the control of schools to general municipal government are presented by Nelson B. Henry and Jerome G. Kerwin in *Schools and City Government*. Although this study relates to cities of 50,000 or more population, many of the findings are also applicable to relationships of school and civil governments in rural areas.

NONGOVERNMENTAL EDUCATIONAL AGENCIES

A number of nongovernmental organizations, foundations, and agencies have particular interest in the quality of educational opportunities in rural areas. Some of the more important of these agencies will be briefly described.

The National Education Association of the United States (1201 16th St. N. W., Washington, D. C.) is a voluntary organization of persons engaged in educational work. Its Department of Rural Education and its Division of Rural Service have been established to facilitate discussion, make studies, and disseminate information relating to rural education; to further the efforts and increase the effectiveness of persons engaged in rural education; and to promote the general advancement of rural education throughout the United States. The Department holds two regular meetings annually and an annual mid-south regional conference on rural life and education. It publishes a yearbook and occasional bulletins. The Educational Policies Commission, created by the National Education Association and the American Association of School Administrators to define guiding policies for American education, has issued a comprehensive statement on rural education, described later in this chapter.

The Julius Rosenwald Fund (4901 South Ellis Ave., Chicago, Illinois) endeavors to improve living conditions through the promotion of education, research, experimentation, and demonstration. It has aided rural education, among other ways, through grants to help in the construction of more than five thousand schools in the South and through publication of a series of readers for rural schools.

The current program of the General Education Board (49 West 49th St., New York) is largely concentrated on the fuller development of the economic and social resources of the South through education and research in the social and natural sciences, with some special consideration of programs in human nutrition, forestry, and rural, social, and economic fields.

The Alfred P. Sloan Foundation, Inc. (30 Rockefeller Plaza, New York) makes grants to the Universities of Kentucky, Florida, and Vermont and to the American Association of Teachers Colleges looking to the improvement of living conditions in rural communities. Special readers have been prepared at these universities for use in rural schools.

The W. K. Kellogg Foundation (Battle Creek, Michigan), among other activities, aids communities in several counties with their health, education, and welfare work; sponsors short summer courses for out-of-school farm youth; and provides funds for 4-H loans.

The Committee on Rural Education at the University of Chicago, financed jointly by the Farm Foundation and the University, conducts research, carries on field activities, offers instruction, holds conferences and workshops, and issues publications in the field of rural education.

The Association of Land-Grant Colleges and Universities (Lyman E. Jackson, Secretary-Treasurer, Pennsylvania State College, State College, Pennsylvania) was established to consider and discuss all questions relating to the success of these colleges. It has issued a report, *Postwar Agricultural Policy,* listed on page 199 of this volume. The work of the land-grant colleges is discussed in Chapter 2.

The American Association for Adult Education (525 West 120th St., New York), established to further the idea of education as a continuing process throughout life, has issued publications relating to the education of adults in rural communities.

The American Council on Education (744 Jackson Place, N. W., Washington, D. C.), made up of representatives of national educational groups and institutional members, has the objectives of promoting scientific inquiry, providing means for consultation, and stimulating experimental activities by educational organizations and institutions. It maintains the Committee on Southern Regional Studies and Education which has as its objective making the findings of research materials on the needs and resources of the South available in forms usable in the schools.

BACKGROUND STUDIES

The most comprehensive recent consideration of the problems of education in rural America is found in the report *The White House Conference on Rural Education, October 3, 4, and 5, 1944.* Called, planned, and directed by the Divisions of Field Service, Rural Service, and Legislation and Federal Relations of the National Education Association, this conference brought together 230 experts in rural education—lay and professional—from forty-three states in every section of the country. Its report contains a wealth of information on the situation and problems of rural education. The report includes papers presented to the conference, group reports, and a charter of education for rural children, which reads as follows:

I. Every rural child has the right to a satisfactory, modern elementary education.

II. Every rural child has the right to a satisfactory, modern secondary education.

III. Every rural child has the right to an educational program that bridges the gap between home and school, and between school and adult life.

IV. Every rural child has the right thru his school to health services, educational and vocational guidance, library facilities, recreational activities, and, where needed, school lunches and pupil transportation facilities at public expense.

V. Every rural child has the right to teachers, supervisors, and administrators who know rural life and who are educated to deal effectively with the problems peculiar to rural schools.

VI. Every rural child has the right to educational service and guidance during the entire year and full-time attendance in a school that is open for not less than nine months in each year for at least twelve years.

VII. Every rural child has the right to attend school in a satisfactory, modern building.

VIII. Every rural child has the right thru the school to participate in community life and culture.

IX. Every rural child has the right to a local school system sufficiently strong to provide all the services required for a modern education.

X. Every rural child has the right to have the tax resources of his community, state, and nation used to guarantee him an American standard of educational opportunity.

Persons "interested in obtaining an over-all picture of existing educational and social conditions in rural America and of recent developments of significance" will find much of value in a volume, *Rural America Today; Its Schools and Community Life,* by George A. Works and Simon O. Lesser. In addition to giving "an account of deficiencies and promising developments in America's rural schools," the authors "have regarded it as an essential part of their task to discuss many phases of rural community life which are closely related to education and to deal with the economic and demographic factors which are responsible for some of the most difficult educational problems rural people face. In the belief that education is a lifelong process, they have also reported upon existing educational facilities in rural areas for older youth and adults." The volume includes much illustrative material describing promising developments in alert rural communities.

A detailed analysis of the social and economic bases of the national interest in education is made by Newton Edwards in *Equal Educational Opportunity for Youth; A National Responsibility.* Data reveal that the adult population of the six major rural problem areas of the United States "has a burden of child support and education much greater than that of any other comparable population group in the nation." The states constituting these problem areas are, in large measure, supplying the population reserves of the nation. Moreover, farm population everywhere carries a heavier educational load than nonfarm population. Youth in large numbers move from farm to city, across state lines, and from region to region. The educational background of these young people is a matter of concern to all communities into which they migrate. "The inequalities of educational opportunity which characterize the American educational system today result primarily from the unequal distribution of the educational load, from regional and community differences in economic well-being, and from long established tradition that the schools should be supported in the main from local and state revenues. . . . Perhaps the most devastating criticism that can be directed against the American educational system is its widespread failure to provide equality of opportunity."

A recent volume that centers attention on emerging educational problems of rural communities is *Education for Rural America* (Floyd W. Reeves, ed.), a series of papers delivered before the Conference on Education in Rural Communities at the University of Chicago in the summer of 1944. This conference, in which a wide variety of rural leaders participated, was held because of a desire "to assist in bringing about a better understanding of the role of education in the improvement of rural life and the life of the nation." The program was arranged "with the thought in mind that the problems of education in rural communities cannot be fully understood without some understanding of the social and economic conditions responsible for the development of such problems" and with an awareness that a number of nonschool agencies, public and private, provide educational opportunities for rural Americans. Although some of the changes in rural education resulting from the war program are steps backward, certain of the effects of the war upon education represent gains of importance. In the transition to a peace economy efforts should be concentrated on resuming the trends in the direction of improved rural education that were interrupted by the war and continuing trends toward better rural education that were accentuated by the war.

School District Organization and Finance

As has already been indicated, the closely related problems of administrative organization and finance are at the root of many of the difficulties of rural education. One remedy generally advocated is to increase the size of the many small administrative units in order to provide a better tax base and, in many instances, to furnish a school population large enough to permit a satisfactory curriculum, adequate supervision, and various special services. Other remedies include increased state and federal aid. In considering educational organization it is necessary to distinguish between administrative units and attendance units. They may be but are not necessarily coterminous; an administrative unit may include one, several, or many schools.

Local School Unit Organization in Ten States, by H. F. Alves and Others, points out that "existing administrative complexities, conflicts of authority, and operating inefficiencies . . . seem to be the concomitants" of the present organization. A far more serious consequence of the existing organization of local school units is inadequate and unbalanced educational opportunity. "There has been a realization that such problems as inadequate schoolhousing, inaccessible schools, restricted curricular offerings, poorly paid and poorly trained personnel can be solved, or at least directly approached, only to the extent that the machinery for the administration of public education —the organization of local school units—operates effectively and economically." The states considered in the study are Arizona, Arkansas, California, Illinois, Kentucky, North Carolina, Ohio, Oklahoma, Pennsylvania, and Tennessee. The study concludes with a chapter on the formulation of a plan for the improvement of public school organization.

A study entitled *Principles and Procedures in the Organization of Satisfactory Local School Units,* by Henry F. Alves and Edgar L. Morphet, suggests procedures and presents forms for collecting and tabulating data and for mapping and charting which may be used in making a study of local school unit organization. It also makes suggestions on evaluating the present situation, proposing improvements in organization, and securing the cooperation and support of the public for proposed changes.

A study by Harold D. Alford, *Procedures for School District Reorganization,* examines and analyzes the statutes of the forty-eight states with respect to education and seeks to discover how they operate, what factors and procedures are responsible for delaying and preventing district reorganization, and what guiding principles should control procedures in a program of reorganization.

Financial Problems Arising from Changes in School District Boundaries, by Neil Ford Garvey, presents an analysis of the legal provisions of the several states pertaining to adjustment of fiscal problems that arise out of changes in territorial pattern or corporate structure of school districts, with general conclusions as to desirable features in a statute designed to control devolution of assets and liabilities of altered districts.

In recent years a number of states have engaged in school district reorganization, utilizing a variety of methods and achieving varying degrees of success in attaining the objective of a small number of administrative districts. Studies or reports describing the problems, programs, and accomplishments in several states are here cited: (1) Edward Allen Bateman, *Development of the County-Unit School District in Utah; A Study in Adaptability;* (2) Iowa State College, *Rural School Reorganization in Iowa;* (3) Calvin Grieder, *School District Reorganization for Colorado;* (4) New York State, *Intermediate Report of the Joint Legislative Committee on the State Education System;* and (5) Kansas Legislative Council, *School District Reorganization; Reorganization in Other States, and Analysis of Problems of Reorganization in Kansas. Rural Education and Rural Life in Missouri,* a report of the Cooperative Study of Rural Life and Education, gives special attention to the problems of the small rural schools and to school service areas.

John K. Norton and Margaret Alltucker Norton consider in *Wealth, Children and Education* the economic ability of the United States to finance education, the studies of relative ability of the states and their efforts to support education, the adequacy of support in relation to ability and effort, and the implications of these matters for social policy and action.

Paul R. Mort and Walter C. Reusser in a more extensive and more technical study of educational finance, *Public School Finance; Its Background, Structure, and Operation,* describe the development and guiding principles of American educational finance, the details of its operation, and trends and needs in state and federal participation in school support.

An Inventory of Public School Expenditures in the United States, by John K. Norton and Eugene S. Lawler, is the most comprehensive study yet made of such expenditures in this country and represents an effort to develop more functional methods of collecting and presenting statistics of school expenditures. In *Unfinished Business in American Education; An Inventory of Public School Expenditures in the United States,* the same authors make available to the general public in popular form, with extensive use of pictures and graphs, the information presented more extensively in their original publication.

A *Research Bulletin* of the National Education Association, "Federal Aid for Education; A Review of Pertinent Facts," presents the case for general federal aid to education. It provides data on the mobility of the population, inequalities of educational opportunity, relative educational responsibilities of the states, relative economic ability of the states to support education, and the financial efforts of the states to support schools. This bulletin supplies a wealth of data on differences among the states in current expenditure per pupil, average salaries paid to teachers, the per-pupil value of school property, average length of school year, high-school enrollments, ratio of school-age children to adults, fertility ratio, income per adult, estimated school revenues per child if each state were to make average effort under a uniform tax program, and actual efforts made to support schools. While data are presented to show differences among the states, they reflect in large part differences between rural and urban areas. In discussing factors underlying differences in economic ability, the bulletin states:

A number of factors have contributed to the widely differing abilities of the states to support schools. There are great differences among the states in the nature and amount of their natural resources. The interplay of economic, social, and political forces has made agriculture generally, and in the Southern states especially, less profitable for the typical family than industrial pursuits. The enormous growth in corporate ownership of wealth has made it difficult for individual states to tax fairly the wealth and income produced within their own boundaries when much of that wealth and income is controlled and exploited by persons or organizations in other states. The shifting of population from farms to cities has taken material wealth as well as human resources from sections in which agriculture is the chief occupation to areas engaged primarily in business and industry.

Still another factor of special significance in recent years has been the program of federal taxation. . . . increases in the amounts of federal revenue actually drawn (not merely collected) from the various states have been relatively greater in most of the poorer states than in most of the wealthier ones.

In *Federal-State Relations in Education,* the Problems and Policies Committee of the American Council on Education and the Educational Policies Commission of the National Education Association issue a warning against the drift toward the federalization of education in the United States. They point out that increased federal action in education is largely a response to profound changes and insistent needs in our society that can be effectively dealt with only through education. In providing funds piecemeal to meet these needs, the federal government has also instituted varying degrees of federal control. They warn that if education in the United States becomes federalized, it will not be because the people have determined upon a policy of gradually shifting predominant educational control from the states and localities to the nation; rather, federalization will result from responses to many small emergencies and from the pressures of many special interests. Federal participation in education is a permanent phenomenon of American life. The important issues have become the directions and the pattern of federal action. The report concludes that:

> Federal educational action in the states should be limited to two functions: financial assistance to permit the establishment of an adequate minimum of educational opportunity for all children and youth and noncoercive leadership exercised by means of educational studies and similar advisory functions.

TEACHERS AND SUPERVISORS

The recruitment, preparation, in-service training, and reimbursement of teachers and supervisors are important factors contributing to the quality of rural schools. These factors are considered in a number of the publications already referred to. Attention is directed particularly to the chapter in Works and Lesser's *Rural America Today*, "The Education of Teachers for Rural Schools," and to the bibliography at the end of that chapter. Rural teachers generally are less well prepared for their tasks than city teachers and receive less outside help with their programs. They operate with textbooks and courses of study designed to meet urban needs and with inadequate equipment and instructional materials. Salary, tenure, and living conditions in rural areas compare unfavorably with the situation prevailing in cities.

"The Rural Teacher's Economic Status" is the subject of a *Research Bulletin* of the National Education Association, issued in January, 1939. It is part of the survey of the Committee on the Economic Status of the Rural Teacher and relates to the financial status of white teachers. It points out, among other things, that the salary situation of rural teachers as a group is unsatisfactory; that conditions of rural teachers in the open country, and especially those in one-teacher schools, are less satisfactory than conditions of teachers in the town districts; that the housing facilities of rural teachers as a group are inadequate; and that the professional qualifications of rural teachers are high enough to justify the payment of larger salaries on the average than these teachers are receiving.

A pamphlet, *A Fair Start in Life for the Country Child*, based on a report entitled *Teachers in Rural Communities*, is also a product of the Committee on the Economic Status of the Rural Teacher. There it is stated that every child is entitled to a teacher who is a friendly neighbor, who is well paid, who can support his family, who is well qualified, and who has a sense of security.

Sister M. Aloysius Crawford is the author of *Preparation of Teachers for Catholic Rural Schools*. The author believes that the major weakness of the Catholic educational system is that religious teachers have seldom had specifically rural preparation. Changing conditions in rural life in America have placed a new task on the rural schools—to prepare rural children to take an intelligent part in organized economic life when they became adults, to participate in economic as well as political democracy.

Educational leadership and adequate supervisory services can do much to improve the quality of education in rural communities. Leadership resources exist in the local school and community. They may also be supplied by the office of the county superintendent, teacher-training institutions, state departments of education, and other outside sources.

The fifteenth yearbook of the Department of Supervisors and Directors of Instruction of the National Education Association, *Leadership at Work,* considers instructional leadership by describing a number of school programs and educational activities behind which such leadership is operating or through which it is being developed.

"The McDonough County and Western Illinois State Teachers College Rural School Supervisory Project" is a progress report by the Project Research Committee on a five-year supervisory project, whose main purpose has been "to attempt to develop an efficient program for training rural teachers in-service in order that rural education might be improved. Every effort is being made to show how an adequate rural school supervisory program can be developed and carried out with the county as the unit."

The volume *Supervision; Principles and Practices in the Improvement of Instruction,* by A. S. Barr, William H. Burton, and Leo J. Brueckner, was written for the purpose of presenting the general problems, principles, and procedures of supervision.

SCHOOL BUILDINGS

Many rural school buildings are entirely inadequate to permit the type of program that these schools should provide. Frequently they are lacking in proper sanitary facilities. Lighting and heating are often primitive. They may not have attractive playgrounds and needed playground equipment.

The ideal of the school building as a community institution is set forth in Engelhardt and Engelhardt's *Planning the Community School*. Prepared at the request of the American Association for Adult Education and with the Association's financial assistance, the volume conceives of the school as a center of adult as well as child education. "A school is never primarily a place, nor even a group of co-operating students and teachers. A school is primarily an idea, of which equipment and personnel are the more or less adequate expression. . . . Public adult education has been, up to now, very badly expressed in the housing provided for it." The authors discuss such matters as the community school auditorium, indoor game spaces, social recreation spaces, cafeterias, workshops for arts and crafts, the library, special discussion and study rooms, community school grounds, and community school design.

Careful planning is essential in the development of new school housing. In order to plan facilities intelligently it is necessary to consider the whole question of service area and to ensure that new buildings are located properly in relation to the communities they should serve. The public works school-building program of the depression years provided many needed buildings; in some instances, however, it contributed to freezing a highly unsatisfactory pattern of administrative units for years to come.

CURRICULUM AND INSTRUCTIONAL MATERIALS

Efforts are being made in many states and communities to adapt the curriculum and instructional materials of rural schools to the particular needs of their pupils. A number of teacher-training institutions are recognizing the need for, and helping in the preparation of, instructional materials that will challenge the interest of rural children. Often, however, the rural schools are held to a program with rigidly established subject and grade divisions that results in an artificial situation, especially in small schools. Although many of the same things should be taught in rural and urban schools, at numerous points curriculum materials need to be adapted in content and organization to rural situations.

The Department of Rural Education of the National Education Association has devoted three recent yearbooks to instructional materials and techniques. The 1938 yearbook, *Newer Types of Instruction in Small Rural Schools,* presents the principles underlying some of the important adaptations of methods and materials of instruction to meet the needs of rural pupils and describes the procedures followed in some outstanding experiments. It deals with specific fields of interest—art, health, language arts, social studies, natural science, and music—as well as with the general principles affecting the organization of the whole curriculum.

In *Child Development and Tool Subjects in Rural Areas,* the yearbook for 1941, the authors of the various chapters follow consistently the idea that the tool subjects will be much more thoroughly and permanently mastered if, by utilization of the environment and experiences of rural children, they are given meaning and are presented as necessary means for attaining desirable ends.

The yearbook for 1943 is entitled *Conservation Education in Rural Schools.* It is pointed out in the foreword that "the ideals, knowledge, and skills of the 13,000,000 rural-school children of our country will have much to do with what happens to our land and its resources now and in the future. Conservation is a prime obligation of American citizenship." The yearbook indicates the major problems of conservation education; gives specific illustrations of what specialists believe rural schools should teach; presents reports from teachers, principals, and supervisors telling what children are doing and learning; and furnishes sources of information which teachers and pupils can consult. Jay N. Darling, in one of the papers included in the yearbook, "Why King Midas Starved," points out that "the road back from Pearl Harbor is short and easy compared to the road back from a continent shorn of its natural resources. . . . Conservation is a science whose principles are written in the oldest legal code in the world—the laws of nature." Ignorance of these laws "has been, and still is, more responsible for the violations than wilful malpractice. It is therefore necessary before any real progress toward conservation can take place that the schools shoulder a large part of the responsible burden." The teachers must be the missionaries in this field. Probably the real job of conservation cannot be done at all "unless the teachers of America, and especially the rural teachers, are willing to take upon themselves the responsibility for the major part of the work which lies ahead."

The twenty-third yearbook of the Department of Elementary

School Principals of the National Education Association, *Creative Schools,* contains much suggestive material on current practices in creative education. An introduction setting forth basic principles is followed by thirty-eight brief articles on such subjects as poetry writing in a 6A language class; our class newspaper; a church Easter; a miniature orchestra; the school museum; a lunchroom decoration project; and housekeeping activities in the kindergarten.

For some time educators and research workers have been aware that the research studies in various fields of natural, physical, and social sciences are one of the great and almost untapped reservoirs of instructional material for schools and colleges. "On the one hand, school leaders recognize that the curriculum needs the enrichment and constant stimulation that comes from current studies of natural and social phenomena. On the other hand, research leaders realize that one of the most effective means of getting something done about their studies is to see them incorporated in the ongoing educational process. The difficulty has been in finding ways and means to unite the interests and talents of both groups." *Channeling Research into Education,* prepared by John E. Ivey, Jr., for the Committee on Southern Regional Studies and Education (which maintains a central office at the University of North Carolina), reports a study "to explore ways and means for insuring the continuous flow of research on southern resources and problems into the educational process, thus stimulating research findings to become a vital factor in the thinking and action of the region." A second publication resulting from the work of the Committee is *Education for Use of Regional Resources: The Report of Gatlinburg Conference II.* The Committee has also issued *Education Helps Build a Region,* a series of articles reprinted from *The High School Journal* of May, 1946. The series is edited by John E. Ivey, Jr. and Harry B. Williams.

The *Teachers College Record* for January, 1940, contains a number of articles relating to the curriculum of rural schools—curriculum planning, social studies and the rural community, music for rural schools, and English in the rural high schools. It also includes articles on supervised correspondence study, education and guidance for teachers, school administration, pupil transportation, and occupational adjustment of rural youth.

GUIDANCE SERVICES

Guidance services are an integral part of the educational program. They are aimed at helping children to make satisfactory adjustments in their personal and social lives and to choose, prepare for, and secure placement in vocations in which they are interested and for which they have aptitude. Although rural teachers do a great deal of individual guidance work, only a small number of rural schools are doing organized work in guidance.

The Department of Rural Education of the National Education Association devoted its 1942 yearbook to *Guidance in Rural Schools.* It represents an effort to bring together for the use of rural educational leaders information on trends and programs of guidance throughout the United States. Rural children need guidance in the same way and for the same reason as children anywhere do. In view of the limited resources available to children of average and below average rural homes, guidance is especially important for them. In almost any rural environment there are materials and experiences that may be used to improve children's physical and mental development. Guidance can help them to find much interest and pleasure in the natural environment. It is also needed to help them to find their places in the world of work.

To assist rural high schools in organizing guidance programs, the Occupational Information and Guidance Service of the United States Office of Education issued in 1940 a bulletin, *Guidance Programs for Rural High Schools,* prepared by Paul W. Chapman. The bulletin presents the point of view that it is the responsibility of every high school to make guidance services an organic part of its program. It reports in some detail on the guidance programs of two high schools and carries an outline of the functions of a complete guidance service for a local school system.

Another study that considers problems of guidance in rural schools is Ruth Strang and Latham Hatcher's *Child Development and Guidance in Rural Schools.* It is designed as "a practical book on guiding rural boys and girls." Among the topics that the authors discuss are conditions that make effective guidance possible, guidance in ongoing activities of the classroom, guidance through groups, and special counseling problems and techniques.

SCHOOLS AND THE COMMUNITY

The concept of the school as a community institution has served as the point of departure for a number of studies and experiments in rural education. Mutual benefits flow from close working relationships between the school and the community it serves. The school program increases in vitality as it draws on the resources of the community. In turn, through its program the rural school can make a major contribution to the quality of rural living. Some of the citations already given contain materials that stress this concept, notably Works and Lesser's *Rural America Today; Its Schools and Community Life,* listed as a background study early in this chapter.

The School and the Changing Pattern of Country Life is a report of the Southern Rural Life Conference—a conference which gave thoughtful consideration to responsibilities of the rural school in relation to "changing patterns in agriculture and industry, in health education and services, in religious life, and in education." It is stated in the foreword:

> Southern rural schools will become . . . community schools of social action when southern teacher-education institutions, state departments of education, and local administrative units become focal points of creative effort in community planning designed to affect the social, economic, physical, cultural, and spiritual development of the people of the rural South. A broader concept of the function of the rural school is needed if the school is to contribute to raising the quality of community living in rural areas. The responsibility for promoting the reorganization of the content and method of community education rests squarely upon teacher-education institutions, state departments of education, and local administrative units.

The Conference acted through four committees, each of which prepared a chapter on a major area of rural life. The four joined to prepare a final chapter, "Suggested Action Programs," to implement their recommendations.

The yearbook of the Department of Rural Education of the National Education Association for 1939 is devoted to the problem of *Community Resources in Rural Schools.* It is pointed out in the foreword that the two fundamental factors in educational progress are the pupil and his environment and that the primary environmental influences are the home and the community. "The discovery and use of community resources are necessary if the school is to assume the role of social agent and if the curriculum is to bring about desirable changes in the pupil and in his community."

Other departments of the National Education Association have also given attention to the school in relation to the community. The Department of Elementary School Principals, in *How to Know and How to Use Your Community,* seeks to assist elementary principals and their faculties to become better acquainted with their communities in order to utilize their resources to improve the instructional program. The papers are organized around the topics of curriculum planning and community life, how to study community life, and utilizing community resources in curriculum planning.

The American Association of School Administrators in its seventeenth yearbook, *Schools in Small Communities,* centers attention on communities of 500 to 5,000, but pays special attention to communities of about 2,500. The yearbook is predicated on the following point of view:

> . . . the small school system should be regarded not merely as a mechanism for maintaining the best educational institutions possible, but it should be conceived as the structure within which it may be possible to develop the best type of rural social organization and the finest rural culture. The small school system should not only make possible the best educational program for young and old (or children and adults), but it should make the school a social center for the community and it should take responsibility for helping to build a better rural community, because the community has an essential part in the educational process.

In its yearbook for 1944, *Rural Schools and the War,* the Department of Rural Education of the National Education Association presents a series of papers relating to educational activities in the war effort and administrative adjustments to facilitate wartime activities in the schools. Throughout, reference is made to the postwar implications of new activities and emphases brought into the educational program as a result of the war. The introduction carries the following statement:

> The best possible basic education for both groups [children who will remain in the country and those who will go to the city] is one that gives the individual an understanding of his community, its environment, its problems, and how to work out the solution to these problems. Those who remain in the rural community can use this understanding of the real problems of life in finding their places in that type of community. Those who go to the city will have learned an approach to the problems of living which they can apply to the problems of urban life.

An analysis of the cooperative relationships between public schools and public health, welfare, recreation, and library agencies, and a framework of policy relating thereto, are presented in a publication of the Educational Policies Commission of the National Education Association, *Social Services and the Schools.*

The Committee on the Community School of the Society for Curriculum Study has sponsored a publication, *The Community School,* which reports on a number of community-school programs. Five are in rural areas. The introductory chapter emphasizes the significance of the community approach in education; an over-all chapter describes community-school programs in various parts of the country; and a final chapter offers an analysis of the educational programs that have been described.

GENERAL DISCUSSIONS

In *Living and Learning in a Rural School,* Genevieve Bowen tells the story of how in Riverside School one teacher, Miss Lee, tried to reconcile her growing understanding of the needs, experiences, interests, and capacities of children with the cramping routine of a prescribed course of study which gave little recognition to the needs and problems of the one-teacher school. The book is written out of wide experience in country teaching.

Modern Education in the Small Rural School, by Kate V. Wofford, is written for those who teach or will teach in such schools. The problems attacked are those that make teaching there different and difficult; the solutions offered are based in a modern philosophy of education and upon experience in the practical application of techniques to classroom situations. The appendices contain suggestions for programs, the constitution for a school club, reporting forms, organization and administration of the library, needed equipment, an emergency kit, and a community survey. *Teaching in Small Schools,* by the same author, is directed to teachers in schools taught by six teachers or fewer, many of which are located in rural areas. It covers such topics as establishing the conditions of teaching and learning, guiding learning and teaching, providing enriching experiences, and understanding and working in the out-of-school environment.

Iman Elsie Schatzmann, in *The Country School at Home and Abroad,* describes rural schools and rural life in Switzerland, Denmark, Sweden, Iceland, England, and Italy and concludes with chapters on problems of rural education in the United States.

A pamphlet, now out of print, which provides a general introduction to problems of rural education and presents a program of action to solve these problems is *Still Sits the Schoolhouse by the Road,* the work of the Committee on Rural Education, appointed in March, 1939, by the American Country Life Association and supported by the Farm Foundation.

Two volumes offer material of especial interest for persons concerned with high schools serving rural areas. R. Emerson Langfitt, Frank W. Cyr, and N. William Newson have collaborated in writing a book, *The Small High School at Work,* which attempts to show how the school, the most important social institution in the community, may serve adolescent youth and contribute to the enrichment of community life. The authors point out what they conceive to be the true functions of the small high school and emphasize the ways it may effectively perform those functions. *Education for* ALL *American Youth* is a statement of policies developed by the Educational Policies Commission of the National Education Association, which stems from a firm conviction that "the extension, adaptation, and improvement of secondary education is essential both to the security of our American institutions and to the economic well-being of our people." Three chapters are written as reports of conditions as they can be in the sixth decade of the twentieth century. One of these three chapters describes the Farmville Community School, a school serving a rural area with a country village as its center. These chapters are written from the point of view that:

Schools should be dedicated to the proposition that every youth in the United States . . . should experience a broad and balanced education which will (1) equip him to enter an occupation suited to his abilities and offering reasonable opportunity for personal growth and social usefulness; (2) prepare him to assume the full responsibilities of American citizenship; (3) give him a fair chance to exercise his right to the pursuit of happiness; (4) stimulate intellectual curiosity, engender satisfaction in intellectual achievement, and cultivate the ability to think rationally; and (5) help him to develop an appreciation of the ethical values which should undergird all life in a democratic society.

At the conclusion of the chapter on the Farmville Community School, it is stated:

We have seen that the keystone of the school program is guidance, a process whereby boys and girls are helped to plan their own lives in the light of all the facts that can be mustered about themselves and the world in which they live and work. Within this process, the Farmville school seeks to provide for each youth a program of learning experiences—a curriculum —which in his judgment and in the judgment of the staff of the school is most likely to meet his particular needs, abilities, and plans. This program includes preparation for a useful occupation, education for citizenship, and personal development for every boy and girl. The entire life of the school is so organized that the fullest cooperation in the education of youth exists between the activities of the schools and activities of other agencies in the Farmville community.

A summary of *Education for* ALL *American Youth* is presented in a publication of the National Association of Secondary-School Principals under the title *Planning for American Youth; An Educational Program for Youth of Secondary-School Age.*

Benson Y. Landis and John D. Willard, in *Rural Adult Education,* present the results of a research project of the American Association for Adult Education undertaken to interpret important rural adult education programs in the United States and suggest measures for improvement.

Good References on Vitalizing Rural Education, compiled by Walter H. Gaumnitz, contains additional references the reader may wish to consult.

PLANNING FOR BETTER SCHOOLS

Much planning for the improvement of educational opportunities in rural areas has been and is being done. Most of the references already cited have carried recommendations, and some have been formalized in policy statements or programs of action to which attention has been called. A few publications concerned specifically with planning and policies are described in this section. Additional references will be found in *Planning for Post-War Education in the United States; An Annotated List of Recent References,* published in 1943 by the United States Office of Education, and *Supplement No. 1,* published in 1945. These bibliographies cite materials published after 1940 and through December, 1944.

In "Equal Access to Education," prepared by Floyd W. Reeves and D. L. Harley for the National Resources Planning Board and included in the Board's *National Resources Development—Report for 1943. Part I, Post-War Plan and Program,* are set forth a series of recommendations which, if followed, "would provide equal access to a justifiable minimum education in the post-war period." Recommendations relate to elementary and high-school education, services for young children, college and university education, the part-time education of adults, the quality of education, the retraining or continued education of men and women demobilized from the armed forces and war industries, work experience for youth, meals at school and supervised work and play projects and other services before and after school hours, school-building program, school district organization, dormitories and transportation services to pupils in rural areas, the services of the United States Office of Education and state departments of education, and the financing of programs recommended.

The United States Office of Education has issued a series of pamphlets with an over-all title, *Planning Schools for Tomorrow,* which covers a variety of topics. One of these pamphlets, *Our Schools in the Post-War World, What Shall We Make of Them?* is designed primarily for the use of citizens' groups interested in the progressive improvement of their local school systems. It gives special attention to needed postwar adjustments.

The Department of Rural Education of the National Education Association issued in 1940 *A Policy for Rural Education in the United States,* a report of its Committee on Program and Policy. The purpose of the statement "is to provide a basis upon which those concerned with the public school program in rural areas can coordinate their activities on a nationwide basis in moving forward toward a more adequate educational program for rural America." The statement covers social and economic factors creating the distinctive problems of rural education, discusses these problems, and suggests procedures for effectuating rural educational policy. The statement of policy "was not formulated as the final and permanent answer to problems of rural education, but rather as a guide in the development of state and local policies. Its greatest usefulness should be as a basis for discussions in teachers' meetings, county institutes, state education departments, normal schools, and teachers colleges, where such discussions interpret and adapt its statements to the situations with which they are concerned."

In 1939 the Educational Policies Commission published its *Educational Policies for Rural America,* in which it states:

Rural children must have educational opportunity equal to that offered in urban sections if the traditional ideal of American education is to be realized. If rural education remains underfinanced and poorly organized, as it is today, there is grave danger that class education will prevail.

. . . .

The problems of rural areas are the problems of the whole country as well. There is no way in which they can be isolated and kept separate from those of urban communities. Whatever affects the rural people adversely is soon reflected in the lives of city dwellers. . . . The welfare of the city is inextricably bound up with that of the country and *vice versa.*

The twenty-third yearbook of the American Association of School Administrators is described by its title, *Paths to Better Schools.* There it is stated:

The place given to education in the postwar period will determine the role of America two decades hence. Educational opportunity, vocational efficiency, effective citizenship, worthy home and community participation, and individual health and happiness—these pillars of American life can be reached only thru a program of education that is modern in method, efficient in organization, adequate in finance, and forward-looking in purpose. America has made great progress along these lines, but much still needs to be done. The purpose of this yearbook has been to indicate improvements which are reasonable goals for the next decade.

References to rural educational needs may be checked through the index.

Rural Schools for Tomorrow, the 1945 yearbook of the Department of Rural Education of the National Education Association, focuses attention on the postwar problems of rural schools "with the idea that local, state, and national leaders should now lay plans for the strengthening of the entire rural school structure and program when peace returns. It is hoped that this publication will be used by thousands of discussion groups thruout the nation as a basis for considering the fundamental social and economic problems of rural people, the implications of these problems for the programs of rural schools, and the practical steps necessary for the improvement of rural education."

The Twenty-Fourth American Country Life Conference, concerned with postwar rural life, issued its proceedings under the title *Farm and Rural Life after the War.* One of its committee reports sets forth "Educational Standards for Rural People." The approach to the topic is broad and covers not only schools, but the church, libraries, discussion in neighborhood and community groups, community councils, farm organizations, extension service, and recreation. The report concludes:

> The problems [facing every community as a consequence of the war] are immediate and future. The social structure is already in existence. Knowledge, understanding and community purpose in action can deal successfully with these problems that are so immediate and so important to the maintenance of the American social community and to the attainment of a higher, a more helpful, and an improved welfare.

PERIODICALS

Developments in public education and the literature of education may be followed in a number of periodicals, a few of which are here listed. *The Elementary School Journal* is published monthly except July and August by the Department of Education at the University of Chicago. *The School Review; A Journal of Secondary Education* is also published monthly except July and August at the University of

Chicago Press. *The Nation's Schools; The Magazine of Better School Administration* is a monthly journal published by the Nation's Schools Publishing Company. *School and Society* is published weekly by the Society for the Advancement of Education. The *National Parent-Teacher* is the official magazine of the National Congress of Parents and Teachers. It has ten issues per year. *The Journal of the National Education Association* is issued monthly September through May. The Research Division of the Association issues a *Research Bulletin* four times yearly; each issue is devoted to some major problem of current interest. Matters of general interest as well as educational happenings of interest in particular states may be followed in the journals of the state education associations.

BIBLIOGRAPHY

The Advisory Committee on Education. *Report of the Committee.* Washington: Government Printing Office, 1938, 243 pp.

Alford, Harold D. *Procedures for School District Reorganization.* Contributions to Education No. 852. New York: Teachers College, Columbia University, 1942, 164 pp. (Selected references at ends of most chapters. General bibliography, pp. 149-50.)

Alves, Henry F. and Edgar L. Morphet. *Principles and Procedures in the Organization of Satisfactory Local School Units.* U. S. Office of Education Bulletin 1938, No. 11. Washington: Government Printing Office, 1939, 164 pp.

Alves, H. F. and Others. *Local School Unit Organization in Ten States.* U. S. Office of Education Bulletin 1938, No. 10. Washington: Government Printing Office, 1939, 334 pp.

American Association of School Administrators. *Paths to Better Schools.* Washington: The Association, 1945, 415 pp. (Selected references by chapters, pp. 260-68.)

——. *Schools in Small Communities.* Seventeenth Yearbook. Washington: The Association, 1939, 608 pp.

American Council on Education, Problems and Policies Committee, and National Education Association of the United States, Educational Policies Commission. *Federal-State Relations in Education.* Washington: The Council, 1945, 47 pp.

American Country Life Conference. "Educational Standards for Rural People," in *Farm and Rural Life after the War.* Proceedings of the Twenty-Fourth American Country Life Conference, Chicago, Illinois, April 11-13, 1944. Champaign, Illinois: Garrard Press, 1944, pp. 72-87.

Barr, A. S.; William H. Burton; and Leo J. Brueckner. *Supervision; Principles and Practices in the Improvement of Instruction.* New York: D. Appleton-Century Co., 1938, 981 pp. (Readings on the historical background of the curriculum, pp. 965-69.)

Bateman, Edward Allen. *Development of the County-Unit School District in Utah; A Study in Adaptability*. Contributions to Education No. 790. New York: Teachers College, Columbia University, 1940, 98 pp. (Bibliography, pp. 95-98.)

Blauch, Lloyd E. *Federal Cooperation in Agricultural Extension Work, Vocational Education, and Vocational Rehabilitation*. U. S. Office of Education Bulletin 1933, No. 15. Washington: Government Printing Office, 1935, 297 pp. (Bibliography pp. 287-97.)

Bowen, Genevieve. *Living and Learning in a Rural School*. New York: Macmillan Co., 1944, 324 pp. (References, pp. 307-14.)

Chapman, Paul W. *Guidance Programs for Rural High Schools*. U. S. Office of Education, Vocational Division, Bulletin No. 203, 1939. Washington: Government Printing Office, 1940, 58 pp.

Cocking, Walter D. and Charles H. Gilmore. *Organization and Administration of Public Education*. The Advisory Committee on Education, Staff Study No. 2. Washington: Government Printing Office, 1938, 183 pp.

The Committee on Rural Education. *Still Sits the Schoolhouse by the Road*. Chicago: The Committee, 1943, 54 pp. Out of print. (Suggested readings, pp. 52-54.)

Cooperative Study of Rural Life and Education. *Rural Education and Rural Life in Missouri*. Supplement to the Ninety-Sixth Report of the Public Schools. Jefferson City, Missouri: State Superintendent of the Public Schools, 1945, 219 pp.

Crawford, Sister M. Aloysius. *Preparation of Teachers for Catholic Rural Schools*. Washington: Catholic University of America Press, 1941, 133 pp. (Bibliography, pp. 125-33.)

Education for Use of Regional Resources; The Report of Gatlinburg Conference II. Sponsored by the Committee on Southern Regional Studies and Education. Washington: American Council on Education, 1945, 129 pp.

Edwards, Newton. *Equal Educational Opportunity for Youth; A National Responsibility*. Washington: American Council on Education, 1939, 189 pp.

The Elementary School Journal. Published by the Department of Education, University of Chicago, monthly September to June, inclusive.

Engelhardt, N. L., and N. L. Engelhardt, Jr. *Planning the Community School*. New York: American Book Co., 1940, 188 pp. (Bibliography, pp. 173-76.)

Garvey, Neil Ford. *Financial Problems Arising from Changes in School District Boundaries*. Urbana, Illinois: University of Illinois Press, 1946, 118 pp. (Bibliography, pp. 112-13.)

Gaumnitz, Walter H. *Good References on Vitalizing Rural Education*. U. S. Office of Education Bibliography No. 66. Washington: Government Printing Office, 1940, 17 pp.

Grieder, Calvin. *School District Reorganization for Colorado.* Boulder, Colorado: Colorado Association of School Boards, 1944, 30 pp.

Henry, Nelson B. and Jerome G. Kerwin. *Schools and City Government; A Study of School and Municipal Relationships in Cities of 50,000 or More Population.* Chicago: University of Chicago Press, 1938, 104 pp.

Iowa State College, Agricultural Experiment Station and Agricultural Extension Service Cooperating. *Rural School Reorganization in Iowa.* Bulletin P69. Ames, Iowa: The College, 1944, pp. 308-52.

Ivey, John E. Jr. *Channeling Research into Education.* Prepared for the Committee on Southern Regional Studies and Education. Washington: American Council on Education, 1944, 187 pp. (Selected source materials on southern resources and problems, pp. 129-87.)

—— and Harry B. Williams, eds. *Education Helps Build a Region.* Chapel Hill: University of North Carolina Press, 1946, pp. 102-71. Reprinted from *The High School Journal,* Vol. XXIX, No. 3, May 1946.

The Journal of the National Education Association. Published by the Association, 1201 Sixteenth St. N. W., Washington, D. C., monthly September to May, inclusive.

Kansas Legislative Council. Research Department. *School District Reorganization; Reorganization in Other States, and Analysis of Problems of Reorganization in Kansas.* Publication No. 130. Topeka, Kansas: The Council, 1944, 51 pp.

Landis, Benson Y. and John D. Willard. *Rural Adult Education.* New York: Macmillan Co., 1933, 229 pp. (Bibliography, pp. 203-23.)

Langfitt, R. Emerson; Frank W. Cyr; and N. William Newson. *The Small High School at Work.* New York: American Book Co., 1936, 660 pp. (Selected references at ends of chapters.)

Mort, Paul R. and Walter C. Reusser. *Public School Finance; Its Background, Structure, and Operation.* New York: McGraw-Hill Book Co., 1941, 569 pp. (Selected references at ends of chapters.)

National Association of Secondary-School Principals. *Planning for American Youth; An Educational Program for Youth of Secondary-School Age.* Washington: The Association (1201 Sixteenth St. N. W.), 1944, 63 pp.

National Education Association of the United States. Committee on the Economic Status of the Rural Teacher. *A Fair Start in Life for the Country Child.* Washington: The Association (1201 Sixteenth St. N. W.), 1939, 15 pp.

——. Department of Elementary School Principals. *Creative Schools.* Twenty-third Yearbook. Washington: The Department (1201 Sixteenth St. N. W.), 1944, 310 pp.

——. ——. *How to Know and How to Use Your Community.* Washington: The Department, 1941-42, 80 pp. (Bibliography, pp. 79-80.)

——. Department of Rural Education. *Child Development and Tool Subjects in Rural Areas.* Yearbook, 1941. Washington: The Department (1201 Sixteenth St. N. W.), 1941, 89 pp. (Bibliography, pp. 85-89.)

——. ——. *Community Resources in Rural Schools.* Yearbook, 1939. Washington: The Department, 1939, 109 pp. (Includes bibliographies.)

——. ——. *Conservation Education in Rural Schools.* Yearbook, 1943. Washington: The Department, 1943, 114 pp. (Bibliography, pp. 99-114.)

——. ——. *Guidance in Rural Schools.* Yearbook, 1942. Washington: The Department, 1942, 127 pp. (References, pp. 123-26.)

——. ——. *Newer Types of Instruction in Small Rural Schools.* Yearbook, 1938. Washington: The Department, 1938, 144 pp. (References at ends of chapters.)

——. ——. *A Policy for Rural Education in the United States.* Washington: The Department, 1940, 47 pp.

——. ——. *Rural Schools and the War.* Yearbook, 1944. Washington: The Department, 1944, 96 pp.

——. ——. *Rural Schools for Tomorrow.* Yearbook, 1945. Washington: The Department, 1945, 152 pp. (Bibliographical footnotes.)

——. Department of Supervisors and Directors of Instruction. *Leadership at Work.* Fifteenth Yearbook. Washington: The Department, 1943, 248 pp.

——. Educational Policies Commission. *Educational Policies for Rural America.* Washington: The Commission, 1939, 19 pp.

——. ——. *Education for* ALL *American Youth.* Washington: The Commission, 1944, 421 pp.

——. ——. *Social Services and the Schools.* Washington: The Commission, 1939, 147 pp.

——. Research Division. *Research Bulletin.* Four issues per year: February, April, October, and December.

——. ——. "Federal Aid for Education; A Review of Pertinent Facts." *Research Bulletin,* Vol. XX, No. 3, September 1942, pp. 119-47.

——. ——. "The Rural Teacher's Economic Status." *Research Bulletin,* Vol. XVII, No. 1, January 1939, 64 pp.

National Parent-Teacher; The P.-T.A. Magazine. Published by the National Congress of Parents and Teachers, 600 South Michigan Ave., Chicago, Illinois, monthly September to June, inclusive.

The Nation's Schools; The Magazine of Better School Administration. Published by the Nation's Schools Publishing Company, 919 North Michigan Ave., Chicago, Illinois, and 101 Park Ave., New York, monthly.

New York State. *Intermediate Report of the Joint Legislative Committee on The State Education System.* Legislative Document (1944) No. 54. Albany, New York: Williams Press, 1944, 377 pp.

Norton, John K. and Eugene S. Lawler. *An Inventory of Public School Ex-penditures in the United States; A Report of the Cooperative Study of Public School Expenditures.* Washington: American Council on Education (744 Jackson Place, N. W.), 1944, 2 vols.

———. ———. *Unfinished Business in American Education; An Inventory of Public School Expenditures in the United States.* Washington: American Council on Education, 1946, 64 pp.

———and Margaret Alltucker Norton. *Wealth, Children and Education,* 2nd ed. New York: Teachers College, Columbia University, 1938, 138 pp. (Bibliography, pp. 131-33.)

Project Research Committee. "The McDonough County and Western Illi-nois State Teachers College Rural School Supervisory Project; A Progress Report at the Middle of a Five-Year Project in Rural School Supervision." *The Western Illinois State Teachers College Bulletin,* Vol. XXIII, No. 2, September 1943, 44 pp.

Reeves, Floyd W., ed. *Education for Rural America.* Chicago: University of Chicago Press, 1945, 213 pp.

Russell, John Dale and Associates. *Vocational Education.* The Advisory Committee on Education, Staff Study No. 8. Washington: Government Printing Office, 1938, 325 pp.

Schatzmann, Iman Elsie. *The Country School at Home and Abroad.* Chicago: University of Chicago Press, 1942, 233 pp. (Bibliography, pp. 215-21.)

School and Society. Published by the Society for the Advancement of Educa-tion, 15 Amsterdam Ave., New York, weekly.

The School Review; A Journal of Secondary Education. Published by the University of Chicago Press, monthly September to June, inclusive.

Smith, Payson; Frank W. Wright; and Associates. *Education in the Forty-Eight States.* The Advisory Committee on Education, Staff Study No. 1. Washington: Government Printing Office, 1939, 199 pp.

Society for Curriculum Study. Committee on the Community School. *The Community School.* Edited by Samuel Everett. New York: D. Appleton-Century Co., 1938, 487 pp. (Annotated bibliography, pp. 463-73.)

Southern Rural Life Conference. *The School and the Changing Pattern of Country Life.* Report of the Conference, sponsored by George Peabody College for Teachers, Vanderbilt University, Scarritt College, Fisk Uni-versity. Nashville, Tennessee: The Conference, 1943, 100 pp.

Strang, Ruth and Latham Hatcher. *Child Development and Guidance in Rural Schools.* New York: Harper & Bros., 1943, 218 pp. (Suggested read-ing, pp. 188-97.)

Teachers College Record. Vol. XLI, No. 4, January 1940. Rural Education Number. New York: Bureau of Publications, Teachers College, Columbia University, pp. 273-376.

U. S. National Resources Planning Board. *National Resources Development —Report for 1943. Part I, Post-War Plan and Program.* Washington: Government Printing Office, 1943. "Equal Access to Education," pp. 68-74, also issued in *The American Teacher*, Vol. XXVII, No. 8, May 1943, pp. 7-14, and in *The High School Journal*, Vol. XXVI, No. 4, May 1943, pp. 110-22.

U. S. Office of Education. *Annual Report for the Fiscal Year . . .* Washington: Government Printing Office.

——. *Biennial Survey of Education in the United States.* Washington: Government Printing Office.

——. *Planning for Post-War Education in the United States; An Annotated List of Recent References.* Washington: The Office, 1943, 8 pp. *Supplement No. 1.* Washington: The Office, 1945, 17 pp.

——. *Planning Schools for Tomorrow. Our Schools in the Post-War World, What Shall We Make of Them?* Office Leaflet No. 17. Washington: Government Printing Office, 1944, 40 pp.

——. *Studies of State Departments of Education.* Bulletin of the Office 1940, No. 6, monographs Nos. 1-16. Washington: Government Printing Office, 1941.

The White House Conference on Rural Education, October 3, 4, and 5, 1944. Washington: National Education Association of the United States (1201 Sixteenth St. N. W.), 1945, 272 pp. (Suggested readings pp. 243-50.)

Wofford, Kate V. *Modern Education in the Small Rural School.* New York: Macmillan Co., 1938, 582 pp.

——. *Teaching in Small Schools.* New York: Macmillan Co., 1946, 399 pp.

Works, George A. and Barton Morgan. *The Land-Grant Colleges.* The Advisory Committee on Education, Staff Study No. 10. Washington: Government Printing Office, 1939, 141 pp.

—— and Simon O. Lesser. *Rural America Today; Its Schools and Community Life.* Chicago: University of Chicago Press, 1942, 450 pp. (Authorities for the facts at ends of chapters.)

2 *THE AGRICULTURAL EXECUTION SERVICE*

2 *THE AGRICULTURAL EXTENSION SERVICE*

AGRICULTURAL EXTENSION is primarily an adult education program serving the needs of the people of rural America. One part of extension work, the 4-H Club program, serves rural youth by encouraging activities that provide education through doing. Extension work is nationwide in scope and is carried on jointly by the Extension Service of the United States Department of Agriculture, the state land-grant colleges, and county governing bodies. In some states the Farm Bureau is the local participating agency. Cooperative programs are formulated in the states but must be approved by the Department of Agriculture before federal funds provided for the programs become available. State officers assist in the selection of local extension workers and generally supervise their activities. Directors of extension employed by the land-grant colleges are responsible for the administration of funds in the states.

George A. Works and Barton Morgan, in a chapter, "Agricultural Extension Work," in their monograph entitled *The Land-Grant Colleges,* point out that efforts to bring to farm people the best scientific knowledge for the improvement of agricultural practices have grown steadily in the United States. Beginning with the early agricultural societies, they have developed through county fairs and farmers institutes and, from the early nineteen-hundreds, through cooperative demonstration projects. More recently a number of federal acts have provided funds and formal organization for agricultural extension work. Its administration, however, has been kept largely grass-roots in approach and techniques. The Smith-Lever Act, 1914, the Capper-Ketcham Act, 1928, the Bankhead-Jones Act, 1935, the additional Extension Act, 1939, and the Bankhead-Flannagan Act, 1945, constitute the landmarks in this legislation.

An idea of the size and nature of the extension program may be gleaned from data presented in the annual reports of the United States Extension Service for 1943 and 1944, *Report of Cooperative Extension Work in Agriculture and Home Economics.* Of $36,739,968 allocated for cooperative extension work for the year ended June 30,

1944, 51.8 per cent was from federal appropriations, 23.0 per cent from state and college funds, 22.2 per cent from county funds, and 3.0 per cent from other local sources. A very high proportion of Extension Service personnel is employed in the counties—as agricultural and assistant agricultural agents, home demonstration agents, and 4-H Club agents. Of the 9,252 Cooperative Extension workers employed on June 30, 1943, 4,431 were agricultural and assistant agricultural agents, 2,211 were home demonstration agents, and 282 were 4-H Club workers. Of these numbers, 540 were Negro workers. Of the 3,075 counties in the United States, 2,941 had men agents and 2,058 had women agents on July 1, 1943. Workers in the counties were assisted by a large group of volunteer workers—948,945 adult extension volunteer leaders and 153,380 boys' and girls' Club leaders in 1943. Cooperative relationships with the communities are also maintained through voluntary extension committees, Farm Bureaus, farm clubs, and other local advisory groups.

COUNTY WORKERS

The county workers give farmers and homemakers a great variety of practical assistance with their problems; they also interpret their needs and points of view and channel the flow of organized planning and thinking of farm people for the benefit of state and federal agricultural policymakers. They take the lead in organizing counties for county program-making, in which farm families, technicians, and administrative workers plan together for the best local use of all government-provided facilities for rural betterment.

The concept of work in the counties has changed with changes in the position of agriculture in the national economy. The county agent began his activities as an itinerant teacher of good farming and improved scientific production methods applicable to the individual farm—improved yields, control of pests, and stock improvement. During World War I, agents undertook promotional activities to increase farm production. In the postwar depression, they broadened their programs to assist individual farmers to improve business methods and solve their marketing problems. In the nineteen-thirties, they extended their activities further in the direction of group work and the adjustment of individual farm plans to national agricultural conditions and policies—to long-range planning for farm living, soil protection and improvement, diversified farming, adjustment of production to needs for farm products, and social, recreational, and cultural needs. Home demonstration agents have directed their attention beyond the improvement of homemaking techniques to wider aspects of family living and household management. More recently, the efforts of county workers have been expanded to include gearing agriculture into national defense and war programs, helping solve emergency problems such as help, machinery, and fertilizer shortages, and giving advisory assistance to returning war veterans who want to farm. Throughout the history of the Service, elasticity of organization and programs has permitted adjustments to local needs and situations.

Extension workers are largely responsible for group and general education programs essential to an understanding of the action programs of other agricultural agencies. The Extension Service cooperates with such agencies as the Soil Conservation Service, the Forest Service, the Rural Electrification Administration, and the Tennessee Valley Authority in the furtherance of their programs. It has helped, for example, in organizing cooperatives, conducting farm forestry demonstrations, and getting the agricultural planning program functioning in the counties.

County workers reach rural people through a variety of methods. These include individual contacts and meetings with organized groups; use of volunteer local leaders especially equipped to conduct demonstrations and lead meetings; distribution of bulletins, discussion pamphlets, and program materials prepared by federal and state offices; issuance of news stories; use of circular letters, radio programs, films, and exhibits; and organization of discussion groups and farmers institutes. Many farm families have received a large amount of help and stimulation. The extent of local cooperation is indicated by the fact that in 1944 more than 620,000 rural leaders helped keep neighbors informed and active in war programs. Many of these persons were in addition to the thousands of local leaders of long standing who assisted on special projects.

Further information as to the programs, activities, and methods of the Extension Service may be found in the annual reports of the Director of Extension Work, currently entitled *Report of Cooperative Extension Work in Agriculture and Home Economics*. Reports of earlier years bore such graphic titles as *Serving American Agriculture* (1933); *On the Front Lines with Agriculture* (1934); *Building Rural Leadership* (1935); *Meeting the Challenge of Agriculture* (1936); *Serving Farm People on Many Fronts* (1937); *For Better Rural Living* (1938); *Leaders on the Land* (1939); and *Security at the Grass Roots* (1940-41). A brief description of the work and relationships of the Service, written by its director, M. L. Wilson, is included in *The Book of the States, 1945-46,* under the title "State-Federal Cooperation in Agricultural Extension Programs."

Gladys Baker, in her book *The County Agent,* describes the typical county agent as follows:

> The county agent is a young man in his middle thirties. He is generally farm reared and serves in his home state but not in his home county. He is usually an agricultural college graduate and has had some previous experience in agricultural work. Often he has been a Smith-Hughes teacher of vocational agriculture. He is active in community affairs, belonging to business as well as to agricultural organizations.

Home demonstration and Club agents have similar backgrounds but are less likely to have had practical experience. Home demonstration agents are apt to be home economics graduates, and Club agents are usually either agricultural or home economics graduates (Works and Morgan, *op. cit.*).

According to the *Report of Cooperative Extension Work . . . , 1944,* there were 45,243 home demonstration clubs with a membership of over one million homemakers. Home demonstration agents, assisted by over two hundred thousand local leaders, brought these groups information on such matters as nutrition, food production and preservation, the care, repair, cleaning, and storage of clothing, improving the arrangement of their homes for convenience and comfort, and educational and recreational activities. The story of home demonstration work in one state, North Carolina, is described in Jane Simpson McKimmon's *When We're Green We Grow.* The author was for many years state director of home demonstration work.

The 4-H Clubs for boys and girls ten to twenty years of age had a membership of 1,692,650 in February, 1943. They were assisted by more than one hundred fifty thousand local leaders. The average Club has from 12 to 15 members, and each Club has an adult leader. The program for these young people centers around practical farm, homemaking, and community projects—raising a farm animal, planting a garden, canning fruits, vegetables, and meats, carrying on a clothing project, and furthering improved practices through the use of demonstration teams. Participants gain social training through group activities. Club members gave major assistance in the war food program, conducted salvage campaigns, sold bonds, and otherwise aided the war effort. There are also rural youth groups for older youth; over fifteen hundred such groups were active in 1944. According to the *Report of Cooperative Extension Work . . . , 1940-41,* during the preceding decade more than one-half the children of Club age growing up on farms in the United States became 4-H Club members. The 1943 enrollment brought to more than ten million the number of young people who had been Club members. Further data on Club work may be found in *Statistical Analysis of 4-H Club Work, 1914-43, with Special Emphasis on 1943,* prepared by Laurel K. Sabrosky, and issued as an Extension Service circular. Examples of publications that have been prepared for use in connection with specific 4-H Club activities are Ruth Lohman's *Teaching Conservation of Wildlife through 4-H Clubs,* and Wilbur R. Mattoon and Erwin H. Shinn's *Forestry for 4-H Clubs.*

STATE AND FEDERAL WORKERS

Subject-matter specialists in various phases of agriculture, homemaking, and rural life make up a large proportion of the state extension staffs. A partial list of the subjects with which these specialists are concerned includes soils, soil conservation, forestry, animal husbandry, dairying, poultry-raising, field crops, horticulture, entomology, plant pathology, agricultural economics, rural sociology, farm management, marketing, rural organization, recreation, clothing, and nutrition. Activities of specialists include supplying information to, and otherwise helping, local agents, holding meetings in various parts of the state to give demonstrations, assisting with the training of volunteer local leaders, and making and publishing studies relating to a great variety of rural problems. State extension specialists numbered 1,675 as of June 30, 1943. There were, in addition, several hundred supervisory and administrative state extension personnel.

As of June 30, 1943, the federal Extension Service employed 169 persons on its Washington staff. This staff is responsible for supervising and coordinating agricultural extension work throughout the nation, approving state plans and budgets, auditing accounts, and stimulating and improving extension activities and methods. Subject-matter specialists and informational employees carry the research findings of the bureaus of the United States Department of Agriculture and the programs of other federal cooperating agencies to the land-grant colleges and the state extension services. The federal office issues the *Extension Service Review,* a monthly publication consisting of short articles and notes on agricultural extension activities throughout the country.

ADDITIONAL REFERENCES

A number of additional publications relating to agricultural extension will be briefly described.

Several works provide historical and background materials for understanding the program. The *Report of the Commission on Country Life,* made in 1909 by the U. S. Country Life Commission, has recently been reprinted. This report urged the establishment of nationalized extension work to be carried on by state colleges of agriculture and "designed to forward not only the business of agriculture, but sanitation, education, home-making, and all interests of country life." Joseph Cannon Bailey, in *Seaman A. Knapp, Schoolmaster of American Agriculture,* describes the contributions of Mr. Knapp in originating and developing extension service ideas and practices. Alfred Charles True has prepared two related histories—*A History of Agricultural Education in the United States, 1785-1925* and *A History of Agricultural Extension Work in the United States, 1785-1923.* The evolution of federal cooperation in extension work is traced in Lloyd E. Blauch's *Federal Cooperation in Agricultural Extension Work, Vocational Education, and Vocational Rehabilitation.* O. B. Martin, in *The Demonstration Work,* describes the philosophy that has motivated extension work from the beginning.

In evaluating the work of the Extension Service in his book *The Land Grant College Movement,* Frederick B. Mumford states that "the nerve center of the agricultural extension service is in the college of agriculture." The program of resident instruction offered by these colleges provides trained workers for the extension program. Their experiment stations carry on the research which makes possible sound technical training in agriculture and furnishes the ideas for improvements that extension workers carry to farmers and rural home-makers.

Russell Lord's *The Agrarian Revival; A Study of Agricultural Extension* is "an account of action teaching in the open country of the United States." It supplies background materials and evaluates agricultural extension as an adult education program.

Edmund deS. Brunner in the foreword to Marjorie Patten's *The Arts Workshop of Rural America* states:

A cultural revival sincerely and authentically American has been going on in rural America during these last dark years. It has reached significant proportions and has turned largely to the agricultural extension services of our state colleges and somewhat to the state universities for help and suggestion. The multiplying activities in drama, art, and music in an ever-growing number of communities have been thus far largely unrecorded. . . . It has seemed wise, therefore, to record the experiences of the states that were among the first to feel the quickening touch of this phenomenon.

C. R. Hoffer and D. L. Gibson's *The Community Situation as It Affects Agricultural Extension Work* is a study of the relation of certain social factors in community situations to success or failure of the various extension projects initiated in a community. The study is focused on the work of the county agricultural agent.

Extension is placed in a larger setting in two recent works. One is a report of the Extension Service and the Office of Foreign Agricultural Relations entitled *The Contribution of Extension Methods and Techniques toward the Rehabilitation of War-Torn Countries.* The other is a volume edited by Edmund deS. Brunner, Irwin T. Sanders, and Douglas Ensminger, *Farmers of the World; The Development of Agricultural Extension.* The papers included in this volume describe extension activities in many parts of the world. The final paper, "The Role of Extension in World Reconstruction," points out that rural adult education with special reference to agriculture and somewhat less to home economics is a worldwide phenomenon. The program must be in harmony with the culture of the people, democratic in operation, simple in conception, and comprehensive in scope.

A monthly periodical first issued in 1945 is *The National County Agent and Extension Review.*

The Extension Service issued in May, 1945, a bibliography, *Publications of Extension Service.*

BIBLIOGRAPHY

Bailey, Joseph Cannon. *Seaman A. Knapp, Schoolmaster of American Agriculture.* New York: Columbia University Press, 1945, 307 pp. (Selected bibliography, pp. 280-90.)

Baker, Gladys. *The County Agent.* Chicago: University of Chicago Press, 1939, 226 pp. (Select bibliography, pp. 214-15.)

Blauch, Lloyd E. *Federal Cooperation in Agricultural Extension Work, Vocational Education, and Vocational Rehabilitation.* Washington: Government Printing Office, 1935, 297 pp. (Bibliography, pp. 287-97.)

Brunner, Edmund deS.; Irwin T. Sanders; and Douglas Ensminger, eds. *Farmers of the World; The Development of Agricultural Extension.* New York: Columbia University Press, 1945, 208 pp.

Hoffer, C. R. and D. L. Gibson. *The Community Situation as It Affects Agricultural Extension Work.* East Lansing, Michigan: Michigan State College Agricultural Experiment Station Special Bulletin No. 312, 1941, 35 pp.

Lohman, Ruth. *Teaching Conservation of Wildlife through 4-H Clubs.* U. S. Department of Agriculture Miscellaneous Publication No. 291. Washington: Government Printing Office, 1938, 34 pp. (Bibliographies, pp. 31-34.)

Lord, Russell. *The Agrarian Revival; A Study of Agricultural Extension.* New York: American Association for Adult Education, 1939, 236 pp. (Recommended reading, pp. 224-26.)

Martin, O. B. *The Demonstration Work.* San Antonio, Texas: Naylor Co., 1941, 257 pp.

Mattoon, Wilbur R. and Erwin H. Shinn. *Forestry for 4-H Clubs.* U. S. Department of Agriculture Miscellaneous Publication No. 395. Washington: Government Printing Office, 1941.

McKimmon, Jane Simpson. *When We're Green We Grow.* Chapel Hill, North Carolina: University of North Carolina Press, 1945, 353 pp.

Mumford, Frederick B. *The Land Grant College Movement.* Columbia, Missouri: University of Missouri Agricultural Experiment Station Bulletin No. 419, 1940, 140 pp.

The National County Agent and Extension Review; The Magazine for Leaders in Agricultural Guidance and Extension. 123 West Madison St., Chicago, Illinois. Monthly.

Patten, Marjorie. *The Arts Workshop of Rural America; A Study of the Rural Arts Program of the Agricultural Extension Service.* New York: Columbia University Press, 1937, 202 pp.

Sabrosky, Laurel K. *Statistical Analysis of 4-H Club Work, 1914-43, with Special Emphasis on 1943.* Washington: U. S. Extension Service Circular No. 427, 1945, 35 pp.

True, Alfred Charles. *A History of Agricultural Education in the United States, 1785-1925.* U. S. Department of Agriculture Miscellaneous Publication No. 36. Washington: Government Printing Office, 1929, 436 pp. (Bibliography, pp. 397-420.)

——. *A History of Agricultural Extension Work in the United States, 1785-1923.* U. S. Department of Agriculture Miscellaneous Publication No. 15. Washington: Government Printing Office, 1928, 220 pp. (Bibliography, pp. 202-18.)

U. S. Country Life Commission. *Report of the Commission on Country Life with an Introduction by Theodore Roosevelt.* Chapel Hill, North Carolina: University of North Carolina Press, 1944, 150 pp. First published as Senate Document No. 705, 60th Cong., 2d sess., [1910?].

U. S. Extension Service. *Extension Service Review.* Washington: Government Printing Office. Monthly.

——. *Publications of Extension Service.* Extension Service Circular No. 425. Washington: The Service, 1945, 35 pp.

——. *Report of Cooperative Extension Work in Agriculture and Home Economics.* Washington: Government Printing Office. Annual.

—— and U. S. Office of Foreign Agricultural Relations. *The Contributions of Extension Methods and Techniques toward the Rehabilitation of War-Torn Countries.* Washington: Government Printing Office, 1946, 239 pp.

Wilson, M. L. "State-Federal Cooperation in Agricultural Extension Programs," in *The Book of the States, 1945-46.* Chicago: The Council of State Governments, 1945, pp. 245-57.

Works, George A. and Barton Morgan. *The Land-Grant Colleges.* The Advisory Committee on Education Staff Study No. 10. Washington: Government Printing Office, 1939, 141 pp.

3 *LIBRARY SERVICE*

LIBRARIES PROVIDE a variety of services to rural people. Some of these services are described in Farmers' Bulletin No. 1847 of the United States Department of Agriculture, *Rural Library Service*. They include, among others, provision of specific information on immediate farm and home problems; background reading to aid in understanding current social, economic, and governmental problems; and recreational reading. Libraries furnish much material for the use of the numerous discussion groups in rural areas throughout the country. They help parents in understanding family problems and supplement and broaden the programs of the rural schools. They make a major contribution to the self-education of adults. Alvin S. Johnson, in *The Public Library—A People's University*, describes the functioning of libraries in the general adult education movement.

The functions that a library may perform are set forth in a leaflet issued by the American Library Association, *Education for the Asking*. A public library is described as a center for self-education, information, and recreation, free to people of all ages, races, beliefs, and occupations. It provides access to books, magazines, pamphlets, and maps, and, more recently, to films and recordings. Public libraries steadily are reaching out to make their services more directly available to users—through branch libraries, deposit stations, and bookmobiles.

Many of the people of rural America, however, do not have access to public library service. According to statistics compiled by the American Library Association in 1944, 34,748,334 persons, or 26 per cent of the total population of the United States, are without such service, and of this number 28,111,286, or 92.7 per cent, are rural residents. (This statement omits Alabama and Texas because separate urban and rural figures are not available for these states.) They constitute 57 per cent of the total rural population. There are 587 counties without any public libraries, and the resources of many small libraries are very inadequate.

These inequalities, the reasons therefor, and suggestions for overcoming them are set forth simply and graphically in a publication of the American Library Association, *The Equal Chance; Books Help to Make It.* Basic among the reasons for unequal service are differences of income among states and between urban and rural areas within states. Sparseness of population is a contributing factor in many rural areas. Still another factor in some states is inadequate leadership and stimulus to cooperation; leadership and stimulation must come largely from state library extension agencies.

Not only are the library resources of the nation very unevenly distributed; there is a comparable unevenness in the distribution of other educational and communications resources—school services, agencies of adult education, bookstores, magazines, daily newspapers, moving pictures, radios, and telephones. Where library resources are abundant, these are also abundant; conversely, where libraries are scarce, these other resources are also scarce. "If the drift from rural areas to urban centers, which has characterized American population trends in the past, continues in the future, as it seems it will, America, in replenishing its great metropolitan centers, will draw upon those areas in which reading facilities are least available and where the benefits which flow from reading have been only partly realized." These conclusions result from an extensive study which is reported in Louis R. Wilson's *The Geography of Reading.*

COUNTY AND REGIONAL UNITS

Among the principal suggestions for improving library service to rural areas is the development of larger units of organization and support. Larger units provide a stronger local tax base and a larger clientele. These, in turn, make possible more extensive and diversified collections of library materials, the employment of trained personnel, and lower per capita administrative costs for a given quality of service.

The greatest success to date in the direction of larger library units is the development of county systems. California was the first state to adopt a county pattern for the whole state. More recently, with state aid, Ohio has developed county service for 62 of its 88 counties, and North Carolina for 83 of its 100 counties. New Jersey also has fairly complete coverage. Thirty-six additional states have some county systems.

Many counties, however, are too small to be satisfactory units of library service; in such instances it is desirable to establish regional systems. Such systems have taken several forms. Vermont, which was well supplied with small, inadequate libraries, has divided the state into four regions, each with its regional library supported primarily by the state. This pattern is spreading to other New England states. Michigan's postwar plan calls for seventeen regional branches of the state library. In the Tennessee Valley area, seven regional library systems have been developed as a result of the need for providing books and periodicals to workers on Tennessee Valley Authority projects. The Authority has stimulated local establishment and improvement of library service and has contracted to have an existing library agency extend service to the area from which the employees come. The state library agency has supplied assistance of various kinds. It is encouraging that as the TVA has finished particular construction programs and withdrawn support, the state has furnished aid to make possible the continuance of the regional systems.

Some 720 counties in the United States now have public library service organized on a county basis or for regions made up of from two to thirteen counties. County, regional, and other new patterns of rural library service are described in Leon Carnovsky's "Library Service to Rural Communities," a chapter in *Education for Rural America*.

A statement of reasons for the establishment of regional and related types of libraries, a description of established regional systems, and a discussion of policy questions relating to regional systems is contained in *Regional and District Libraries,* issued by the Library Extension Board of the American Library Association. There it is stated:

In a large unit library system, each community branch is kept fresh and live through frequent exchange of books, and any book in the system is made available as needed. The services of an able librarian and specialists in various fields, as adult education or work with children, are shared. Even a very small community has an "open channel to specialized services." By pooling library resources over a large area, everyone shares in a library service that can actually be an educational force.

In a county or regional library system, books and other reading materials are taken to all parts of the service area from a headquarters library. They are distributed through branch libraries located in community centers; through service stations located in stores, filling stations, schools, and homes; and by bookmobiles, trailers, or buses that make regular trips to various parts of the service area. The smaller lending collections are frequently exchanged so that readers may have fresh materials.

The methods used to operate county library systems in Ohio are described in Mildred W. Sandoe's *County Library Primer*. This volume also contains much illustrative material—forms, standards, statistics, and a recommended list of adult books for bookmobile and branch collections.

State Library Agencies

The vitality of library service depends in large degree upon the quality of leadership provided by the state library agency. In many communities adequate library service depends also upon state grants-in-aid. Forty-seven states have set up official state library extension agencies to serve local communities. These agencies vary widely in form of organization, resources, services, and quality of leadership. Nineteen states make appropriations to aid in the development of large units of library service, and many more give some form of aid. Many states now have, also, carefully prepared plans for the development of adequate library service for their states; such plans often provide for the organization of the state on a regional basis for library service.

A discussion of state functions in library service and information on their status is presented by Julia Wright Merrill in "State Responsibility for Public Library Development," an article in *The Book of the States, 1945-46*. *The State Library Agency; Its Functions and Organization* and *State Grants to Public Libraries* are publications of the Library Extension Board of the American Library Association. The first of these publications describes the present functions and form of organization of state library agencies (data presented on individual states), makes recommendations as to desirable types and the principles that should govern all types, and indicates ways and means of achieving the desired organization. The second presents the case for state aid, describes the state-aid situation, discusses policy matters, and indicates steps to be taken in securing state aid. Results of state aid reported by state leaders include rapid spread of library service to persons previously without it, encouragement of units large enough to be effective, stimulation of local efforts and appropriations, strengthening of existing libraries, and improvement of personnel. Current information on amounts of state aid and a mimeographed directory of state library extension agencies may be obtained from the American Library Association, 50 East Huron St., Chicago, Illinois.

THE FEDERAL GOVERNMENT AND LIBRARIES

The whole relationship of the federal government to library service is canvassed by Carleton B. Joeckel in *Library Service,* a study prepared for the Advisory Committee on Education. The study concludes that the federal government (1) should synthesize and correlate its own departmental library functions, should expand and extend its technical and bibliographic services to the maximum limit of their potential usefulness, and through its library agency in the Office of Education should take an active part in the development of library service throughout the nation; (2) should cooperate in the development of some type of regional library service; and (3) should provide financial aid in order to establish a national minimum standard of library service.

The federal government gave much direct aid to libraries throughout the United States under the program of the Work Projects Administration. An evaluation of this assistance and a discussion of its implications for future federal library aid are contained in Edward Barrett Stanford's *Library Extension under the WPA; An Appraisal of an Experiment in Federal Aid.*

LIBRARY EXTENSION

Various aspects of library extension are discussed in a volume, *Library Extension; Problems and Solutions,* Carleton B. Joeckel, editor, made up of the papers presented before the Library Institute at the University of Chicago in August, 1944. One group of papers is concerned with the problem of the organization of library service at the level of local government; other papers consider the role of the state in library extension and state and federal aid. Integrated with the discussion are a number of papers that describe similar problems in other areas of public service. In his introduction the editor states that the papers indicate substantial approval of three principal conclusions, which may be translated into a simplified national library plan containing the following essential elements:

1. A system of perhaps not more than one thousand strong local public library units, embracing the entire territorial area of the United States.
2. Forty-eight effective state library agencies, with sufficient state aid within each state to insure a basic library program.
3. A nation-wide minimum level of library service sustained by grants-in-aid by the federal government.

SETTING LIBRARY STANDARDS

The Committee on Postwar Planning of the American Library Association has developed standards for the various phases of library service, which are set forth in *Post-War Standards for Public Libraries*. A summary of these recommendations is contained in a pamphlet, *Standards and Planning for Public Libraries*. The Committee recommends units of library service large enough to provide essential services and efficient administration. Such units should be able to provide a minimum of $25,000 per year for the support of the library. There should be a state library agency that plans and helps to develop statewide public library service. There should be state grants-in-aid to supplement local appropriations or to provide minimum service. The recommended annual per capita expenditure to assure limited or minimum service is $1.00; reasonably good service, $1.50; superior service, $2.00. (The per capita expenditure for public libraries for the entire population of the United States in 1941 was 42 cents; for the population served, 58 cents.)

For the country as a whole there is less than one book (0.87) per capita available in public libraries. Figures for many rural areas would be much lower. The Committee recommends standard sizes of book collections as follows—3.0 volumes per capita for service areas of 6,000–10,000 population; 2.5 for areas of 10,000–35,000 population; 2.0 for 35,000–100,000; and 1.75 to 1.0 for larger populations. A minimum stock is 6,000 volumes regardless of the population served. A library collection should reflect the basic library objectives of education, information, aesthetic appreciation, recreation, and research; should include books, pamphlets, periodicals, newspapers, maps, pictures, films, recordings, and music scores; should meet the needs of readers of all ages and of varied interests and educational backgrounds; should make available the best literature of civilization, books in all fields of knowledge, and books for children and young people; should represent all sides of controversial subjects; and should be kept alive and up to date.

Other recommendations of the Committee on Postwar Planning relate to library government, library staff, and buildings.

A summary of the planning for libraries engaged in by the American Library Association, its various boards and committees, and affiliated and related organizations is contained in Louis R. Wilson's *Library Planning*. This memorandum indicates the plans libraries have formulated for their future development, and further problems or areas of librarianship that should be studied with a view to formulating plans to insure the maximum contribution of libraries to reconstruction in the postwar era.

ADDITIONAL REFERENCES

Libraries belong to and serve citizens. Citizen interest and action in extending and improving library service are therefore of primary importance. Practical suggestions as to what the rural leader can do to secure information on available state library service and to promote effective service for his community are set forth in *Rural Public Library Service,* a pamphlet of the American Library Association.

A description of what library service does and can mean to rural adults is contained in Marion Humble's *Rural America Reads; A Study of Rural Library Service.*

It is pointed out in the introduction to *The Library in the Community,* made up of a series of papers presented before the Library Institute at the University of Chicago, 1943, edited by Leon Carnovsky and Lowell Martin, that the quality that distinguishes American public libraries from all others is their close identity with the community. This series of papers, prepared by a group of social scientists and social planners, describes the social structure of the several types of community in the United States in relation to library service.

Public Libraries in the Life of the Nation, by Beatrice Sawyer Rossell, was prepared to give young people an idea of the opportunities open to them in urban, rural, school, and special libraries. Concerned primarily with library service at the local level, it is also useful in giving a brief, comprehensive view of the significance of public libraries in American life.

Current developments in library service may be followed in several periodicals. The *A.L.A. Bulletin,* the official organ of the American Library Association, carries news of the Association, addresses of conference speakers, articles by official representatives of the Association, and brief professional communications. The Association is the professional organization that provides leadership for librarians and furthers the extension of library services throughout the country. The *Library Quarterly* is a journal of investigation and discussion published by the Graduate Library School of the University of Chicago. It carries reviews of current publications. *The Library Journal* is a semimonthly publication containing articles and book notes.

BIBLIOGRAPHY

A.L.A. Bulletin. Published by the American Library Association, 50 East Huron St., Chicago, Illinois, monthly except August; semimonthly in October and December.

American Library Association. *Education for the Asking.* Chicago: The Association, 6 pp.

——. *The Equal Chance; Books Help to Make It.* Chicago: The Association, 1943, 32 pp.

——. *Rural Public Library Service.* Chicago: The Association, 1945, 12 pp.

——. *Standards and Planning for Public Libraries.* Based on *Post-War Standards for Public Libraries.* Chicago: The Association, 1944, 12 pp.

——. Committee on Postwar Planning. *Post-War Standards for Public Libraries.* Chicago: The Association, 1943, 92 pp. (Bibliographical footnotes.)

——. Library Extension Board. *Regional and District Libraries.* Compiled by Julia Wright Merrill. Rev. ed. Chicago: The Association, 1942, 41 pp.

——. ——. *State Grants to Public Libraries.* Compiled by Julia Wright Merrill. Rev. ed. Chicago: The Association, 1942, 69 pp.

——. ——. *The State Library Agency; Its Functions and Organization.* Organization data compiled by Julia Wright Merrill. 5th ed. Chicago: The Association, 1945, 42 pp.

Carnovsky, Leon. "Library Service to Rural Communities," in *Education for Rural America.* Chicago: University of Chicago Press, 1945, pp. 143-59.

—— and Lowell Martin, eds. *The Library in the Community; Papers Presented before the Library Institute at the University of Chicago, August 23-28, 1943.* Chicago: University of Chicago Press, 1944, 238 pp. (Selected reading list, pp. 224-32.)

Humble, Marion. *Rural America Reads; A Study of Rural Library Service.* New York: American Association for Adult Education, 1938, 101 pp.

Joeckel, Carleton B. *Library Service.* Washington: Government Printing Office, 1938, 107 pp.

——, ed. *Library Extension; Problems and Solutions.* Chicago: University of Chicago Press, 1946, 260 pp.

Johnson, Alvin S. *The Public Library—A People's University.* New York: American Association for Adult Education, 1938, 85 pp.

The Library Journal. 62 West 45th St., New York, semimonthly September to June, inclusive; monthly July-August.

Library Quarterly. Chicago: University of Chicago Press, 5750 Ellis Ave., Chicago, Illinois.

Merrill, Julia Wright. "State Responsibility for Public Library Development," in *The Book of the States, 1945-46.* Chicago: The Council of State Governments, 1945, pp. 366-70.

Rossell, Beatrice Sawyer. *Public Libraries in the Life of the Nation*. Chicago: American Library Association, 1943, 105 pp. (Bibliography, pp. 103-5.)

Sandoe, Mildred W. *County Library Primer*. New York: H. W. Wilson Co., 1942, 221 pp. (Bibliography, pp. 133-37.)

Stanford, Edward Barrett. *Library Extension under the WPA; An Appraisal of an Experiment in Federal Aid*. Chicago: University of Chicago Press, 1944, 284 pp. (Bibliography, pp. 269-84.)

U. S. Department of Agriculture. *Rural Library Service*. Farmers' Bulletin No. 1847. Washington: Government Printing Office, 1940, 27 pp.

Wilson, Louis R. *The Geography of Reading; A Study of the Distribution and Status of Libraries in the United States*. Chicago: American Library Association and the University of Chicago Press, 1938, 481 pp. (Selected bibliography, pp. 443-60.)

——. *Library Planning; A Working Memorandum*. Chicago: American Library Association, 1944, 93 pp. (References, pp. 85-93.)

4 *THE CHURCH*

THE CHURCH occupies an important place in rural life. Churches have the allegiance of large numbers of people and provide them spiritual, social, and recreational satisfactions. They can be a factor in rural progress, and their vitality reflects and also influences the vitality of rural community life.

PRESENT STATUS

In a chapter "The Rural Church and Its Problems," in his volume *Rural Sociology and Rural Social Organization*, Dwight Sanderson discusses trends relating to the rural church—its finances, program, organization, ministerial leadership, the results of competition from overchurching, and the evidences of church cooperation. He cites numerous statistics, principally from surveys of village-centered agricultural communities made by E. deS. Brunner and his associates in the nineteen-twenties and thirties, and draws conclusions therefrom. (Citations to these studies are given in Chapter 12. Citations to several other publications of Brunner relating to the rural church appear at the end of the present chapter.) The data generally seem to indicate a decline in the rural church. The number of churches both in the open country and in villages is being gradually reduced. The rate of reduction is somewhat greater in the open country than in villages, and increasing numbers of farm families are attending village churches. While the total number of church members increased from 1924 to 1936, the increase was not so great as the increase in population. Church attendance declined. Causes of rural church decline include a declining population in many rural counties, too great a number of churches in many communities, and increased church costs and lack of financial resources to meet them.

The chief function of the church in the past has been Sunday preaching, but interest is gradually shifting toward an educational program, character building in nature. Newer-type programs call for ministers and buildings suited to the accomplishment of these programs. More effort needs to go into training Sunday school teachers and leaders for youth work. The minister must do more pastoral work and carry his share of leadership in civic movements for community improvement.

Enrollments in village and country Sunday schools are small, on the average. Although graded lessons have been available for a number of years, most rural Sunday schools are using the same lessons for all ages. It is desirable to have larger Sunday schools with enough pupils to permit grading. In some places school buses are being used to transport children to larger Sunday schools.

Organizations for various groups in rural churches are not especially strong. Young people's societies have declined in number and membership in recent years. There are women's organizations such as the Ladies' Aid and the Women's Missionary Society in only a few more than half the rural churches. Men's clubs are few in number, as are organizations for boys and girls.

In discussing ministerial leadership, Sanderson points out that village pastors have much better training than pastors of country churches. Resident ministers are also more often college or seminary graduates than are those who do not reside in the communities they serve. Small country churches with nonresidential ministers have the poorest leadership.

A major handicap of many rural ministers is their lack of knowledge of agriculture and country life, a knowledge which is essential for them to understand the problems and attitudes of their parishioners. As yet very few theological seminaries give any special training for the rural ministry. ... To meet this situation there has been established in the last three years a conference of the theological seminaries and the colleges of agriculture, which has aroused considerable interest among both parties and which promises much for ruralizing the point of view of the seminaries and giving new standing to recruiting prospective rural pastors in the agricultural colleges. Many state agricultural colleges also hold summer short courses for town and country ministers, with the cooperation of denominational boards and state councils of churches.[1]

Rural pastors are also poorly paid in comparison to members of other professions. Short tenure is another handicap.

The financial condition of rural churches generally is poor, as a result largely of their excessive number and small membership. While the number of churches is decreasing somewhat, the process is slow. Sanderson points out that rural schools and rural churches are in similar positions relative to financial aid and that there are like reasons for equalizing church support.

---

[1] This excerpt and the one on page 51 are reprinted by permission from *Rural Sociology and Rural Social Organization* by Dwight Sanderson, published by John Wiley and Sons, Inc.

This has been partially accomplished by so-called home missionary aid from city to rural churches, but in too many instances this has been used chiefly to maintain competing churches. The problem goes much further and deeper. The city church depends quite largely upon members and clergy who have come from the country, and without them it would lose much of its vitality. If it is just to tax the cities for the support of rural schools, is it not equally fair for them to help in maintaining the rural churches through an equalization of church funds, so that the rural minister may have an adequate standard of living, may be able to purchase the books he needs, and educate his children?

A forward step taken by several of the leading Protestant denominations, under the leadership of the Home Missions Council, is the setting up of a master list of communities in which home mission aid is being given to competing churches. Representatives of state or county councils of churches then work with the local churches to close unnecessary churches. Local churches, themselves, are taking action to form united or community churches of various types. They are also developing cooperative programs which result in greater service at less cost.

Rockwell S. Smith, in *The Church in Our Town; A Study of the Relationship between the Church and the Rural Community,* points out that the church is the strongest voluntary agency in rural society. But rural churches tend to be competitive. They have inadequate economic resources for pastor and program and are not likely to command the best pastoral leadership. It is important to pull programs and churches into a single religious effort for the whole community. The author suggests ways in which this end may be accomplished. This book has been written especially for churchmen. It is about the church as a group among groups and utilizes materials from the fields of rural sociology and agricultural economics as they bear upon the work of the rural church.

The Church in Rural Life, by David Edgar Lindstrom, "touches the present socio-economic situation as it affects the farm family." Two emphases stand out: " (1) the insistence that economic and social security must be stabilized and assured for the farmer if the best in rural and national life is to be preserved; and (2) that all institutions and particularly the church in the whole of society must work tirelessly toward that end; the institutions must be a means and not an end in this struggle for security."

Mark A. Dawber states in his introduction to *Rebuilding Rural America* that "we must put an end to the waste and chaos and bring the wild, competing forces that are disrupting rural life into the

service of harmony, cooperation and community friendship. . . .
This is the real challenge . . . which the church must meet: to create
a new motive for life." This book gives considerable attention to the
place of cooperatives in rural communities.

Luigi G. Ligutti and John C. Rawe's *Rural Roads to Security* is
written "for the purpose of presenting some of the steps that must be
taken to rebuild our land, our homes, our democracy, our culture, and
our religion." They hold that "what could easily have endured as a
nation of secure and free, landowning people, through an intelligent
'agriculture' on our two billion acres, has become a nation of servile
dependents."

CONFERENCE REPORTS

The reports of several national conferences and convocations on
the problems of the rural church contain valuable materials. *The
Rural Church Today & Tomorrow* and *The Church and the Agricultural Situation* cover two such conferences held in 1936. Each
publication contains a number of papers bearing upon the relationship of the church to fundamental social and economic problems of
rural communities. *What Emphasis for the Church in Town and
Country?* is a report of the National Convocation on the Church in
Town and Country held in 1943. It contains the papers and commission reports of a meeting attended by 450 persons from forty-one
states of the United States and from Canada. The convocation came
into being because prominent laymen asked for it, because of considerable sentiment among ministers and laity that the church at large
should know more about the contributions of the church in small
communities, and because of a desire to offer more opportunity for
ministers and lay leaders of town and country churches to meet and
consider their special needs and interests.

The Town and Country Committee expects, through the Convocation,
to increase cooperation among rural churches; to bring together the leaders
of the rural church and of rural community agencies; to improve the administration of the rural church; to help to stimulate the development of a
Christian philosophy of rural life.

A second convocation, held in 1944, was attended by 645 persons from
twenty-five or more denominations living in forty states and Canada.
The publication *Urgent Tasks of the Church in Town and Country*
contains the papers presented at the meeting, digests of commission
reports, and general actions of the convocation. There were papers on

such subjects as the church in the rural life movement, the mission of soil conservation, social issues in rural life and agriculture, the rural minister as a modern homesteader, and how young people may become farm owners.

Three reports relating to the church and land tenure in different parts of the United States have resulted from conferences sponsored by the Land Tenure Committee of the Town and Country Committee of the Home Missions Council and the Federal Council of Churches of Christ in America in cooperation with the Farm Foundation. Each report is made up of a series of papers. The first conference was held in cooperation with the Committee on Land Tenure in the Corn Belt, in October, 1940, and resulted in the publication *The Church and Land Tenure*. The second meeting was held in cooperation with the Southwestern Regional Land Tenure Committee, in May, 1941; it was reported in *The People, the Land and the Church in the Rural South*. The third report included papers resulting from a series of conferences in western states in 1943 and was published under the title *The People, the Land, and the Church in the Rural West*.

The Southern Rural Life Conference in its report *The School and the Changing Pattern of Country Life* devotes a chapter to the present status of, and trends in, the rural church. Major problems relate to awakening needed vision and getting statesmanlike planning; securing necessary support; securing reasonably Christian economic and social conditions in rural areas; serving the whole population, including the neediest and minority groups; using all the resources of all the churches to help build the new rural America; securing worthy buildings and equipment; and securing skilled and devoted leadership.

Special Studies and Reports

Youth Work in the Rural Church, by Mark Rich and Others, was written to answer numerous questions about program planning in the rural church. It was conceived along interdenominational lines and can be used by leaders and young people in classes in local church or summer conferences.

A study of the effect of the war on the churches of one community is described in Lowry Nelson's *Red Wing Churches during the War*. It concludes that these churches do not seem to have grasped the significance of recent world events and raises the question of where leadership may be expected to develop.

Rural Life in a Peaceful World is a statement of principles and method adopted at the wartime meeting of the Executive Committee and Advisory Board, National Catholic Rural Life Conference, January 12, 1944. Actions advocated include reform of tenancy laws and strengthening of measures that encourage ownership of family-type farms, a living wage and social security benefits for farm workers, fair prices for farm products, the extension of cooperatives, and improved social services and rural institutions.

Hoosier Churches; A Study of the Rural Congregational Christian Churches of Indiana is a study published by the Indiana Congregational Christian Conference in cooperation with the Town and Country Department, Church Extension Division, Board of Home Missions, Congregational Christian Churches.

In *Life in the Larger Parish,* Margaret J. Harris tells the story of how Van Hornersville, New York, provided religious instruction through the creation of the larger parish .

The land-grant colleges have made a number of studies of the rural church in various states and of special rural-church problems. These have been issued as experiment station or extension service bulletins.

B. H. Cain's book *The Church Ministering to Rural Life* is based on the experience of the author as pastor and superintendent of rural churches and discusses the work of the Commission on Rural Life of the United Brethren Church.

The Christian Mission among Rural People was prepared primarily for the use of rural missionaries and ministers. It is appropriate also for the use of those training for these callings and for persons responsible for determining mission and church policy and program.

The Christian Rural Fellowship has issued two reprints of interest to those concerned with the rural church. One, *The Holy Earth,* by L. H. Bailey, was originally published in 1915. The other is *The Story of John Frederic Oberlin,* by Augustus Field Beard, published in 1909.

PERIODICALS

The Christian Rural Fellowship Bulletin, published monthly by the Christian Rural Fellowship, carries articles on rural problems related to the church.

Town and Country Church is published nine times a year by the Committee on Town and Country, Home Missions Council of North America, the Federal Council of Churches of Christ in America, and the International Council of Religious Education. It carries brief items on what people are doing in local congregations and communities in order to help put the workers in the small community in touch with numerous activities. The issue of September, 1945, contains "Man's Relation to the Land; A Statement of Principles which should underlie our national, state and individual actions," signed by Protestant, Catholic, and Jewish leaders.

Religious Education for March–April, 1945, carries a symposium, "Religious Education in Rural America."

Current publications relating to the rural church are frequently noted in the quarterly journal *Rural Sociology.*

The Rural Church; A Publication for Religious Leaders of the Middle West is published by Garrett Biblical Institute, Evanston, Illinois, an institution especially interested in training ministers for rural churches. For a number of summers the Institute has conducted an interdenominational school for rural leaders.

Some periodical publications of particular church groups directed to rural problems are here listed. *Land and Home* is the monthly publication of the National Catholic Rural Life Conference. The *Rural Lutheran* is issued six times yearly. The *Methodist Rural Fellowship Bulletin* is issued three times a year. *The Rural Messenger* is the quarterly publication of the National Council of the Episcopal Church, Division of Domestic Missions.

Social Action, published monthly by the Council for Social Action of the Congregational Christian Churches, carries in its issue for May 15, 1945, "Adventures in Rural Community Action," by Shirley E. Greene, which seeks "to illustrate by actual case studies the basic nature of rural social problems, the need for a philosophy and program of rural social change and the outlines for a technique of rural community action."

BIBLIOGRAPHY

Bailey, L. H. *The Holy Earth.* New York: The Christian Rural Fellowship (156 Fifth Ave.), 1943, 117 pp. Reprinted in cooperation with the author. Copyright 1915.

Beard, Augustus Field. *The Story of John Frederic Oberlin.* New York: The Christian Rural Fellowship, 1946, 100 pp. Reprinted with the permission of the Pilgrim Press. Copyright 1909.

Brunner, Edmund deS. *The Church and the Agricultural Crisis.* Boston: Pilgrim Press, 1928, 48 pp. (Bibliography, pp. 45-48.)

——.*Industrial Village Churches.* New York: Institute of Social and Religious Research, 1930, 193 pp.

——.*The Larger Parish, a Movement or an Enthusiasm?* New York: Institute of Social and Religious Research, 1934, 95 pp.

Cain, B. H. *The Church Ministering to Rural Life.* Dayton, Ohio: The Home Mission and Church Erection Society, The Church of the United Brethren in Christ, [1941], 104 pp. (Bibliography, pp. 103-4.)

The Christian Mission among Rural People. New York: Rural Missions Cooperating Committee of the Foreign Missions Conference of North America, 1945, 334 pp. (Bibliography, pp. 318-29.)

The Christian Rural Fellowship Bulletin. Monthly publication of the Christian Rural Fellowship, 156 Fifth Ave., New York.

The Church and the Agricultural Situation. A Report of the National Conference on the Rural Church, Iowa State College, Ames, Iowa, November 23-25, 1936. Under the auspices of the Home Missions Council and the Council of Women for Home Missions, 105 East 22nd St., New York. With the cooperation of the Agricultural Extension Service of the Iowa State College. 85 pp.

Dawber, Mark A. *Rebuilding Rural America.* New York: Friendship Press, 1937, 210 pp. (Reading list, pp. 205-10.)

Greene, Shirley E. "Adventures in Rural Community Action." *Social Action,* May 15, 1945, pp. 4-32.

Harris, Margaret J. *Life in the Larger Parish.* New York: Committee on Town and Country, Home Missions Council of North America and the Federal Council of the Churches of Christ in America, 1944, 89 pp. (Bibliography, pp. 86-89.)

Hoosier Churches; A Study of the Rural Congregational Christian Churches of Indiana. Indiana Congregational Christian Conference in cooperation with Town and Country Department, Church Extension Division, Board of Home Missions, Congregational Christian Churches, New York, 1943, 51 pp. (Some reading suggestions, p. 51.)

Land and Home. Monthly publication of the National Catholic Rural Life Conference, 3801 Grand Ave., Des Moines, Iowa.

Land Tenure Committee of the Town and Country Committee of the Home Missions Council and the Federal Council of Churches in Cooperation with the Farm Foundation. *The Church and Land Tenure.* Chicago: Farm Foundation, 1940, 102 pp.

——. *The People, the Land and the Church in the Rural South.* Chicago: Farm Foundation, 1941, 232 pp.

——. *The People, the Land, and the Church in the Rural West.* Chicago: Farm Foundation, 1943, 172 pp.

Ligutti, Luigi G. and John C. Rawe. *Rural Roads to Security; America's Third Struggle for Freedom.* Milwaukee: Bruce Publishing Co., 1940, 387 pp. (Selected bibliography, pp. 361-78.)

Lindstrom, David Edgar. *The Church in Rural Life.* Champaign, Illinois: Garrard Press, 1939, 145 pp. (Revised edition issued in 1946.)

"Man's Relation to the Land; A Statement of Principles which should under-lie our national, state and individual actions." *Town and Country Church,* September 1945, pp. 1-3.

Methodist Rural Fellowship Bulletin. Published three times yearly at Town Hall, Pennsylvania.

National Catholic Rural Life Conference. *Rural Life in a Peaceful World.* Des Moines, Iowa: The Conference (3801 Grand Ave.), 26 pp.

Nelson, Lowry. *Red Wing Churches during the War.* The Community Basis for Postwar Planning, No. 7. Minneapolis: University of Minnesota Press, 1946, 21 pp.

"Religious Education in Rural America: A Symposium." *Religious Education,* March–April 1945, pp. 67-91.

Rich, Mark and Others. *Youth Work in the Rural Church.* St. Louis, Missouri: Bethany Press, 1940, 112 pp. (Sources of information, pp. 107-12.)

The Rural Church; A Publication for Religious Leaders of the Middle West. Garrett Biblical Institute, Evanston, Illinois. (Issues per year?)

The Rural Church Today & Tomorrow; A Report of the National Conference on the Rural Church. Under the auspices of the Home Missions Council and the Council of Women for Home Missions, 105 East 22nd St., New York, 90 pp. (Bibliography, pp. 83-85.)

Rural Lutheran. Bimonthly. Subscriptions to O. G. Salveson, Business Manager, Flandreau, South Dakota.

The Rural Messenger. Quarterly publication of the National Council of the Episcopal Church, Division of Domestic Missions, 281 Fourth Ave., New York.

Rural Sociology. East University, Louisiana, Louisiana State University Press. Quarterly.

Sanderson, Dwight. "The Rural Church and Its Problems," in *Rural Sociology and Rural Social Organization.* New York: John Wiley & Sons, 1942, pp. 308-43. (References, pp. 342-43.)

Smith, Rockwell S. *The Church in Our Town; A Study of the Relationship between the Church and the Rural Community.* New York: Abingdon-Cokesbury Press, 1945, 190 pp. (Bibliography, pp. 185-88.)

Southern Rural Life Conference. "The Rural Church," in *The School and the Changing Pattern of Country Life.* Report of the Southern Rural Life Conference Sponsored by George Peabody College for Teachers, Vanderbilt University, Scarritt College, Fisk University. Nashville, Tennessee: The Conference, 1943, pp. 47-58.

Town and Country Church. Published nine times a year by the Committee on Town and Country, Home Missions Council of North America, the Federal Council of the Churches of Christ in America, and the International Council of Religious Education, 297 Fourth Ave., New York.

Urgent Tasks of the Church in Town and Country; A Report of the National Convocation on the Church in Town and Country, Elgin, Illinois, November 14-16, 1944. New York: Committee on Town and Country, Home Missions Council of North America, the Federal Council of the Churches of Christ in America, and the International Council of Religious Education (297 Fourth Ave.), 1945, 88 pp.

What Emphasis for the Church in Town and Country? A Report of the National Convocation on the Church in Town and Country, Columbus, Ohio, September 6-8, 1943. New York: Committee on Town and Country, Home Missions Council of North America and the Federal Council of the Churches of Christ in America (297 Fourth Ave.), 1943, 103 pp.

5 *MEDICAL CARE AND HEALTH SERVICES*

ADEQUATE medical, hospital, and health services are essential to the well-being of rural America. Large sectors of the rural population at present either lack entirely or suffer from a serious shortage of one or more needed services. Many rural counties have no physicians and no dentists. Others have only older practitioners. In one-third of the counties of the United States, counties that are predominantly rural, there are no hospitals of any type. Of the more than 3,000 counties, only 60 per cent have full-time public health service. This situation is partly responsible for the fact that farm boys drafted for World War II were rejected for physical defects to a greater extent than boys in any other major occupational group and, again, for the fact that maternal and infant death rates are high in many of the most rural states.

A number of factors contribute to the lack of medical and health services in rural areas. Among these factors are the high percentage of rural people with low incomes, the great variability in farm income from year to year, sparsity of population in many rural regions, the distances people must travel to secure the services of physicians and hospital care, poor roads and other deficiencies of transportation, in some instances lack of understanding of elementary health facts, and the lack of adequate enabling legislation for the establishment of public health units.

The situation of rural areas relative to health and medical care, the reasons for the situation, and actions taken and plans projected to improve it are described in a report, *Better Health for Rural America; Plans of Action for Farm Communities,* issued in October, 1945, by the Interbureau Committee on Post-War Programs of the United States Department of Agriculture. Another publication, *Medical Care and Health Services for Rural People,* also covers the general range of problems rural people face in obtaining medical care and health services, outlines the essentials of a rural health service, describes plans and proposals for developing an integrated health service for all the people, and sets forth possible lines of action to develop a constructive program of medical and health services for rural America. This publication resulted from a conference sponsored by the Farm Foundation in the spring of 1944, which brought together representatives of farm organizations, governmental agencies, and other groups interested in exploring the problem of rural health and medical care services and the efforts that are being made by governmental and private agencies toward solving it. A paper presented by Frederick D. Mott before the National Conference on Rural Health sponsored by the American Medical Association in 1946, "A Public Health Program for Rural Areas," appearing in *Public Health Reports* for April 26, 1946, presents pertinent data on the health and medical care situation of rural areas. A number of statements in subsequent paragraphs are based upon the information contained in these three sources.

A publication covering the medical care and health problems of a major rural section of the United States is *Medical Care and Health Services for Farm Families of the Northern Great Plains,* a report of a conference held in 1945 by the Subcommittee on Health of the Northern Great Plains Council. The purpose of the conference was "to pool available information regarding present health and medical facilities available in the plains region, to learn what needs are not now being met, and to initiate action among rural people looking toward a solution of their rather serious health and medical care predicament." The Subcommittee is concerned with health and medical care problems common to Kansas, Montana, Nebraska, North Dakota, South Dakota, and Wyoming, and is working toward the establishment of state and county health planning committees.

A publication of the United States Department of Agriculture, *What Farm Families Spend for Medical Care,* by Jean L. Pennock and Grace M. Angle, presents data on medical care expenditures of farm families at different income levels, medical care expenditures as they affect individual farm families, and rural-urban differences in medical care expenditures.

MEDICAL, DENTAL, AND NURSING PERSONNEL

There are great disparities in the availability of medical, dental, and nursing personnel in various parts of the country. In 1940, the national ratio of physicians to population was about 1 to 800; in three states, however, there were more than 1,500 persons per physician and in twenty-one more than 1,000. There are also great variations in the distribution of physicians within states as between urban and rural areas. Specialists, particularly, are concentrated in large cities and in wealthy communities.

It is pointed out in *Better Health for Rural America* that in view of the time it takes for a rural doctor to travel to see patients "a ratio of about one physician to 1,000 people, or even fewer, is probably necessary, if rural people are to enjoy a true parity of physicians' services with city people. Yet, in the thousand most rural and isolated counties just before the war, there were so few doctors that each one had to serve 1,700 people, while in the big city areas there was a doctor for each 650 people."

Maldistributions of dentists and nurses are equally or even more marked. "Although there probably ought to be 1 dentist for not more than every 1,500 people, most rural areas have hardly a third of this ratio. Before the war, there was 1 dentist to every 1,400 persons in the cities but only 1 to every 4,200 in the rural sections." In 1940 in the rural state of Mississippi there was only 1 active nurse for approximately 1,600 people, whereas in industrial Massachusetts there was 1 for each 250 people. Before the war in one state each public health nurse served an average of over 11,000 people as compared with fewer than 4,000 in another.

Facts relative to the trend of supply of physicians in rural areas are presented in an article by Joseph W. Mountin, Elliott H. Pennell, and George S. Brockett, "Location and Movement of Physicians, 1923 and 1938," in *Public Health Reports,* February 16, 1945. The combined effect of physician recruitment, migration, and losses from the profession in this period resulted in gains for both large and small cities and in losses for rural communities. Failure of rural areas to attract and retain their share of new practitioners resulted in a disproportionate number of older physicians in these areas. In 1923 the median age of rural physicians was four years above that for physicians in large cities; by 1938 the difference was ten years.

The situation of rural areas relative to services of physicians and rural-urban contrasts are also described in Bernhard J. Stern's *American Medical Practice in the Perspectives of a Century,* one of the monographs prepared for the Committee on Medicine and the Changing Order established by the Council of the New York Academy of Medicine in 1942. The monograph summarizes the data of many recent studies.

HOSPITAL FACILITIES

The hospital situation of rural areas is described in *Better Health for Rural America.* "Over 1,250 of the 3,070 counties in our Nation are without a single satisfactory general hospital. Over 700 of these counties have populations exceeding 10,000 people." It is suggested that for adequate service there should be about 4.5 general hospital beds per 1,000 persons, but that a variation between rural and urban areas is permissible in view of the number of cases of illness among rural people that are and should be referred to city hospitals for care. "While in the cities . . . 5.0 or more beds per 1,000 persons may be necessary, in the rural areas 3.5 or 4.0 general beds per 1,000 are probably adequate. The fact is that today most rural areas do not have even 2.0 beds per 1,000." County hospitals generally are smaller and less well equipped than city hospitals and lacking in "free" beds for the people who cannot pay for care.

Rural areas are also in a serious situation as regards hospital facilities for tuberculosis or mental disease and clinical and laboratory facilities. A satisfactory standard for care of tuberculars is 2.5 beds for every death from tuberculosis per year. "Yet in the 28 States that are over half rural there are only 0.9 TB beds for every death occurring from this disease, compared with a ratio of 1.8 beds per death in the 20 most urban States." To care for cases of mental disorder a standard of 5 beds per 1,000 persons is suggested; "the predominantly rural States have only 3.4 beds per 1,000, compared with 5.6 beds per 1,000 in the most urban States." "Public clinics or 'health centers' where people can come for diagnosis or treatment without necessarily being hospitalized, are practically unknown in rural areas" and "scientific laboratory facilities and well-trained technicians for helping the doctor to diagnose disease are scarce. . . ."

Joseph W. Mountin; Elliott H. Pennell; and Vane M. Hoge, in their study *Health Service Areas: Requirements for General Hospitals and Health Centers,* "have attempted to project a plan for an integrated scheme of hospitals and related facilities to cover every section of the nation. Certain concepts of service that are fairly well accepted by students of the subject and by practical hospital administrators are fitted into the existing structure of voluntary and public hospitals." They suggest that for adequate hospital service the country be divided into 760 districts offering varying types of service—126 primary districts, 528 secondary districts, and 106 isolated districts. Their plan would involve provision of some 165,000 new general hospital beds. They also suggest a plan for health centers that would furnish facilities for all agencies concerned with communitywide health services—400 administrative and 800 neighborhood units for cities of 25,000 or more, 6,000 combination administrative and service units for small cities and towns, and 7,000 units for remote rural areas. The report carries maps showing counties, districts, and regional areas and tables showing selected statistics for these areas, estimates of hospital beds needed, and estimates of health centers needed.

The federal Hospital Survey and Construction Act of August 13, 1946, authorizes the appropriation of $3,000,000 to assist the several states in surveying the need for hospital construction and developing programs for the construction of such public and other nonprofit hospitals as will, in conjunction with existing facilities, afford the necessary physical facilities for furnishing adequate hospital, clinic, and similar services to all their people. It also authorizes the appropriation of $375,000,000 over a five-year period to construct public and other nonprofit hospitals in accordance with such programs.

The nearly twenty years of experience of the Commonwealth Fund in the construction, organization, and operation of small community hospitals is described in *Small Community Hospitals,* by Henry J. Southmayd and Geddes Smith. The Fund has helped to build thirteen rural institutions and has given each of them advisory and consultant service. The objective has been to provide services measuring up to accepted standards at a cost that could be met by ordinarily prosperous rural communities. "The record shows that a rural community of 50,000 or 100,000 people, even if it spreads across county lines, *will* make effective use of a single central institution." There is still a definite gap, however, between the care offered in such hospitals and the best medical care to be had in almost any large city. The authors point out the need for much more experimentation with hospital services to small communities.

SANITATION

A national inventory of needs for rural sanitation facilities, described in an article by C. H. Atkins in *Public Health Reports* for July 28, 1944, may be summarized as follows: (1) Safe water supplies and sanitary methods of excreta disposal are essential for the protection of public health, and properly constructed and equipped wells and sanitary privies should be provided as the minimum facilities for this purpose; (2) approximately 50,000,000 people in the United States must utilize private water supplies and excreta disposal facilities; (3) although considerable progress has been made in the provision of safe water supplies and sanitary facilities for the rural population, about 5,294,000 rural homes now need new or improved water supplies and 5,100,000 rural homes need sanitary privies; (4) these rural sanitation needs should be met through intensive educational programs, enactment and enforcement of adequate sanitary ordinances, the full utilization of such local, state, and federal funds as may be available for this type of work, and the assignment of sufficient personnel to rural sanitation to carry on the necessary educational work and to give technical supervision to the construction and maintenance of water supplies and excreta disposal facilities.

In 1941 representatives of a number of federal governmental agencies and a representative of the Conference of State Sanitary Engineers organized a Joint Committee on Rural Sanitation for the purpose of developing uniform recommendations based upon sound field experience to insure safe water supplies and adequate measures for the disposal of sewage in rural and suburban areas. The Committee recommendations relative to sewage disposal appeared in *Public Health Reports* for March 12, 1943, under the title "Recommendations of Joint Committee on Rural Sanitation—Rural Sewage Disposal." They have also been made available in a reprint. They point out that the safe disposal of all human and domestic wastes is necessary to protect the health of families and the community and to prevent the occurrence of nuisances. *Rural Water-Supply Sanitation,* issued as Supplement No. 185 to the *Public Health Reports,* covers the sanitation aspects of "small water supplies used by one or possibly several families and by rural schools, recreational areas, camps, and similar developments which are without access to a public water-supply system." While both sets of recommendations have been prepared primarily to establish a uniform approach for various federal agencies concerned with the respective problems, it is hoped that they will also prove useful to state and local health authorities, other local governmental agencies, and individuals.

Forrest B. Wright's *Rural Water Supply and Sanitation* "is written for those who wish to gain a practical knowledge of water supply, sewage disposal, plumbing, and sanitation for rural homes and farms." The author has aimed to provide the reader with information that will permit him "to take the fullest advantage of the possible water sources provided by nature. . . ." He should be able "to plan and construct a safe, convenient, and sanitary sewage disposal system, and should be able to service and keep in repair his plumbing and sewage-disposal systems at a minimum expense."

Municipal and Rural Sanitation, by Victor M. Ehlers and Ernest W. Steele, is a condensed work on environmental sanitation.

NUTRITION

A bulletin of the National Research Council, *Inadequate Diets and Nutritional Deficiencies in the United States; Their Prevalence and Significance,* sets forth the results of a large number of dietary surveys and nutritional appraisals made during recent years. It also includes a considerable amount of previously unpublished material. A number of surveys of rural communities are considered. Every nutritional survey in the past decade has revealed that the consumption of diets below the recommended standards is widespread in the United States. When the results of certain of these surveys were re-evaluated against the recommended schedule of the Food and Nutrition Board of the National Research Council, it was found that fewer than one-fifth of the families in the United States had food supplies in 1936 that met the Council's recommendations with respect to the seven nutrients studied. About one-fourth of the farm families were in this category.

Through the activities of many national, state, and local official and nonofficial agencies and commercial organizations, people generally are becoming increasingly aware of nutritional needs and ways of meeting them. Publications on various phases of food and nutrition problems and their solution have been produced in the federal government by the Children's Bureau; the Office of Education; and the Bureau of Human Nutrition and Home Economics and the War Food Administration of the Department of Agriculture; in the states by the state extension services and education, health, and other departments; and at the local level by a variety of public and private health and educational agencies. The Nutrition Division of the United States Office of Defense Health and Welfare Services has issued a pamphlet, *Democracy Means All of Us,* which describes how communities can organize to study and meet community needs, with special suggestions for developing nutrition programs in wartime. The National Planning Association has issued *A Food and Nutrition Program for the Nation; A Report of the Subcommittee of the Agriculture, Business, and Labor Committees on National Policy.*

PUBLIC HEALTH SERVICES

It is pointed out by Frederick D. Mott in "A Public Health Program for Rural Areas" that "the whole pattern of rural deaths and rural disease is more like that found in the Nation as a whole in 1900 than is the corresponding urban pattern. . . . The picture still has some resemblance to the situation when infectious diseases and the results of grossly inadequate sanitation were prevalent everywhere. The implications are clear; organized preventive services in rural communities must be strengthened and must be broadened."

Direct public health services are administered largely by local health units. In 1942, however, there were still 1,242 counties without full-time county or district health departments. Competent authorities agree that a $2 per capita annual expenditure is needed to provide satisfactory public health services. In rural counties expenditures are hardly 50 cents annually.

An effective organization and program of public health work "can promote good sanitation, farm safety, the prevention and control of acute communicable diseases or venereal infection or tuberculosis, the care of expectant mothers and of infants, the protection of children in and out of school, the improvement of nutrition, the education of all people about healthful living." These objectives are stated in *Better Health for Rural America*.

Larger cities generally have well-developed maternal and child health programs, but the programs in most small towns and villages are limited. In approximately one-fourth of the counties of the United States there is no public health nursing service, in almost three-fourths monthly prenatal clinics are not available, and in two-thirds there are no monthly child health conferences. Only one-fourth of the counties have all three of these types of service. Very few small communities have outpatient clinics to which children can be taken, and few have a pediatrician available for local consultation. Although all cities of 100,000 population and over have developed systems of medical inspection of school children, this service is inadequately developed in the smaller communities and in rural areas. The health activities and functions of schools are described in a chapter, "The Schools and Rural Health," in *Rural America Today,* by George A. Works and Simon O. Lesser.

Welfare, recreation, public works, and other local government departments also provide various services related to health. The vitality of health programs depends largely upon proper coordination and the full use of resources at the community level. It is important to secure cooperation among physicians, hospitals, official health agencies, and other government departments conducting programs. In some areas, cities, counties, and townships are offering duplicating services. In some states legislative authorization is lacking to permit adjacent communities or counties to pool their health service resources in order to reduce overhead expense, provide a wider tax base, and furnish more effective services.

State and federal governmental agencies also provide a variety of health services and serve to stimulate the work of local agencies. All states have health departments with fairly well-defined functions. Many health activities are also carried on by other state agencies. Among their activities, state health departments provide leadership and coordination for local agencies, establish and enforce minimum standards, carry on research and educational activities, provide central laboratory services, publish vital statistics, and provide a variety of direct services, particularly in rural areas. They also route federal funds destined for local health departments to these departments. The agricultural experiment stations and the extension services in a number of states have issued bulletins and pamphlets relating to various problems of medical care and health service in their respective states.

In the federal government the principal health agency is the United States Public Health Service; a large number of other agencies also participate to some degree in public health or medical care activities. The program of the Farm Security Administration to promote group medical care for farmers is described later in this chapter. The FSA has also given impetus to rural sanitation activities through farm inspections and an environmental sanitation program. The work of the Children's Bureau, which includes health activities, is described in Chapter 9. The work of the Public Health Service and the program of services conducted by the Department of Agriculture for migratory farm workers are described in the paragraphs that follow.

The United States Public Health Service carries on research in the causes and the methods of prevention and control of disease; exercises control over biologic products; under the Public Health Service Act of 1944 (which codifies public health legislation and embodies provisions of Title VI of the Social Security Act) assists states, counties, health districts, and other political subdivisions of states in establishing and maintaining adequate public health services, including the training of personnel; works to prevent the introduction of disease from abroad and the spread of disease within the country; and disseminates health information. An annual appropriation not to exceed $30,000,000 is authorized to carry out the provisions of the Public Health Service Act of 1944 to assist states and their political subdivisions in establishing and maintaining adequate public health services. The Public Health Service also carries on, in cooperation with the states and their subdivisions, programs for the control of tuberculosis and the control of venereal disease. It conducts research in cancer control. These and other facts relating to the work of the United States Public Health Service are set forth in *United States Government Manual—1947*. Detailed reports on the various programs of the Public Health Service are contained in its *Annual Report*.

The health program of the Department of Agriculture for migratory farm workers has been of special interest to rural people. The program has been supported with federal funds; local personnel and facilities have provided preventive and therapeutic medical and related services. In view of total rural health needs, this program may be described as very limited. It has, however, provided a large volume of needed services to a disadvantaged group. It has also served as a demonstration, and it is believed that it has awakened the interest of many local health agencies to the special problems of farm labor health needs. The program is described in an article by F. D. Mott and M. I. Roemer, "A Federal Program of Public Health and Medical Services for Migratory Farm Workers," in *Public Health Reports*, March 2, 1945.

The Social Security Act, passed in 1935, gave great impetus to the development of public health activities and a national health program. It is pointed out by Wilson G. Smillie, in *Public Health Administration in the United States*, that the Act revolutionized the work of the United States Public Health Service and the United States Children's Bureau. In the period from 1935 to 1940, the number of full-time health departments increased fourfold, state health departments were put on an effective basis, child health activities were developed in an adequate manner, and increased facilities were provided for the training of all types of public health personnel. This book presents a comprehensive analysis of various phases of public health organization and procedure. It contains a chapter on rural health administration.

The message of the President and other materials relating to a national health program are contained in *National Health Act of 1945*, a report to the Committee on Education and Labor of the United States Senate on S. 1606, a bill to provide for a national health program. The bill, not enacted into law, provided for strengthening the program of federal aid for local public health services, maternal- and child-health services, and medical care of needy persons. It also provided for a system of prepaid personal health service benefits.

Persons wishing information on the development of, and present situation in, governmental health activities should consult Harry S. Mustard's *Government in Public Health*.

Bernhard J. Stern, in *Medical Services by Government; Local, State, and Federal,* offers an inventory of the medical services that are provided directly and indirectly by governmental agencies.

VOLUNTARY AGENCIES

Voluntary agencies make large contributions to the national health program. It is pointed out in the foreword to *Voluntary Health Agencies; An Interpretive Study,* by Selskar M. Gunn and Philip S. Platt, that "the voluntary health movement has had its fullest flowering in the United States." It has paralleled the development of tax-supported services and reaches into nearly all parts of the country to help in the prevention and control of disease. The volume by Gunn and Platt presents the results of a study of this movement undertaken under the auspices of the National Health Council to determine the soundness of the voluntary programs and the problems involved in their execution. The National Health Council, located at 1790 Broadway, New York, serves as a clearing house for twenty-one voluntary health organizations.

Although the programs of many voluntary groups and professional associations reach into rural communities, they are generally less effective there than in cities. The work of the American Public Health Association, it is believed, has special implications for rural residents. This Association is a professional society of 9,000 public health workers. It has made a major contribution through the development of standards for service and personnel which have largely guided the public health movement of the country. The Association works principally through a number of standing committees.

In 1945, the Subcommittee on Local Health Units of the American Public Health Association made its report, *Local Health Units for the Nation,* under the direction of its chairman, Haven Emerson. Work for this report had been carried on since 1942. Developed by a committee of state and local public health administrators, the report "is addressed to the home-town folks of continental United States, and more particularly to their elected officers of local government. . . . Its purpose is to suggest a way to cover a free society with full time health services at the community level." The report points out that approximately 40,000,000 persons in the United States today lack full-time local health protection. Health services, whether full- or part-time, are provided by 18,000 or more counties, cities, towns, villages, and districts. The committee suggests a new administrative pattern for providing local health services. Guided by the

principles of complete coverage with basic minimum full-time service, units with enough population (50,000 or more) to support and
justify staffs of full-time professionally trained persons, and expenditures of approximately $1 per capita, the committee shows how all
these objectives can be realized through the establishment of 1,197
local health units. These units may be single-county, multi-county,
county-district, or city. The committee has enlisted the cooperation
of the several state health officers in its work, and the officers of thirty-
seven states and the District of Columbia have approved in principle
or accepted as desirable and practicable the number and boundaries
of units of local health administration suggested in the report. Most
of the other state health officers have given their approval with certain reservations. The report gives for each state tabular and descriptive materials to show present and suggested personnel and costs for
local health services and a map of the proposed units.

Closely related to the report just described is *Desirable Minimum
Functions and Organization Principles for Health Activities,* an official declaration of the Association.

Other activities of the American Public Health Association which
would seem to have special interest for rural residents are its stimulation of local communities to appraise their public health work and
its sponsorship of a national health program. The *Appraisal Form
for Local Health Work,* which grew through successive revisions from
a preliminary edition in 1925 of 40 pages to 180 pages in the edition
of 1938, was first adapted to cities and later to rural areas. Its successor
has been the *Evaluation Schedule,* first drafted in 1929 and repeatedly
revised. Communities interested in evaluating their health work may
obtain information from the Association. *Health Practice Indices,
1943-1944* contains a collection of charts showing accomplishments
in various fields of health service for 243 communities in thirty-two
states as determined from evaluation schedules. The Association
went on record at its Second Wartime Public Health Conference in
October, 1944, in favor of a national program which would make
available for all the people of the United States adequate medical
care of all essential types. The administration of this program would
be decentralized; the program would be supported by compulsory
insurance plus taxation, or by taxation alone. The official statement with reference to the program appears in the *American Journal
of Public Health* for December, 1944.

The Committee on the Hygiene of Housing of the Association has
adopted *Basic Principles of Healthful Housing.* Its publication *Hous-*

ing for Health contains a number of papers most of which are directed to urban situations; a few, however, are of general interest. The Committee has also issued *An Appraisal Method for Measuring the Quality of Housing.*

HEALTH INSURANCE

Various plans of group health insurance, hospitalization insurance, and the like have been developed to ease the payment of medical and related services and to secure more nearly adequate services to persons in the lower income groups. One of the largest voluntary group medical care programs in the world is that of the Farm Security Administration for borrower families. By 1943, plans had been put into operation in over a thousand counties in forty-one states and Puerto Rico. The Department of Agriculture has also sponsored in five counties experimental plans of group health insurance open to all farm families. An evaluation of the two types of plans, a description of other plans developed under private sponsorship, and suggestions of possible immediate action for farm families desiring improved medical services are presented in *Better Health for Rural America.* A publication of the Farm Security Administration, *Group Medical Care for Farmers,* describes the program of that organization. *The Experimental Health Program of the United States Department of Agriculture* has been issued as a monograph of the Subcommittee on Wartime Health and Education of the Committee on Education and Labor of the United States Senate. Functions of the FSA were merged into the Farmers Home Administration by Act of August 14, 1946.

In *Medical Care and Health Services for Rural People* will also be found a wealth of material describing government-sponsored and private prepayment insurance programs in operation which are helping to solve the health problems of a number of rural communities, as well as descriptions of the plans and programs of action of a number of organizations. Brief descriptions are included, among others, of medical care programs of the Farm Security Administration and the experimental programs sponsored by the United States Department of Agriculture; the health association for the Sandhills Region of Nebraska; the municipal doctor plan in operation in Manitoba, Canada; the cooperative health association of Taos County, New Mexico (subsidized by FSA); the medical service plan for the State of Michigan; the plan in operation at the Mary Imogene Bassett Hospital in Cooperstown, New York; the Blue Cross hospital plans, seventy-seven of which are in operation in the United States; and the six-county district organization in southeastern Missouri (subsidized by FSA).

A basic source of information on health care plans which gives a considerable amount of attention to the problems of rural areas is *America Organizes Medicine,* by Michael M. Davis.

The Story of Blue Cross is a Public Affairs Pamphlet prepared by Louis H. Pink which describes the hospitalization insurance plan which in 1944 had some 16,000,000 enrolled, 500,000 of them farm people. The Blue Cross is endeavoring to extend its services to country people through cooperation with farm organizations, local marketing associations, local banks and newspapers, and other agencies serving rural people.

The Interbureau Coordinating Committee on Post-War Programs of the United States Department of Agriculture outlines in *Experimental Rural Health Program* how a community may go about planning such a program, what it should include, and what it may cost.

As a result of the demand for information concerning the economics of medical services, a Joint Committee of the Twentieth Century Fund and the Good Will Fund; and Medical Administration Service, Inc., has published *How to Organize Group Health Plans,* prepared for the Committee by Martin W. Brown, Katharine G. Clark, and Perry W. Taylor.

A pamphlet designed to aid in the solution of problems of policy and procedure in connection with medical group practice is Dean A. Clark and Katharine G. Clark's *Organization and Administration of Group Medical Practice.*

A nationwide health insurance program that would make good medical and hospital facilities available to every person in the country regardless of ability to pay has been developed by a Health Program Conference group of twenty-nine well-known physicians, economists, and administrators; this program is presented in *Principles of a Nation-wide Health Program.*

A program of health insurance developed by the Canadian Federation of Agriculture will also be of interest to persons in the United States. The Federal Department of Pensions and National Health asked the Federation to submit the principles it felt should be incorporated in a national health insurance plan. A committee was established to draft the principles, which were approved by the Executive Committee of the Federation and presented to the Advisory Committee on Health and Insurance at Ottawa, October 13,

1942. They are set forth with discussion in *Health on the March; A Pamphlet on National Insurance Planning for Canada.*

HEALTH EDUCATION

Health education for the prevention and control of disease and for the development of people healthy in body and mind is an essential part of a public health program. *Health Education of the Public,* by W. W. Bauer and Thomas G. Hull, is a practical manual in this field. The techniques used in conducting a health education program are described by Ira V. Hiscock and Others in *Ways to Community Health Education.* An account of adult health education programs in the United States is contained in Frank Ernest Hill's *Educating for Health.*

The function of the schools in a rural health program is discussed in a number of references. The chapter on the schools and rural health in George A. Works and Simon O. Lesser's *Rural America Today; Its Schools and Community Life* has already been mentioned. The Twentieth Yearbook of the American Association of School Administrators, *Health in Schools,* presents a long-range view of the school's part in health education and the role therein of the administrator. This volume complements *Health Education; A Guide for Teachers in Elementary and Secondary Schools and Institutions for Teacher Education,* issued by a Joint Committee on Health Problems in Education of the National Education Association and the American Medical Association. The United States Office of Education has issued *Physical Fitness through Health Education for the Victory Corps,* which contains curriculum material for teachers and suggestions for administrative action. The Office has also issued *Food for Thought; The School's Responsibility in Nutrition Education* and *Nutrition Education in the Elementary School* to assist in making nutrition education more effective. A project developed with the objective of improving the diets of rural people through work in the schools, conducted by the Bureau of Educational Research of the University of Kentucky with financing from the Sloan Foundation, is described in "The Sloan Experiment in Kentucky" by Maurice F. Seay and Leonard E. Meece. Ruth E. Grout is the editor of a *Handbook for Health Education; A Guide for Teachers in Rural Schools,* which presents methods and materials developed in connection with a school health educational project in Cattaraugus County, New York. The American Association for Health, Physical Education, and Recreation, a department of the National Education Association, maintains an information service on health materials. Among its bibliographies is *Some Recent Publications Pertinent to Health in the Rural School Program,* issued June 1, 1943. National sources of material on health education, in addition to the resources of state and city health departments and other local community agencies, are listed in the August, 1944, issue of the *American Journal of Public Health.*

Suggested School Health Policies; A Charter for School Health is a statement issued in 1945 by the National Committee on School Health Policies, a committee of representatives from a number of professional groups. "The purpose of this document is to provide a clear, comprehensive, printed statement of the consensus of well-informed professional opinion concerning many specific school policies which directly or indirectly affect the health of children and adults. It is implied that the adoption of these policies by any elementary or secondary school or any school system will improve the health status both of the students in the school and of the communities in which they are located."

Community Organization for Health Education is a publication of the American Public Health Association which describes a number of examples of such organization initiated under different kinds of leadership.

SOME GENERAL PUBLICATIONS

A summary of health conditions in the United States and a broad program to provide equal access to health are contained in the National Resources Planning Board's *National Resources Development —Report for 1943: Part I. Post-War Plan and Program.*

Health Care for Americans, a Public Affairs Pamphlet prepared by C.-E. A. Winslow, serves as an introduction to the problem by exploring such questions as: Can America afford good health care? Why is our medical care inadequate? What kind of health program do we need?

Administrative Medicine, Haven Emerson, editor, contains a chapter by Harry S. Mustard, "Local Health Administration: Rural." Harry S. Mustard's, *An Introduction to Public Health* is designed to orient the student in the field of public health and furnish a background of information. *Rural Health Practice* by the same author is intended particularly for health officers and their associates in rural areas and small cities.

Two early studies, on which are based present-day analyses of medical care needs, were carried out by the Committee on the Costs of Medical Care and by the United States Public Health Service in its national health survey of 1935-36. *Medical Care for the American People; The Final Report of the Committee on the Costs of Medical Care* summarizes the results of a five-year program and gives specific recommendations for action. The research staff of the Committee produced twenty-six reports on fact-finding studies. The national health survey was executed by the Public Health Service with the aid of Work Projects Administration grants. It included among other things a house-to-house canvass of sickness and medical care among approximately 700,000 households or 2,500,000 persons in 83 cities and 37,000 households or 140,500 persons in 23 primarily rural counties in three states. Publications are listed in the United States Public Health Service's *National Health Survey; List of Publications,* a reprint from *Public Health Reports.*

For further references to publications in the field of health and medical care, attention is called to *Rural Health and Medical Care; A Selected List of References,* compiled by Marion E. Wheeler, Librarian, Lincoln Branch, United States Department of Agriculture Library. A committee of the National Health Library has compiled a bibliography of basic books for the public health worker which has been published in the *American Journal of Public Health,* January, 1944. Information on more than two hundred organizations is contained in *Prepayment Medical Care Organizations,* by Margaret C. Klem.

Current developments in medical care programs, legislative proposals for medical and health care, reports on matters concerning hospitals and medical care, and the like may be followed in the *American Journal of Public Health and the Nation's Health,* the monthly journal of the American Public Health Association; in *Public Health Reports,* issued weekly by the United States Public Health Service; in *Public Health Economics; A Monthly Compilation of Events and Opinions,* issued by the School of Public Health of the University of Michigan; in *Hospitals; The Journal of the American Hospital Association,* published monthly; and in *The Journal of the American Medical Association,* published weekly.

BIBLIOGRAPHY

American Association for Health, Physical Education, and Recreation. *Some Recent Publications Pertinent to Health in the Rural School Program.* Washington: The Association (1201 16th St. N. W.), 1943, 5 pp.

American Association of School Administrators. *Health in Schools.* Twentieth Yearbook of the Association. Washington: The Association (1201 16th St. N. W.), 1942, 544 pp. (References on health education, pp. 353-63.)

American Journal of Public Health and the Nation's Health. Monthly publication of the American Public Health Association, 1790 Broadway, New York.

American Public Health Association. *Community Organization for Health Education.* A Report of the Committee on Community Organization for Health Education. Cambridge, Massachusetts: The Technology Press, 1941, 120 pp.

——. *Desirable Minimum Functions and Organization Principles for Health Activities; An Official Declaration of the American Public Health Association, Adopted October 9, 1940, and Supplemented by the Executive Board, December 10, 1941, and January 29, 1943,* 12 pp. (Reprinted from the *American Journal of Public Health.*)

——. "Medical Care in a National Health Program; An Official Statement of the American Public Health Association adopted October 4, 1944." *American Journal of Public Health,* Vol. XXXIV, No. 12, December 1944, pp. 1252-56. (Also issued as a reprint.)

——. Committee on the Hygiene of Housing. *An Appraisal Method for Measuring the Quality of Housing; A Yardstick for Health Officers, Housing Officials and Planners. Part I. Nature and Uses of the Method.* New York: The Association, 1945, 71 pp.

——. ——. *Basic Principles of Healthful Housing.* 2nd ed. New York: The Association, 1939, 32 pp.

——. ——. *Housing for Health. Papers Presented under the Auspices of the Committee.* Lancaster, Pennsylvania: Science Press Printing Co., 1941, 221 pp.

——. Subcommittee on State and Local Health Administrators of the Committee on Administrative Practice. *Health Practice Indices, 1943-1944.* 3rd ed. New York: The Association, 1945, 87 pp.

Atkins, C. H. "National Inventory of Needs for Sanitation Facilities IV.. Rural Sanitation." *Public Health Reports,* Vol. LIX, No. 30, July 28, 1944, pp. 969-78.

Bauer, W. W. and Thomas G. Hull. *Health Education of the Public; A Practical Manual of Technic.* 2nd ed. Philadelphia: W. B. Saunders Co., 1942, 315 pp. (Bibliographies.)

Brown, Martin W.; Katharine G. Clark; and Perry W. Taylor. *How to Organize Group Health Plans.* New York: Joint Committee of the Twentieth Century Fund and the Good Will Fund; and Medical Administration Service, Inc. (1790 Broadway), 1942, 72 pp.

The Canadian Federation of Agriculture. *Health on the March; A Pamphlet on National Insurance Planning for Canada.* Ottawa: The Association (304 Booth Building), 1943, 31 pp.

Clark, Dean A. and Katharine G. Clark. *Organization and Administration of Group Medical Practice.* New York: Joint Committee of the Twentieth Century Fund and the Good Will Fund; and Medical Administration Service, Inc., 1941, 109 pp.

Committee of the National Health Library. "Suggested Five Foot Shelf of Basic Books for Public Health Workers." *American Journal of Public Health,* Vol. XXXIV, No. 1, January 1944, p. 74.

Davis, Michael M. *America Organizes Medicine.* New York: Harper & Bros., 1941, 335 pp. (References, pp. 302-20.)

Ehlers, Victor M. and Ernest W. Steele. *Municipal and Rural Sanitation.* 3rd ed. New York: McGraw-Hill Book Co., 1943, 449 pp. (Bibliography at end of most chapters.)

Emerson, Haven. *Local Health Units for the Nation.* New York: Commonwealth Fund, 1945, 333 pp.

The Experimental Health Program of the United States Department of Agriculture. Monograph No. 1 of the Subcommittee on Wartime Health and Education of the Committee on Education and Labor, United States Senate. Washington: Government Printing Office, 1946, 166 pp.

Grout, Ruth E., ed. *Handbook of Health Education; A Guide for Teachers in Rural Schools.* Garden City, New York: Doubleday, Doran & Co., 1936, 298 pp.

Gunn, Selskar M. and Philip S. Platt. *Voluntary Health Agencies; An Interpretive Study.* New York: Ronald Press Co., 1945, 364 pp.

Health Program Conference. *Principles of a Nation-wide Health Program.* New York: Committee on Research in Medical Economics (1790 Broadway), 1944, 34 pp.

Hill, Frank Ernest. *Educating for Health: A Study of Programs for Adults.* New York: American Association for Adult Education, 1939, 224 pp.

Hiscock, Ira V. and Others. *Ways to Community Health Education.* New York: The Commonwealth Fund, 1939, 306 pp. (Suggested reading at end of each chapter.)

Hospitals; The Journal of the American Hospital Association. 18 East Division St., Chicago, Illinois, monthly.

Joint Committee on Health Problems in Education of the National Education Association and the American Medical Association. *Health Education; A Guide for Teachers in Elementary and Secondary Schools and Institutions for Teacher Education.* 2nd revision. Washington: National Education Association (1201 16th St. N. W.), 1941, 368 pp. (Bibliography, pp. 311-61.)

The Journal of the American Medical Association. 535 North Dearborn St., Chicago, Illinois, weekly.

Klem, Margaret C. *Prepayment Medical Care Organizations.* 3rd ed. Washington: Government Printing Office, 1945, 148 pp.

Medical Care and Health Services for Rural People; A Study Prepared as a Result of a Conference Held at Chicago, Illinois, April 11-13, 1944, Sponsored by the Farm Foundation. Chicago: Farm Foundation, 1944, 226 pp.

Medical Care for the American People; The Final Report of the Committee on the Costs of Medical Care. Publications of the Committee on the Costs of Medical Care No. 28. Chicago: University of Chicago Press, 1932, 213 pp.

Mott, Frederick D. "A Public Health Program for Rural Areas." *Public Health Reports,* Vol. LXI, No. 17, April 26, 1946, pp. 589-98.

—— and M. I. Roemer. "A Federal Program of Public Health and Medical Services for Migratory Farm Workers." *Public Health Reports,* Vol. LX, No. 9, March 2, 1945, pp. 229-49.

Mountin, Joseph W.; Elliott H. Pennell; and George S. Brockett. "Location and Movement of Physicians, 1923 and 1938—Changes in Urban and Rural Totals for Established Physicians." *Public Health Reports,* Vol. LX, No. 7, February 16, 1945, pp. 173-85.

——; ——; and Vane M. Hoge. *Health Service Areas: Requirements for General Hospitals and Health Centers.* Public Health Bulletin No. 292. Washington: Government Printing Office, 1945, 68 pp. (Selected bibliography, pp. 11-12.)

Mustard, Harry S. *Government in Public Health.* New York: Commonwealth Fund, 1945, 219 pp. (References at ends of chapters.)

——. *An Introduction to Public Health.* 2nd ed. New York: Macmillan Co., 1944, 283 pp. (Suggested readings at ends of chapters.)

——. "Local Health Administration: Rural" in Haven Emerson, ed., *Administrative Medicine.* New York: Thomas Nelson & Sons, 1941.

——. *Rural Health Practice.* New York: The Commonwealth Fund, 1936, 603 pp. (Bibliography at end of each chapter.)

National Committee on School Health Policies of the National Conference for Cooperation in Health Education. *Suggested School Health Policies; A Charter for School Health.* 2nd ed. New York: Health Education Council (10 Downing St.), 1945, 46 pp. (Selective source bibliography, pp. 43-46.)

National Health Act of 1945. Report to the Committee on Education and Labor Relating to the Bill (S. 1606) to Provide for a National Health Program. Senate Committee Print No. 1, 79th Cong., 1st sess. Washington: Government Printing Office, 1946, 36 pp.

National Planning Association. *A Food and Nutrition Program for the Nation; A Report by a Subcommittee of the Agriculture, Business, and Labor Committees on National Policy.* Planning Pamphlets No. 46. Washington: The Association (800 21st St. N. W.), 1945, 35 pp.

National Research Council. *Inadequate Diets and Nutritional Deficiencies in the United States; Their Prevalence and Significance.* Report of the Committee on Diagnosis and Pathology of Nutritional Deficiencies, Food and Nutrition Board. Washington: Bulletin of the National Research Council, No. 109, November 1943, 56 pp. (References, pp. 48-56.)

Northern Great Plains Council. Subcommittee on Health. *Medical Care and Health Services for Farm Families of the Northern Great Plains. Proceedings of the Subcommittee ... during a Conference Held in the Student Union Building, The University of Nebraska, May 17, 18 and 19, 1945.* Lincoln, Nebraska: The University of Nebraska, 1945, 84 pp.

Pennock, Jean L. and Grace M. Angle. *What Farm Families Spend for Medical Care.* U. S. Department of Agriculture Miscellaneous Publication No. 561. Washington: Government Printing Office, 1945, 18 pp.

Pink, Louis H. *The Story of Blue Cross; On the Road to Better Health.* Public Affairs Pamphlet No. 101. New York: Public Affairs Committee (30 Rockefeller Plaza), 1945, 32 pp.

Public Health Economics; A Monthly Compilation of Events and Opinions. Published by the School of Public Health, University of Michigan, Ann Arbor, Michigan. (Successor to *Medical Care.*)

"Recommendations of Joint Committee on Rural Sanitation—Rural Sewage Disposal." *Public Health Reports,* Vol. LVIII, No. 11, March 12, 1943, pp. 417-48. (Also issued as Reprint No. 2461.)

Rural Water-Supply Sanitation; Recommendations of the Joint Committee on Rural Sanitation. Supplement No. 185 to the *Public Health Reports.* Washington: Government Printing Office, 1945, 56 pp.

Seay, Maurice F. and Leonard E. Meece. "The Sloan Experiment in Kentucky. The Second Progress Report of an Experiment in Applied Economics." *Bulletin of the Bureau of School Service, College of Education, University of Kentucky,* Vol. XVI, No. 4, June 1944, 131 pp.

Smillie, Wilson G. *Public Health Administration in the United States.* 2nd ed. New York: Macmillan Co., 1941, 553 pp. (Bibliographies.)

Southmayd, Henry J. and Geddes Smith. *Small Community Hospitals.* New York: Commonwealth Fund, 1944, 182 pp.

Stern, Bernhard J. *American Medical Practice in the Perspectives of a Century.* New York: Commonwealth Fund, 1945, 156 pp.

——. *Medical Services by Government; Local, State, and Federal.* New York: Commonwealth Fund, 1946, 208 pp.

U. S. Department of Agriculture. Interbureau Committee on Post-War Programs. *Better Health for Rural America; Plans of Action for Farm Communities.* Washington: Government Printing Office, 1945, 34 pp.

——. ——. *Experimental Rural Health Program.* Washington: 1942, 19 pp.

U. S. Division of Public Inquiries. Government Information Service. Bureau of the Budget. *United States Government Manual—1947.* 1st ed. Washington: Government Printing Office, 1946, 718 pp.

U. S. Farm Security Administration. *Group Medical Care for Farmers.* Washington: Government Printing Office, 1941, 14 pp.

U. S. National Resources Planning Board. "Equal Access to Health," in *National Resources Development—Report for 1943: Part I. Post-War Plan and Program.* Washington: Government Printing Office, 1943, pp. 60-67.

U. S. Office of Defense Health and Welfare Services. *Democracy Means All of Us: How Communities Can Organize to Study and Meet Community Needs with Special Suggestions for Developing Nutrition Programs in Wartime.* Washington: The Office, 1942, 30 pp.

U. S. Office of Education. *Food for Thought; The School's Responsibility in Nutrition Education.* Education and National Defense Series Pamphlet No. 22. Washington: Government Printing Office, 1941, 32 pp.

——. *Nutrition Education in the Elementary School.* Nutrition Education Series Pamphlet No. 1. Washington: Government Printing Office, 1943, 35 pp. (Bibliography, pp. 33-35.)

——. *Physical Fitness through Health Education for the Victory Corps.* Victory Corps Series Pamphlet No. 3. Washington: Government Printing Office, 1943, 98 pp. (References at ends of chapters.)

U. S. Public Health Service. *Annual Report of the . . . for the Fiscal Year . . . .* Washington: Government Printing Office.

——. *National Health Survey; List of Publications.* Reprint No. 2384 from *Public Health Reports,* Vol. LVII, No. 22, May 29, 1942, pp. 834-41.

——. *Public Health Reports.* Weekly.

Wheeler, Marion E., compiler. *Rural Health and Medical Care; A Selected List of References.* Lincoln, Nebraska: U. S. Bureau of Agricultural Economics, 1944, 27 pp.

Winslow, C.-E.A. *Health Care for Americans.* Public Affairs Pamphlet No. 104. New York: Public Affairs Committee (30 Rockefeller Plaza), 1945, 32 pp. (For further reading, p. 31.)

Works, George A. and Simon O. Lesser. "The Schools and Rural Health," in *Rural America Today; Its Schools and Community Life.* Chicago: University of Chicago Press, 1942, pp. 189-214. (Authorities for the facts, pp. 212-14.)

Wright, Forrest B. *Rural Water Supply and Sanitation.* New York: John Wiley & Sons, 1939, 288 pp. (Bibliography, p. 282.)

6 *WELFARE SERVICES*

PUBLIC WELFARE activities may be generally described as tax-supported activities carried on by national, state, and local governments for the prevention and treatment of dependency, delinquency, crime, and physical and mental handicaps. Among the groups of persons assisted are the aged; the unemployed; dependent, neglected, and maladjusted children; criminals and delinquents; the blind, the deaf, the crippled, and the tuberculous; and the mentally defective, the feeble-minded, and the epileptic. Among the types of activities included are general assistance or relief; old-age assistance; aid to the needy blind; aid to dependent children; the operation of institutions such as homes for children, almshouses, hospitals for the insane, and hospitals for the needy chronically ill; the inspection and licensing of privately operated institutions; family case work; child placement and supervision of foster homes; supervision of children and adults on probation; aid to veterans; aid to transients; legal aid; and psychiatric services. A description of the nature, development, programs, and problems of public welfare is contained in an article by Howard L. Russell, "Public Welfare," in the *Social Work Year Book, 1945.*

A number of welfare functions are also carried on by private voluntary groups or agencies. Rural people, with a tradition of self-sufficiency, have depended largely upon family, neighborhood, and community resources for mutual aid. Voluntary programs that are organized on a nationwide basis are largely concentrated in urban centers and have spread in varying degrees to smaller communities and rural areas. Religious and fraternal agencies supply services in many smaller communities. An idea of the variety of services that national voluntary agencies perform may be obtained from an examination of the list of such agencies carried in the *Social Work Year Book, 1945,* pp. 515-84. Information is given as to the membership, purpose, and activities of each. Reference may also be made to an article by David H. Holbrook, "National Associations in Social Work," which appears in the *Year Book.*

Welfare problems and activities change with changes in social and economic conditions, in the public's awareness of needs, and in the feeling of responsibility for meeting them. During the depression period, for example, emphasis tended to be placed on financial aid for the needy; in the war and postwar periods, the emphasis has largely shifted to the social service aspects of welfare work. Over the years the concept of public responsibility for welfare services has broadened, and the trend has been toward developing a program of assistance and services to all needy people.

It will simplify the later discussion to distinguish at this point between public assistance and social insurance. These two programs have both similarities and differences. Both seek to provide a minimum degree of economic security. Social insurance programs, which include workmen's compensation, unemployment compensation, and old-age and survivors insurance, make payments from funds built up by contributions of employers and employees. The insured employee has a contractual right to share in the funds collected, and payments are made at a fixed rate without regard to other resources of the insured. Public assistance is provided from public appropriations and is related to the degree of need and the special requirements of the recipient.

Social insurance programs have assumed large proportions, especially since the passage of the federal Social Security Act in 1935, yet substantial groups are still not covered by existing programs, and payments under these programs frequently are insufficient to meet vital needs. Agricultural workers are one of the large groups not covered by unemployment compensation and old-age and survivors insurance.

GOVERNMENTAL WELFARE ACTIVITIES

Public welfare services originally were largely the responsibility of local governments. The trend, however, especially since 1933, has been toward placing responsibilities with the higher levels of government and toward supervision of local activities by the states and the federal government. In most states today, general poor relief is chiefly a responsibility of the townships, counties, or cities. In some states, the state government contributes to such relief and does some supervising of its administration. The care of the insane, mental defectives, the blind and deaf, and felons is now almost entirely a state function. In recent decades, the federal government has established institutions to care for prisoners, lepers, insane federal employees and residents of the District of Columbia, and sick federal employees. With the establishment of the Federal Emergency Relief Administration, in 1933, the federal government assumed the most important role in public assistance through an extensive program of work and home relief.

This agency was succeeded in 1935 by the Works Progress Administration (later the Work Projects Administration), through which the federal government administered a large work relief program. The Social Security Act of 1935 has made the federal government a participant in large assistance and insurance programs. Social insurance programs are administered by state and federal governments; workmen's compensation is a state-administered program; unemployment compensation is a federal-state program; old-age and survivors insurance is entirely federally administered.

Federal public welfare functions are distributed among a number of agencies, the most important of which, for rural people, are the Federal Security Agency, the Farm Security Administration, the Agricultural Extension Service, and the Veterans Administration. Certain of the activities of the Federal Security Agency, the Farm Security Administration, and the Veterans Administration are briefly described in the following paragraphs. The work of the Children's Bureau, located in the Federal Security Agency, is discussed in Chapter 9; the work of the Extension Service is described in Chapter 2. The descriptions are based on statements appearing in the *United States Government Manual—1947*, unless otherwise noted.

Federal Security Agency. The Federal Security Agency carries on a variety of health, welfare, social insurance, and educational activities. Chief among its welfare activities are assistance programs for the needy aged, dependent children, and the needy blind; a program of old-age and survivors insurance; and a program of unemployment compensation.

The benefits available under the three assistance programs of the federal government—aid for the needy aged, dependent children, and the needy blind—extend to rural as well as urban residents. They require state action and are based on state plans which are federally approved and state administered, or state supervised and county administered. The Social Security Act defines the scope of federal financial participation; the state plan may be broader. Federal participation is restricted to persons who are needy, who are not inmates of public institutions, who receive money payments, and who meet certain eligibility conditions. These conditions preclude federal sharing in old-age assistance to persons under age 65, or to children age 18 and over, or age 16 and over if not attending school. Federal contributions range from more than one-half to as much as two-thirds of the state's payments. The federal government does not participate in that portion of a payment that is over $45 for old-age assistance and aid to the blind, and over $24 for the first child aided and $15 for each additional child in the home for aid to dependent children.

Old-age and survivors insurance provides monthly benefits for insured workers and their wives when they reach the age of 65, as well as for children under 16 years of age, or 18 if they are attending school. Monthly benefits are also provided, under specified conditions, for widows and children or aged dependent parents of deceased workers. Eligibility for benefits depends upon employment for a specified minimum period of time in occupations covered by the Social Security Act. Agriculture is one of the occupations not included in this program. Total monthly benefits payable range from a minimum of $10 to a maximum of $85. Benefits are paid out of a fund accumulated in the United States Treasury from the tax contributions of workers and their employers.

Federal unemployment compensation activities are designed to facilitate the enactment and administration of unemployment compensation laws by the states. States record wage credits toward unemployment benefits, determine benefit rights and eligibility, collect contributions, and pay benefits. States having approved laws receive federal grants to pay necessary administrative costs, and employers within those states receive certain credits against federal taxes collected from employers of eight or more workers on some day in each of 20 weeks of the year. Agriculture is not included in the federal unemployment compensation program.

The *Social Security Bulletin* for August, 1945, is devoted to summarizing the accomplishments of the social security program during the first ten years of its operation. It bears the title "Ten Years of Social Security" and is made up of brief articles on various phases of the program and summary statistics.

The Office of Vocational Rehabilitation in the Federal Security Agency cooperates with the states in providing vocational rehabilitation to prepare for, and place in, remunerative employment persons who are vocationally handicapped because of a permanent disability caused by accident, disease, or congenital defect. State boards of vocational education carry on the functions of the program; each board has a division of vocational rehabilitation with a full-time director and professional staff. The federal Office is responsible for the establishment of standards, for technical assistance to the states, and for certification of federal funds for grants-in-aid to the states upon the approval of state plans meeting the requirements of the federal act.

Farm Security Administration. The Farm Security Administration in the United States Department of Agriculture operates a program of assistance to farm families. The FSA has aided nearly 900,000 farm families who have lacked other sources of adequate credit by loans to purchase machinery, equipment, livestock, seed, feed, fertilizer, and other farm and home supplies needed to make a living and to increase production of essential food and fiber. Among borrowers are more than 17,700 veterans of World War II. Loans are made for periods up to five years at an interest rate of 5 per cent. They are accompanied by technical guidance from supervisors trained in farm and home management. Aid to borrower families to help them secure medical, dental, and hospital care through setting up group health services in cooperation with local physicians and dentists is described in Chapter 5.

Small loans also are made to low-income farmers for group purchase and use of farm machinery and purebred sires. The FSA makes loans to a limited number of capable farm tenants, sharecroppers, and farm laborers to enable them to buy family-type farms. By June 30, 1946, loans had been approved for nearly 41,500 families for the purchase of such farms. Loans are repayable over a period of forty years at 3 per cent interest. These loans may also be made to veterans of World War II if they are qualified by experience or training to carry out successfully the undertakings required of them under the loans. In the seventeen western states, the FSA makes loans and supplies technical assistance to farmers and ranchers for the construction or repair of water facilities, such as ponds, windmills, pumps, storage tanks, and irrigation ditches, which they need in order to make better use of their land resources. Functions of the FSA have been merged into the Farmers Home Administration by Act of August 14, 1946.

Veterans Administration. The Veterans Administration is responsible for extending relief to veterans and to dependents of deceased veterans, as provided for by various acts of Congress. These laws make provision for compensation, pensions, vocational rehabilitation, and education; the guarantee of loans for purchase or construction of homes, farms, and business property; readjustment allowance for veterans who are unemployed; government life insurance, death benefits, adjusted compensation, emergency and other officers' retirement pay; and physical examinations, hospital and out-patient treatment, and domiciliary care.

State Welfare Services. There are one or more state welfare agencies in every state, but patterns of organization for state welfare activities vary greatly. The trend is toward consolidating public welfare services in a single department; in many states, however, they are scattered among a variety of agencies. R. Clyde White, in *Administration of Public Welfare,* lists the following as the services that belong in a coordinated state department of public welfare—"services for the insane, epileptic, feeble-minded, delinquents, criminals, invalids, aged persons, able-bodied unemployed, dependent or neglected children. For the unemployed, the aged, widows, orphans, and the industrially injured, the social insurance system is the first line of defense, but when persons are not protected by any of the social insurances or have exhausted their rights to benefits, they fall back upon the public welfare system as the second line of defense. By 1939 the undeniably public welfare services had been completely, or almost completely, coordinated in fourteen states. . . . " Publications of state welfare departments are described in "Reports and Periodicals of State Welfare Departments," in *Public Welfare* for October, 1945.

Types of state welfare activities may be illustrated by those carried on in New York State. As listed in the annual report of the State Department of Social Welfare for 1943, they include supervising the administration of public assistance by local public welfare agencies; supervising public and private agencies that provide foster care and other child welfare services; supervising and inspecting public and private welfare institutions for the sick, the aged, children, and dependent adults; licensing boarding homes for the foster care of children; issuing permits for the day care of children; maintaining a record for every child in foster care; maintaining a register of all blind persons and providing various services to the blind; investigating and acting upon applications for the incorporation of charitable institutions and agencies in the state; supervising the establishment of emergency welfare services in local public welfare districts; and operating five state institutions.

Many of the activities of state welfare agencies, as the above list suggests, are of direct help in local welfare administration. State agencies help local administration through supplying leadership and stimulating and supporting local leadership, through providing the special services of trained workers and special clinical services, through assistance in research and program planning, through supervision of activities, particularly those which receive state aid, to assure that standards of service are maintained, and through the issuance of research and other reports. State welfare agencies provide liaison between federal and local programs and assist in securing cooperation from other state agencies with programs that should be integrated with welfare activities at the local level.

Most direct public welfare services, other than institutional services, are rendered by the staff of a local governmental unit or by a local administrative unit of a federal or a state agency. The type of local organization depends on state legislation, and counties, townships, towns, and cities exercise only such powers as the state constitution or the legislature delegates to them. The federal Social Security Act offers inducements to make old-age assistance, aid to dependent children, and assistance to the blind universal. The amount of assistance, however, has remained a matter for local decision, and standards of services to needy persons are largely fixed by local public opinion.

A description of the administration of public welfare activities at the federal, state, and local levels is contained in R. Clyde White, *Administration of Public Welfare,* a volume that has already been mentioned. This work also discusses methods of treatment and management problems in welfare programs. Marietta Stevenson, in *Public Welfare Administration,* describes the organization of public welfare and discusses administrative principles and problems.

COMMUNITY WELFARE ACTIVITIES

The administration of welfare activities in rural communities is described in the introduction to Part I of *Rural Public Welfare; Selected Records,* by Grace Browning. In general, county welfare departments are responsible for administering old-age assistance, aid to dependent children, and aid to the blind. Frequently they administer local and state general relief funds. In many states such departments provide certain services to delinquent, dependent, neglected, and handicapped children. Local welfare departments may carry on a variety of additional activities, such as acting as probation officer, furthering recreation programs, and handling intake to almshouses and infirmaries. Other local government agencies also frequently carry on various welfare activities. In most states the juvenile court is responsible for the care of neglected and dependent children, and this court may also have a variety of other welfare functions. Other local officials who may provide welfare or closely related services are the probation officer, the prosecuting attorney, the sheriff, the constable, educational authorities, overseers of the poor, the township trustee, the town selectman, and the county commissioner.

Other general statements in Browning's *Rural Public Welfare* provide excellent materials for an understanding of the rural welfare situation. The introduction (pp. 91-100) to the welfare records contained in Part II (which relate to worker, client, and community) stresses the importance for the social worker of understanding the rural economy and rural culture. The introduction (pp. 315-47) to Part III (rural social resources) describes various resources available to the social worker in the rural community—the family group, the church, the school, special educational resources, recreation, organization for health and medical care, employment services, federal, state, and local relief resources—and points to the need for coordinating these resources.

The community aspects of rural social work are also presented in Gertrude V. Withers' *Effective Rural Social Work through Community Organization*. This author believes that the frontier of social welfare work is in rural and semirural areas. The rural worker needs not only all the basic case-work and group-work skills, but in addition a high degree of skill in community organization. The pamphlet shows by concrete example how the worker may increase her usefulness to clients, broaden community interest and understanding, and build a foundation for long-range social planning through developing and organizing community resources.

In response to a demand from communities that are organizing, or would like to organize, planning and coordinating councils to deal with local problems of health, family and child welfare, and recreation, Community Chests and Councils, Inc. has prepared a pamphlet, *Health and Welfare Planning in the Smaller Community*. Such councils can be useful in coordinating public and private welfare activities, in bringing needs to public attention, and in extending and improving programs. The pamphlet is intended as a practical guide to setting up such councils in those small communities where a number of welfare agencies have been developed.

Rural Case Work Services, by Marjorie J. Smith, makes clear through description of a number of welfare cases in rural and small-town communities the need for individual treatment in the handling of cases.

The County Worker's Job; What It Is and What It Takes, by Josephine Strode, is a collection of articles appearing in the *Survey Midmonthly.*

A work that offers concrete suggestions for developing social work activities in rural communities is Josephine C. Brown's *The Rural Community and Social Case Work.*

Chapter XI of Works and Lesser, *Rural America Today,* is titled "The Schools and Rural Social Welfare" and is devoted to a discussion of rural welfare problems, programs, and agencies and the relationship of the schools thereto.

A volume that will prove useful to anyone wishing to investigate welfare and related needs and services of his community is Joanna C. Colcord's *Your Community; Its Provision for Health, Education, Safety, and Welfare.* "This outline contains suggestions for groups of persons desirous of securing a rounded picture of their own community, especially as to the provision which that community makes to conserve the health and safety and to promote the education and general welfare of its inhabitants. . . . It suggests . . . the type of information that might be assembled and studied by intelligent citizens and citizens-to-be, in order to have a background from which to attack the problem of supplying community lacks and improving existing services."

A pamphlet designed to orient rural case workers is *Rural Routes to Community Understanding,* issued by the Social Work Publicity Council. It consists of an exchange of letters between two workers in rural communities in which they discuss some of their problems.

EXTENDING SOCIAL SECURITY PROGRAMS

In a monograph prepared for the Social Science Research Council, under the title *Social Insurance and Agriculture; A Memorandum Presenting Suggestions for Research and a Bibliography,* William S. Hopkins gives primary attention to the question of extending unemployment and old-age and survivors insurance. The monograph contains a background statement on the capacity of agriculture to support a social insurance program and the probable consequences of programs for social insurance coverage.

It is the conclusion of Carl C. Taylor in an article, "Rural Social Programs," in *Social Work Year Book, 1945* that "the extension of the provisions of the Social Security Act to include farmers in all benefits appears . . . to hold out the major prospect for establishing a universal public welfare program in rural areas. At the present time farm people are recipients of only a small share of these benefits. . . . There are no insurmountable difficulties in the way of extending social security programs to farm people. The present obstacles are the administrative details of collecting payments from self-employed farmers who do not receive regular income, and the fact that probably the majority of farm people know little or nothing about the social

security program." This article discusses various rural social programs
—those of the Agricultural Extension Service and the Farm Security
Administration among others—and points out rural welfare needs.

It is pointed out in the *Report of the Secretary of Agriculture, 1944*
that "proposals are now being made to extend the program [of social
security] to the self-employed including farmers, and to expand the
benefits for medical and hospital care. Farm people themselves must
decide whether or not they want to participate. They can have the
benefits of the present social security program, and of an expanded
program, if they want them." The Social Security Board has been
working closely with a group in the United States Department of
Agriculture giving careful consideration to how the social security
program can be modified so as to include farmers if they want to be
included. They believe that the principal obstacle to extending the
program to farmers is that they do not understand it.

The *9th Annual Report, Fiscal Year 1943-44* of the Social Security
Board carries this conclusion relative to farm people:

> Farm people in the United States face the future with far less protection
> from organized measures for social security than any other major segment
> of our population. Standards of assistance, especially general assistance,
> are characteristically lower in rural States and communities than elsewhere,
> and health resources are inadequate in many rural areas. In Selective Service
> examinations, boys classified as "farmers" had a higher rejection rate for
> physical incapacity than any other occupational group. Work accidents
> are common on farms, yet farm workers are seldom covered by workmen's
> compensation laws. Nor do farm families, despite their relatively low income
> levels, have the protection of old-age and survivors insurance or unemploy-
> ment insurance.

The report presents recommendations for extending and strengthening tested principles of social insurance and assistance.

Section five of the *Annual Report of the Federal Security Agency
for the Fiscal Year 1945* outlines a recommended plan for social
security which includes a comprehensive basic national system of
social insurance and a comprehensive program of public assistance.
Social insurance should cover "all major risks to economic independence and all workers and their dependents to whom such risks apply.
Such a program would include insurance against wage loss in periods
of disability and against costs of medical care, as well as old-age and
survivors insurance and unemployment insurance, relating benefits
to past earnings with provision for additional benefits for dependents." A program of public assistance on a state-federal basis, with pay-

ments financed from state and federal funds, "would be available to any needy person in the United States irrespective of the reason for need or the place of residence. Such a program would be designed to remove the great disparities which now exist in the treatment of various classes of needy persons and in the treatment of persons who are in like circumstances but live in different parts of the country. It would also be designed to remove serious present inequities in the relative burdens borne by States and localities in financing public assistance." Old-age and survivors insurance would cover "all gainful workers, including agricultural and domestic employees, public employees and employees of nonprofit organizations, and self-employed persons, including farmers." The Federal Unemployment Tax Act should extend "to all employers of one or more in covered industries and to as many other excepted employments as is administratively feasible." There should be federal grants-in-aid to states "for general assistance to any needy person, irrespective of cause of need, as well as for old-age assistance, aid to the blind, and aid to dependent children."

Social Security for Farm People; Questions and Answers is a publication of the United States Department of Agriculture and the Social Security Board, prepared at the suggestion of leaders of farm organizations. It lists questions raised by farm people and attempts to answer them in brief space. It covers such topics as what farm people would pay for coverage under the old-age and survivors insurance program, what benefits farm people would receive if they were covered by the existing program, how they would become eligible for benefits, and what reports and records they would be required to keep.

A comprehensive investigation of welfare needs and policies to meet them is contained in the report of the United States National Resources Planning Board, *Security, Work, and Relief Policies; Report of the Committee on Long-Range Work and Relief Policies.* This report describes the evolution of public aid programs, what they accomplish, and financial, economic, and administrative aspects of public aid. A summary of the Committee's recommendations on general policy and its specific proposals appeared under the title *After the War—Toward Security.* A brief statement on postwar planning for social security is presented in the Board's *National Resources Development—Report for 1943,* under the heading "Equal Access to Economic Security."

Maxwell S. Stewart's *Jobs and Security for Tomorrow* is a Public Affairs Pamphlet based on the two reports of the National Resources

Planning Board and the seventh annual report of the Social Security Board.

A *Joint Statement on Social Security by Agriculture, Business and Labor* appears in Planning Pamphlet No. 33 of the National Planning Association. As stated in the foreword:

The proposed income maintenance program provides for the creation of a single national social insurance system under which, in return for contributions made, the vast majority of the people would be entitled to receive certain money payments in the event of interruptions of earning power due to old age, unemployment, illness or disability, and death of a breadwinner. To provide security for those who may be ineligible for benefits even under an expanded social insurance program or whose minimum needs cannot be met by the normal social insurance benefit, the *Statement* outlines the steps necessary to develop a more effective and more constructive general public assistance program.

A report by Murray R. Benedict, *A Retirement System for Farmers,* Planning Pamphlet No. 49 of the National Planning Association, carries a "Statement of the Agriculture Committee on National Policy on Old-Age, Survivors', and Disability Insurance for Farm People." The statement points out that "farm people already bear some of the costs of providing social insurance for nonfarm workers," that farm areas "support a larger proportionate number of the very young and the aged than do urban areas," and that "rural counties and states are helping to carry an increasingly heavy burden in the care of the aged under noncontributory old-age assistance programs." Great numbers of aged rural people who are supported under such programs "could be better served at less public expense through an orderly, contributory program which would enable them to build up rights to assured incomes in old age, widowhood, or disability." The Committee recommends, among other things, that:

The old-age and survivors' insurance provisions in the social security legislation of the federal government be broadened to include self-employed farmers, croppers, and farm wage-workers along lines substantially similar to those outlined in this report [by Mr. Benedict].

The Committee recognizes "the need for unemployment insurance, or other measures to stabilize the employment and incomes of wage-workers in agriculture," but it is not yet prepared to recommend specific measures. It recommends that the problem "be given active study with a view to developing a workable solution."

Unemployment Compensation in the Post-War Period; Suggestions for Expanding and Perfecting State Unemployment Compensation

Systems and a Digest of State and Federal Provisions is a publication of the Council of State Governments which contains suggestions designed to assist the states in appraising the adequacy of their systems, so that with a minimum of dislocation and distress they may do the best possible job of industrial reconversion.

War and Post-War Social Security; The Outlines of an Expanded Program consists of a series of papers by Arthur J. Altmeyer and Others covering such matters as principles, goals, and specific programs.

GENERAL REFERENCES, BIBLIOGRAPHIES, PERIODICALS

The addresses before a National Conference on Social Security sponsored by the Chamber of Commerce of the United States are presented in a publication *Social Security in America.*

The report of Sir William Beveridge, *Social Insurance and Allied Services,* a survey with recommendations relating to the situation in Great Britain, has been widely discussed in the United States. It is summarized in a Public Affairs Pamphlet by Maxwell Stewart, *The Beveridge Plan.* A more recent publication of Sir William's, *Full Employment in a Free Society,* analyzes the causes of unemployment and their cure. His assumptions as to employment in the earlier report are fundamental to the successful functioning of his social insurance program.

Dorothy C. Tompkins' *Plans for Security* is a bibliography of planning for security in Australia, Canada, Great Britain, and the United States, which contains references to pamphlet and periodical materials.

A list of over eight hundred titles of books, pamphlets, articles, addresses, and periodical sources on the Social Security Act and the programs administered under it is contained in a publication prepared by the Social Security Board Library and published under the title *Some Basic Readings in Social Security.*

Current developments in public welfare may be followed in a number of periodical publications. *Public Welfare* is the monthly journal of the American Public Welfare Association. *Social Service Review,* a quarterly devoted to the scientific and professional interests of social work, is edited by the faculty of the School of Social Service Administration at the University of Chicago. *The Compass* is the publication of the American Association of Social Workers, issued six times yearly. The *Survey Graphic* and the *Survey Midmonthly,* issued monthly, carry articles, book reviews, and news notes of interest to social workers. Current data on the operations of the social security program, the results of research and analysis pertinent to the program, and the legislative history of proposals in Congress relating to social security are reported in the *Social Security Bulletin,* published monthly by the Federal Security Agency. The Agency also publishes an annual supplement to the *Bulletin,* the *Social Security Yearbook. The Child,* monthly publication of the United States Children's Bureau, is devoted to child welfare matters. The *Proceedings of the National Conference of Social Work,* selected papers presented before the annual sessions of the Conference, gives a cross section of events, developments, and thinking about social work. The *Social Work Year Book* "is presented as a concise encyclopedia descriptive of organized activities in social work and related fields." It is issued biennially and consists of (1) signed articles written by authorities and (2) directories of national agencies, governmental and voluntary, in the field of social work. Each article carries a bibliography. The directories describe the activities of the agencies listed.

BIBLIOGRAPHY

Altmeyer, Arthur J. and Others. *War and Post-War Social Security; The Outlines of an Expanded Program.* Washington: American Council on Public Affairs (2153 Florida Ave.), 1942, 89 pp.

Benedict, Murray R. *A Retirement System for Farmers.* Planning Pamphlet No. 49. Washington: National Planning Association (800 21st St. N. W.), 1946, 44 pp.

Beveridge, Sir William H. *Full Employment in a Free Society.* New York: W. W. Norton & Co., 1945, 429 pp.

——. *Social Insurance and Allied Services.* New York: Macmillan Co., 1942, 299 pp.

Brown, Josephine C. *The Rural Community and Social Case Work.* New York: Family Welfare Association of America (122 East 22nd St.), 1933, 165 pp. (Suggested reading, pp. 157-65.)

Browning, Grace. *Rural Public Welfare; Selected Records, with Introductory Notes and Comments.* Chicago: University of Chicago Press, 1941, 578 pp. (Selected bibliography, pp. 547-66.)

The Child. Monthly journal of the U. S. Children's Bureau, Federal Security Agency, Washington, D. C.

Colcord, Joanna C. *Your Community; Its Provision for Health, Education, Safety, and Welfare.* New York: Russell Sage Foundation (130 East 22nd St.), 1941, 281 pp. (List of references, pp. 241-51.)

Community Chests and Councils, Inc. *Health and Welfare Planning in the Smaller Community.* New York: Community Chests and Councils, Inc. (155 East 44th St.), 1945, 27 pp.

The Compass. Published six times yearly by the American Association of Social Workers, 130 East 22nd St., New York.

Council of State Governments. *Unemployment Compensation in the Post-War Period; Suggestions for Expanding and Perfecting State Unemployment Compensation Systems and a Digest of State and Federal Provisions.* Chicago: The Council (1313 East 6oth St.), 1944, 77 pp.

Holbrook, David H. "National Associations in Social Work," in *Social Work Year Book, 1945,* pp. 274-80. (Bibliography, p. 280.)

Hopkins, William S. *Social Insurance and Agriculture; A Memorandum Presenting Suggestions for Research and a Bibliography.* Pamphlet Series No. 5. Washington: Committee on Social Security, Social Science Research Council (726 Jackson Place, N. W.), 1940, 93 pp. (Bibliography, pp. 38-93.)

National Planning Association. *Joint Statement on Social Security by Agriculture, Business and Labor.* Planning Pamphlet No. 33. Washington: The Association (800 21st St. N. W.), 1944, 36 pp.

Proceedings of the National Conference of Social Work, Selected Papers. New York: Columbia University Press, annual.

Public Welfare. Monthly journal of the American Public Welfare Association, 1313 East 6oth St., Chicago, Illinois.

"Reports and Periodicals of State Welfare Departments." *Public Welfare,* Vol. III, No. 10, October 1945, pp. 233-34.

Russell, Howard L. "Public Welfare," in *Social Work Year Book, 1945,* pp. 351-63. (Bibliography, pp. 362-63.)

Smith, Marjorie J. *Rural Case Work Services.* New York: Family Welfare Association of America (122 East 22nd St.), 1943, 62 pp.

Social Security Bulletin. Monthly publication of the Federal Security Agency. Washington: Government Printing Office.

Social Security in America; Addresses, National Conference on Social Security Sponsored by Chamber of Commerce of the United States. January 1944, 103 pp.

Social Security Yearbook. Publication of the Federal Security Agency. Washington: Government Printing Office.

Social Service Review. A quarterly journal edited by the faculty of the School of Social Service Administration, University of Chicago. Chicago: University of Chicago Press.

Social Work Publicity Council. *Rural Routes to Community Understanding.* New York: The Council (130 East 22nd St.), 1940, 19 pp.

Social Work Year Book, 1945; A Description of Organized Activities in Social Work and in Related Fields. Eighth Issue. Russell H. Kurtz, ed. New York: Russell Sage Foundation (130 East 22nd St.), 1945, 620 pp.

Stevenson, Marietta. *Public Welfare Administration.* New York: Macmillan Co., 1938, 352 pp. (Bibliography, pp. 333-43.)

Stewart, Maxwell S. *The Beveridge Plan*. Public Affairs Pamphlet No. 79. New York: Public Affairs Committee, Inc. (30 Rockefeller Plaza), 1943, 31 pp.

——. *Jobs and Security for Tomorrow*. Public Affairs Pamphlet No. 84. New York: Public Affairs Committee, Inc., 1943, 31 pp.

Strode, Josephine. *The County Worker's Job; What It Is and What It Takes*. New York: Survey Associates, Inc. (112 East 19th St.), 40 pp.

Survey Graphic and *Survey Midmonthly*. Monthly publications of Survey Associates, Inc., 112 East 19th St., New York.

Taylor, Carl C. "Rural Social Programs," in *Social Work Year Book, 1945*, pp. 384-89. (Bibliography, p. 389.)

"Ten Years of Social Security." *Social Security Bulletin*, Vol. VIII, No. 8, August 1945, 56 pp.

Tompkins, Dorothy C. *Plans for Security*. Berkeley, California: Bureau of Public Administration, University of California, 1943, 11 pp.

U. S. Department of Agriculture. *Report of the Secretary of Agriculture, 1944*. Washington: Government Printing Office, 1944, 196 pp.

—— and U. S. Social Security Board. *Social Security for Farm People; Questions and Answers*. Washington: Government Printing Office, 1946, 14 pp.

U. S. Division of Public Inquiries. Government Information Service. Bureau of the Budget. *United States Government Manual—1947*. 1st ed. Washington: Government Printing Office, 1946, 718 pp.

U. S. Federal Security Agency. *Annual Report of the Federal Security Agency for the Fiscal Year 1945, Section Five, Social Security Board*. Washington: Government Printing Office, 1945, 117 pp.

U. S. National Resources Planning Board. *After the War—Toward Security*. Washington: Government Printing Office, 1942, 61 pp.

——. "Equal Access to Economic Security," in *National Resources Development—Report for 1943. Part I, Post-War Plan and Program*. Washington: Government Printing Office, 1943, pp. 75-81.

——. *Security, Work, and Relief Policies; Report of the Committee on Long-Range Work and Relief Policies*. Washington: Government Printing Office, 1942, 640 pp.

U. S. Social Security Board. *9th Annual Report, Fiscal Year 1943-44*. Washington: Government Printing Office, 1944, 82 pp.

——. Library. *Some Basic Readings in Social Security*. Social Security Board Publication No. 28, Revised. Washington: Government Printing Office, 1942, 74 pp.

White, R. Clyde. *Administration of Public Welfare*. New York: American Book Co., 1940, 527 pp. (Selected bibliography, pp. 511-17.)

Withers, Gertrude V. *Effective Rural Social Work through Community Organization*. Chicago: American Public Welfare Association (1313 East 60th St.), 1942, 42 pp. (Bibliography, p. 42.)

Works, George A. and Simon O. Lesser. "The Schools and Rural Social Welfare," Chapter XI in *Rural America Today; Its Schools and Community Life*. Chicago: University of Chicago Press, 1942, pp. 242-66.

7 HOUSING

Housing for farm families presents special problems in designing, construction, and financing. In addition to providing a home for the farm family, the farmhouse serves as the business office for the farm enterprise. In the farmhouse the homemaker must carry on many activities needing space and special equipment. The farm home may serve as the center of social life for the family to a greater extent than the home in the city. There are special problems in supplying heat, light, water, and sanitary facilities in the farmhouse; more of such services must be provided on an individual basis in the country than in the city. There is greater need for storage space in the farm than in the city home. Rural regions, like cities, suffer from the shortcomings of an inefficient housebuilding industry. The rural home builder is at a special disadvantage in hiring the skilled workers needed in house construction. The financing of housing ties in directly with the financial status of the whole farm operation and with the position of agriculture in the national economy. It is also related to the way in which the householder derives his income; problems of housing finance are quite different for farm owners and operators, tenants attached to farms, migratory workers, part-time farmers, and nonfarm rural residents who make their living in the city.

Data on the condition of farm housing are contained in the Farm Housing Survey of 1934, the Housing Census of 1940, and several less extensive recent surveys. A brief statement of housing needs, based on these data, is contained in *The Need for Rural Housing*, by Emma G. Holmes and Grace M. Angle. The median market value of owner-occupied farm homes in 1940 was $1,028. In the North the median was $1,450; in the West, $1,084; and in the South, $600. The median monthly rental of tenant-occupied farmhouses was $4.72. Crowding is more general in rural than in urban homes. In 16 per cent of the farm homes as compared with 9 per cent of the urban, there were, in 1940, more than 1.5 persons per room. In the South and in the Mountain States more than 25 per cent were in this category. A generally accepted standard is that the number of rooms available for living quarters should equal the number of people occupying the home. Closet space in farm homes is apt to be inadequate or entirely lacking.

In 1940, only 18 per cent of the farm homes had running water in the house; another 11 per cent had hand pumps in the kitchen. Almost four-fifths had outside toilets, and over 9 per cent had no toilet facilities whatever. Slightly more than one-fourth had a kitchen sink with drain. Two-thirds had no electric lights, and only 10 per cent had central heating. Only 15 per cent had mechanical refrigerators. Nearly two and a half million of the more than seven million farm homes were in need of major repairs.

Similar data are presented in a publication of the Interbureau Coordinating Committee on Post-War Programs of the United States Department of Agriculture, *The Need for Rural Housing,* which also suggests some causes of the rural housing problem and ways of meeting the housing need.

HOUSING ACTIVITIES OF THE FEDERAL GOVERNMENT

Federal governmental activities in the interest of rural housing improvement are carried on principally by the Extension Service, the Bureau of Human Nutrition and Home Economics, the Farm Security Administration, the Farm Credit Administration, the National Housing Agency, and the Rural Electrification Administration. The activities of the REA are described in Chapter 10.

The Extension Service provides information, instruction, and demonstrations concerning planning, financing, construction, and improvement of houses and other farm buildings. Building-plan books and bulletins furnish information on planning, modernizing, water supply, plumbing, heating, decorating, and the like. The land-grant colleges in many states have issued bulletins designed to meet various rural housing needs in their respective states.

The Bureau of Human Nutrition and Home Economics in the Department of Agriculture makes surveys, conducts research, and issues information on rural housing problems. Mention has been made of the Farm Housing Survey of 1934, in which the Bureau participated. *The Need for Rural Housing,* by Holmes and Angle, referred to above, is a Bureau publication. Another example is *Housing Requirements of Farm Families in the United States,* by Maud Wilson, "prepared as an aid to designers and property owners in planning low-cost farmhouses." This publication covers such matters as construction and orientation, room uses, entrance protection, doors and windows, heating, sanitary facilities, storage facilities, basement use, dining areas, business area, provisions for child care, indoor sleeping arrangements, and provision for leisure activities. It points out regional variations in housing requirements of farm families. Still another example of a Bureau publication is *Minimum Adequate Standards for Farm Dwelling and Household Equipment.*

The Farm Security Administration in the Department of Agriculture aids rural housing through loans to a limited number of capable tenants, sharecroppers, and farm laborers to enable them to buy family-type farms. When necessary these loans include funds to repair the existing house or to construct a new dwelling. Under this program, through 1941, over 11,000 new farm homes had been built and nearly 12,000 had been repaired. Since 1941, as a result of the war, this program has been greatly curtailed. Other housing activities of the FSA have included building homes on resettlement projects, housing in camps for migratory farm workers, defense trailers and houses, and dormitory units for war workers. The housing activities of the FSA are described in articles in recent volumes of the *Housing Yearbook,* issued by the National Association of Housing Officials.

The Farm Credit Administration in the Department of Agriculture has the general purpose of providing a complete and coordinated credit system for agriculture by making long-term and short-term credit available to farmers. It lends funds for home construction on the same basis that it lends funds for farm purchase, provided the loan is secured by the entire farm and the residence is suited to its operation.

On November 1, 1946, credit facilities and services of the Farm Security Administration and the emergency crop and feed loan division of the Farm Credit Administration were merged into a new agency, the Farmers Home Administration.

Other credit facilities of the federal government that are available to help in home financing are the Federal Home Loan Bank System and the Home Owners' Loan Corporation. The Federal Housing Administration insures private lending institutions against loss on loans secured by mortgages on one- to four-family dwellings or on large-scale rental housing projects and on loans for property repair and improvement. All of these agencies and the Federal Public Housing Authority are currently consolidated in the National Housing Agency.

LOCAL HOUSING AUTHORITIES

Public housing activities of the federal government are centered in the Federal Public Housing Authority. Under the United States Housing Act of 1937, as amended, the federal government provides subsidies to local housing authorities to ensure low rentals in housing constructed to rehouse low-income families living in slums. The local housing authorities are public corporate bodies established by resolution of the governing body of a city or county, in accordance with state law. They have full power to acquire property and to plan, construct, and operate housing and related facilities for families of low income. They may borrow up to 90 per cent of their capital from the national Authority. They must fulfill specific conditions established by law. According to the *Housing Directory, 1946-1947*, there were 479 regional, county, and municipal authorities; only 34 of these, however, had been established to engage exclusively, or almost exclusively, in rural or farm housing. The *Directory* lists only 7 authorities with active rural programs; in others, programs are deferred. The rural housing program of the Federal Public Housing Authority is described in its publication *Homes for Farm Families*.

More detailed information as to the organization and activities of federal agencies concerned with housing may be obtained in the *United States Government Manual—1947* and in the annual reports issued by the agencies.

The *Housing Directory, 1946-1947* lists official housing administrative agencies for twelve states—agencies whose principal function is to regulate or to plan, finance, construct, or manage housing. In some other states there are public agencies devoted primarily to housing but having only investigatory or advisory powers. In her extensive study, *State Housing Agencies,* Dorothy Schaffter presents a detailed description of the history of state housing agencies and points out that the conspicuous gap in public housing activities occurs in the states. A final chapter of conclusions and recommendations is based on the belief that the state must become an active participant if public housing is to approximate the success of other social programs, such as education and health. In discussing rural and village housing, she suggests that state housing agencies might well concentrate attention in this area, which thus far has received relatively little attention from any source. Small cities and villages and rural areas must be assured of a reasonable degree of independence in the control of their own housing programs; they also need more state assistance and control than large cities.

General References

The National Association of Housing Officials has issued a report, *Housing for the United States after the War,* prepared by the Association's Committee on Postwar Housing and approved in principle and issued by the Board of Governors of the Association. The section on rural housing points out that "farm housing is directly related to the use of land for agricultural production. . . . Farm housing needs vary with variations in characteristics of farm families and farm workers. . . . The need for farm housing is determined by economic land use studies and analyses of rural population as to social characteristics, and in relation to farm economic resources. While the types and designs of farm housing will be substantially different from those of urban housing, standards of healthfulness, convenience, and livability should be no less. . . . Proper planning of educational, cultural, and other community facilities is an essential part of the comprehensive planning that must underlie an effective rural housing program." In discussing problems of financing, the report states:

> From the point of view of private mortgage finance, the farm home is not considered a good risk for a separate loan, since the loan is justified only by the success of the business of farming. Private funds for farm housing, therefore, are available only indirectly. As a result, there is little hope of improving the quality of housing for low-income farmers through the operation of private finance alone. Federal assistance is needed to provide: more effective use of various forms of farm credit; a method for making available to rural housing the benefits of such direct loans and subsidies as may be necessary to serve low-income families, but through procedures suited to the nature of rural housing and to the needs of rural families; and utilization of the educational facilities of the Department of Agriculture in fostering sound maintenance methods.
>
> Obviously, housing should not be subsidized in uneconomic farm areas. On the contrary, rural housing plans should be integrated with the efforts of states, counties, and the Department of Agriculture to promote sound use of farm land and the shifting of farm families from areas where it is impossible to make a satisfactory living from the land.

The Twentieth Century Fund has published the results of an extensive survey of the housing situation in a volume entitled *American Housing; Problems and Prospects*. Major sections of the book are devoted to the production of housing, marketing of housing, and conclusions and recommendations of the Housing Committee of the Fund. In discussing rural and farm housing, the point is made that home financing and production facilities suitable for urban conditions are rarely adaptable to the rural situation. However, "in rural housing, as in urban, the greatest hope of improvement lies in the development of a more efficient housebuilding industry which will give consumers better houses at lower cost." It is suggested that there may be special opportunities for the wide use of prefabricated construction in rural areas. Specific recommendations of the Committee relating to rural housing are as follows:

1. That the existing means for aiding farm housing through the Farm Credit Administration, the Farm Security Administration, and Rural Electrification Administration be continued; that, for the purposes of co-ordinating and developing rural housing policy, there be established in the Department of Agriculture an Intradepartmental Housing Committee; and that the strictly farm housing functions now residing in the National Housing Agency be transferred to appropriate agencies in the Department of Agriculture. Since its loan funds and expenses are provided by the government, the Farm Security Administration could continue to finance disadvantaged farmers who cannot get credit from business credit agencies. The FSA is also the logical agency to assist or administer programs involving federal subsidies such as those of local or regional farm housing authorities. The Farm Credit Administration is a business-credit agency, partly owned by farmers, borrowing funds from investors and operating on a self-supporting business basis without Congressional appropriation. However, it should assist in educational programs to improve housing conditions among its borrowers. It should also give sympathetic consideration to loans for financing new houses or improvements that are appropriate to the borrower's financial condition and within his reasonable capacity to repay. Production credit associations and banks should be urged to make intermediate term loans for financing farm housing improvements that are justified by sound credit policies and the borrower's capacity to repay.

2. That the proposed Committee co-ordinate all housing research functions now being carried on in the several bureaus of the Department of Agriculture and promote decentralized housing research through the State Agricultural and Mechanical Colleges.

3. That the new agency, through the state extension services and the county and home extension agents, enlarge and strengthen education programs among farm families, emphasizing adequate but economically sound housing standards and assisting farm families in obtaining suitable housing at the lowest possible cost.

4. That, as an experiment, provision be made for sale to farmers on a conditional sale basis of surplus demountable houses acquired under the wartime housing program.

5. That an extensive rural house repair and modernization program be instituted, utilizing methods based on the experience of Rural Electrification Administration and the Electric Home and Farm Authority.

6. That the Federal Home Loan Bank Board, Federal Housing Administration and the farm housing agencies co-operate to reduce and eliminate the gap in credit facilities between farm and urban housing.

Two pamphlets based on the survey of the Twentieth Century Fund may be cited. The Fund has issued *Building America's Houses*, which points out basic troubles and indicates ways to their solution. Public Affairs Pamphlet No. 96, *Houses for Tomorrow*, by Thomas

R. Carskadon, is a summary of principal findings and recommendations of the Fund survey.

Farm Housing—A Case Study, issued by the National Committee on Housing, contains the proceedings of a conference held in May, 1945, on the problems of farm housing in the State of Kentucky. "While the conference sought concrete plans to improve the housing of Kentucky's 280,000 farm families, its discussions may be said to have nation-wide interest and value." Farms in the state "range from the very successful to the very poor, and the housing of farm families is in keeping. Agriculture is both specialized and diversified. For these reasons Kentucky farm housing presents a cross-section of conditions and a wide range of problems, the study of which may prove helpful to other areas." On the national problem of farm housing, the study states:

Of the Nation's more than six and a half million farm families an estimated 4,300,000 are ill-housed, half of them in dwellings which are beyond repair. Farm housing thus presents a problem of huge proportions, complicated further by the fact that unlike urban housing it has received scant attention and less study until very recent months.

Minimum Requirements for Farmhouses is a pamphlet issued by the United States Department of Agriculture, based on conclusions reached after extensive study by technicians representing agencies in the Department which have had firsthand experience with rural housing problems and have gained considerable knowledge of the kind of homes farm people want.

W. K. Williams' *Farm Buildings from Home-Grown Timber in the South* is a recent Farmers' Bulletin of the United States Department of Agriculture. It carries a bibliography of publications on the construction of farm buildings and related subjects.

Two studies of subsistence homesteads include materials of value to persons interested in rural housing. Russell Lord and Paul H. Johnstone are the editors of a volume entitled *A Place on Earth; A Critical Appraisal of Subsistence Homesteads.* Paul W. Wager is the author of *One Foot on the Soil; A Study of Subsistence Homesteads in Alabama.*

The building industry has evinced interest in rural housing and has issued publications relating thereto. One such publication is *Engineered Low-Cost Farm and Village Homes,* by the National Homes Foundation, which includes a number of floor plans, information as to building materials, a list of federal agencies concerned with rural housing and information on their functions, and a list of trade associations in the home-building industry that can supply information about home-building products.

Persons interested generally in problems of housing will find an authoritative discussion in Edith Elmer Wood's *Introduction to Housing; Facts and Principles.*

A pamphlet by Catherine Bauer, *Housing in the United States; Problems and Policy,* provides a discussion of the social, economic, and civic problems of housing and of emerging progressive principles that should aid in their solution.

Bibliographies and Periodicals

Rural Housing; A Selected List of References Prepared for Postwar Planning Groups in the Great Plains Region, compiled by Marion E. Wheeler, lists bibliographies, general references, census publications, and references on cost and standard of living, financing, foreign legislation and experience, housing standards (plans, materials, modern conveniences), index and scales, and landscaping.

Two additional bibliographies on housing are United States National Housing Agency's *Reading List on Housing* and Elizabeth L. Carey's *Bibliography on Public Housing and Related Subjects for the Use of Teachers and Students,* a publication of the United States Federal Public Housing Authority.

Current developments in housing may be followed in the *Journal of Housing,* the monthly publication of the National Association of Housing Officials. The *Housing Yearbook,* published by the Association, contains authoritative articles summarizing accomplishments in the housing field and a directory of housing agencies—national, state, regional, and local. Over the years the *Yearbook* has carried a number of articles dealing with rural housing.

Publications of the Committee on the Hygiene of Housing of the American Public Health Association are described in Chapter 5.

BIBLIOGRAPHY

Bauer, Catherine. *Housing in the United States; Problems and Policy.* Montreal: International Labour Organisation, 1945, 28 pp. Reprinted from the *International Labour Review,* Vol. LII, No. 1, July 1945.

Carey, Elizabeth L. *Bibliography on Public Housing and Related Subjects for the Use of Teachers and Students.* Washington: U. S. Federal Public Housing Authority, 1945, 11 pp.

Carskadon, Thomas R. *Houses for Tomorrow.* Public Affairs Pamphlet No. 96. New York: Public Affairs Committee (30 Rockefeller Plaza), 1944, 32 pp.

Holmes, Emma G. and Grace M. Angle. *The Need for Rural Housing.* Washington: U. S. Bureau of Human Nutrition and Home Economics, April 1944, 10 pp.

Journal of Housing. Monthly publication of the National Association of Housing Officials, 1313 East 60th St., Chicago, Illinois.

Lord, Russell and Paul H. Johnstone, eds. *A Place on Earth; A Critical Appraisal of Subsistence Homesteads.* Washington: U. S. Bureau of Agricultural Economics, 1942, 202 pp.

National Association of Housing Officials. *Housing for the United States after the War.* Publication No. N193. Chicago: The Association, 1944, 65 pp.

——.*Housing Directory, 1946-1947.* Chicago: The Association, 1946.

——. *Housing Yearbook,* 1935-44. Chicago: The Association, 1935-44.

National Committee on Housing. *Farm Housing—A Case Study; Proceedings of the Conference Sponsored by the Committee for Kentucky in Association with University of Kentucky, National Committee on Housing, Inc., Lexington, Kentucky, May 25-26, 1945.* New York: The Committee (512 Fifth Ave.), 1946, 77 pp.

National Homes Foundation. *Engineered Low-Cost Farm and Village Homes.* Washington: The Association (515 Union Trust Building), 23 pp.

Schaffter, Dorothy. *State Housing Agencies.* New York: Columbia University Press, 1942, 808 pp. (Bibliography, pp. 689-783.)

Twentieth Century Fund. Housing Committee. *American Housing; Problems and Prospects.* The Factual Findings by Miles L. Colean; The Program by the Housing Committee. New York: The Fund, 1944, 466 pp. (Bibliography, pp. 441-55.)

——. *Building America's Houses.* Twentieth Century Pamphlet No. 1. New York: The Fund, 1945, 12 pp.

U. S. Bureau of Home Economics. *The Farm Housing Survey.* Miscellaneous Publication No. 323. Washington: U. S. Department of Agriculture, 1939, 42 pp.

U. S. Bureau of Human Nutrition and Home Economics. *Minimum Adequate Standards for Farm Dwelling and Household Equipment.* Washington: The Bureau, 1943, 6 pp.

U. S. Bureau of the Census. *Sixteenth Census of the United States: 1940. Housing . . .* Washington: Government Printing Office, 1943, 4 Vols. in 13 Parts.

——. *Sixteenth Census of the United States: 1940. Population and Housing. Families; Characteristics of Rural-Farm Families, Regions and Divisions.* Washington: Government Printing Office, 1943, 82 pp.

U. S. Department of Agriculture. *Minimum Requirements for Farmhouses Recommended by the United States Department of Agriculture.* Miscellaneous Publication No. 475. Washington: Government Printing Office, 1941, 8 pp.

——. Interbureau Coordinating Committee on Post-War Programs. *The Need for Rural Housing*. Rev. ed. Washington: The Committee, July 1943, 17 pp.

U. S. Division of Public Inquiries. Government Information Service. Bureau of the Budget. *United States Government Manual—1947*. 1st ed. Washington: Government Printing Office, 1946, 718 pp.

U. S. Federal Public Housing Authority. *Homes for Farm Families; The Rural Housing Program of the ... Authority*. Washington: The Authority, 1945, 5 pp.

U. S. National Housing Agency. Information Service. *Reading List on Housing*. Washington: The Agency, 1945, 18 pp.

Wager, Paul W. *One Foot on the Soil; A Study of Subsistence Homesteads in Alabama*. University, Alabama: Bureau of Public Administration, University of Alabama, 1945, 230 pp.

Wheeler, Marion E. *Rural Housing; A Selected List of References Prepared for Postwar Planning Groups in the Great Plains Region*. Lincoln, Nebraska: U. S. Department of Agriculture, Library, Lincoln Branch, January 1944, 28 pp.

Williams, W. K. *Farm Buildings from Home-Grown Timber in the South*. U. S. Department of Agriculture, Farmers' Bulletin No. 1975. Washington: Government Printing Office, 1945, 18 pp. (Publications on the Construction of Farm Buildings and Related Subjects, p. 18.)

Wilson, Maud. *Housing Requirements of Farm Families in the United States*. Bureau of Home Economics, Miscellaneous Publication No. 322. Washington: Government Printing Office, 1939, 40 pp. (References, p. 39.)

Wood, Edith Elmer. *Introduction to Housing; Facts and Principles*. Washington: U. S. Housing Authority, 1939, 161 pp.

8 RECREATION

RURAL AREAS have many recreational advantages, such as open space for outdoor sports, opportunities for nature study, a spirit of neighborliness, and in many localities a long record of community activities. Many areas also suffer from such disadvantages as lack of funds, isolation, long working hours, lack of leadership, lack of physical facilities in schools, churches, or elsewhere, and lack of libraries and other cultural resources. One of the results of technological advancement should be increased leisure for rural people, with opportunities for recreation that will bring personal satisfactions and improved individual and community life.

Recreation may be defined as any voluntary leisure-time activity that gives immediate satisfaction to the participant. The range of recreational activities is wide, but the important element in recreation is the satisfaction of the participant rather than the particular activities carried on. Major groups into which recreational activities fall are described by George D. Butler in an article "Recreation" in the *Social Work Year Book, 1945,* as arts and crafts, drama and music, nature and gardening, social recreation, athletics and sports, and camping. A variety of activities is included in each of these major categories.

ELEMENTS IN A RECREATION PROGRAM

Among the elements necessary for an effective recreational program are area, facilities, organization, leadership, activities, and programs.

The area requirements for recreation agreed upon by the National Resources Planning Board are set forth in a section, "Public Works and Recreational Land," in the Board's report *Public Works and Rural Land Use.* The needs of urban people include playfields and neighborhood playgrounds within easy walking distance of all children, playfields and neighborhood centers not over one and a half miles distant from all residents, parks and other areas of natural and man-made beauty so distributed that all may enjoy them occasionally, protection of urban and suburban streams and other waters from pollution and "uglifying" uses, and parkways along waterways and connecting major recreational areas. For the holiday and week-end use of urban people and those living in intensively cultivated rural sections, there is need of public areas for picnicking, water sports, day and overnight camping, hiking, and other such activities.

While the needs of rural America for recreational areas are somewhat different, rural residents need something roughly equivalent to the parks and playgrounds of city dwellers, provision for such activities as baseball, softball, and tennis, and provision for group activities such as picnics, music and dramatics, competitive sports, festivals, pageants, and dancing.

There is need for extensive public holdings for the vacation use of the entire population, for adequate ocean, lake, and river frontage publicly owned, and for public ownership of areas of distinctive beauty or of historic, prehistoric, and scientific significance. In addition, there is need for public parkways, trails and trailways, routes of water travel, wayside areas, and border strips along highways.

Recreation facilities and equipment are needed for a large variety of outdoor and indoor activities. General types of outdoor facilities include game courts and fields and facilities for various sports; structures such as bleachers, stadiums, pavilions, outdoor theaters, recreation piers, and swimming pools; equipment such as fireplaces, picnic facilities, and playground apparatus; and special areas such as athletic fields, bathing beaches, golf courses, bridle paths, boating areas, camps, concert areas, farm plots, gardens, parking fields, picnic areas, and putting greens. Indoor facilities are also needed for many kinds of recreational activities. Many communities have buildings designed and built exclusively for recreational uses. Schools, libraries, churches, and other public and private buildings also provide recreational facilities. In rural communities the school is most frequently the indoor recreational center, and there is a growing tendency to plan and construct school buildings with a view to their use as recreation centers by both school and nonschool groups.

Effective leadership is essential to the success of a recreation program. The need for variety in play and for acquiring skill makes play leadership as important in rural as in urban areas. Rural areas provide a rich and potentially stimulating play environment, but leadership is frequently lacking. There is increasing recognition on the part of various groups of the need for trained recreation leaders, and efforts are being made to meet it. The state agricultural colleges are providing more recreation training for teachers, 4-H Club leaders, and county agents. In a number of states the extension service has employed full- or part-time workers in rural recreation and community organization. Youth-serving agencies, the Farm Bureau, the Farmers Union, the Grange, rural churches, and other agencies are giving formal training for recreation leaders in many communities.

Opportunities for recreation are provided by public agencies, voluntary agencies not for profit organized on a community or wider basis, and commercial recreation and amusement interests.

FEDERAL ACTIVITIES

The principal federal governmental agencies furthering recreational opportunities of interest to rural people are the National Park Service, the Forest Service, and the Extension Service, although a number of other agencies also are instrumental in providing opportunities for leisure-time activities.

The national park system, administered by the National Park Service in the United States Department of the Interior, as of June 30, 1945, contained 22,201,880 acres (*Annual Report of the Director, National Park Service . . . Fiscal Year Ended June 30, 1945*). It includes some outstanding scenic and scientific sites, especially in the western states; historic and prehistoric sites throughout the nation; and recreational areas of regional and national appeal. The Service makes these areas readily accessible by roads and trails, provides transportation and hotel accommodations for park visitors, and in many areas maintains a nature guide service. The approximate average number of visitors annually in the five-year period 1941-45 was 11,581,823. The Park Service has also administered recreational demonstration areas, which, as of June 30, 1943, numbered forty-six and contained 360,392 acres. An act of June 6, 1942, authorized transfer of these areas to other jurisdictions, and most have since been transferred. The recreational areas are intended to provide group camps, cabins for family use, and facilities for water sports, picnicking, hiking, and other day uses.

In the Park, Parkway, and Recreation Study Act of 1936, Congress directed the Secretary of the Interior through the National Park Service to make a study of recreational programs and lands throughout the United States which are or may be chiefly valuable for recreation, and to cooperate with other federal, state, and local agencies in planning for coordinated and adequate public park, parkway, and recreational area facilities. The Park Service has cooperated with appropriate agencies in formulating statewide recreation plans and in making special studies of park use and attendance, fees and charges, legislation, organization, camping, hiking, and winter sports. It has published a report, *A Study of the Park and Recreation Problem of the United States,* which reflects the preliminary findings of state studies and presents the recommendations of the Service for a coordinated nationwide park and recreational land plan for the United States.

In the years 1937 through 1941, the National Park Service issued a *Yearbook, Park and Recreation Progress,* which brought together the current views of leaders in the park and recreation field. The 1942 and 1943 numbers of the *Yearbook* were issued by the National Conference on State Parks.

The National Park Service has issued many other useful publications. Among these is *Information Relating to the National Park System.* For information on publications, including pamphlets on individual national parks, inquiries may be addressed to the Service.

The Forest Service in the United States Department of Agriculture has prepared recreational plans for all national forests and coordinates its work with that of other agencies. According to a pamphlet issued by the Service, *The Work of the U. S. Forest Service,* there are 154 national forests covering an area of 179,000,000 acres. Recreational users in 1940 numbered 16,000,000 persons in addition to 22,000,000 who drove over forest roads. The national forests contain more than 5,000 camp and picnic grounds, winter-sports areas, organization camps, and resorts developed for public use. Good roads and trails make these areas readily accessible. The Forest Service issues a variety of publications, some of which are concerned with recreation. It published an extensive bibliography on this subject in 1938, *Forest Recreation: A Bibliography,* and has also published a volume *Forest Outings,* prepared by thirty foresters.

In many communities social and recreational activities are an important part of the program of the Extension Service of the United States Department of Agriculture. Such activities include community singing, plays, games, camping, debates, reading, picnics, and folk dancing. Over a four-year period the Service cooperated with the National Recreation Association in conducting training institutes for rural leaders. Some eighty thousand volunteer leaders received training in these institutes. The large number of summer camps conducted in the 4-H Club program provide leadership training to rural youth in games, music, and other recreational activities. The Extension Service also conducts summer camps for rural women. The organization and activities of the Extension Service are described in some detail in Chapter 2.

The program of the Future Farmers of America, sponsored by the

Vocational Education Division of the United States Office of Education for public high-school students of vocational agriculture, includes organized recreational activities. Leadership in local chapters is provided by the teachers of vocational agriculture. A number of state associations have permanent state camps, and organized training for leadership is part of the summer camp program. Similar groups for rural Negro youth are known as the New Farmers of America.

A publication of the Office of Education, *Planning Schools for Tomorrow; The Schools and Recreation Services,* is concerned primarily with "the school's responsibility in providing or in helping to provide recreational opportunities for the children and youth of the community."

The work of the United States Children's Bureau is described in some detail in Chapter 9, but mention should be made here of two of its publications bearing on rural recreation. A *Handbook for Recreation Leaders,* by Ella Gardner, is based on experience with recreation programs in rural areas. It is designed to be used in planning programs and in selecting games and other recreational materials for use in the home and by club and community groups. *Development of a Leisure-Time Program in Small Cities and Towns,* by the same author, is concerned with community planning for leisure-time activities. It covers such items as securing sponsors, obtaining the cooperation of local agencies, planning and conducting the survey meeting, starting the program, and standards for playgrounds and other recreational facilities.

The programs of a number of other federal agencies contribute to public recreation. Among these may be mentioned the Federal Communications Commission, established to help make available to the people of the United States wire and radio communication service with adequate facilities at reasonable charges; the Soil Conservation Service, which provides recreational facilities in a number of areas; the Fish and Wildlife Service, which has developed a limited number of recreational facilities; the Bureau of Biological Survey, which provides some picnicking and day-camping facilities; and the Bureau of Reclamation, which administers limited recreational facilities on its water storage projects. The Bureau of Reclamation has published *Columbia Basin, Joint Investigations: Problem 25, Rural Recreation Areas.* The problem is stated as follows:

To locate and plan the layout and improvement of rural parks and recreational grounds within the project area. Attractive spots, quickly and conveniently accessible, and without high agricultural utility insofar as practicable, seem to be indicated.

Recreation was featured in the programs of the emergency agencies of the depression period and in the defense and war programs of the federal government. Recreational facilities for local use were developed in many areas through the public works and relief work programs of the Public Works Administration and the Work Projects Administration. The WPA also trained thousands of community and recreation leaders and issued a number of publications in the recreation field. Its *American Recreation Series* consists of fifty-two booklets, one for each state and one each for Alaska, Hawaii, Puerto Rico, and the Virgin Islands. Its series of recreation circulars contains one entitled *Rural Recreation Area,* which suggests a plan for a twenty-acre area to serve the recreational needs of a rural community. A publication, *Community Recreation Programs: A Study of WPA Recreation Projects,* presents a general survey of the WPA recreation program. Eduard C. Lindeman, for four years consulting director of the division of recreation of the WPA, has set down in *Leisure—A National Issue* not the detail of the WPA program "but how this experience may be utilized for future planning purposes."

The Civilian Conservation Corps and Public Recreation is one of the series of illustrated pamphlets that the CCC issued to describe various phases of its work.

Several publications of the Office of Civilian Defense, in the Office for Emergency Management, and of the division of recreation, Office of Community War Services, in the Federal Security Agency have valuable materials for community groups interested in recreational activities. OCD publication No. 3624, *Recreation in War Time; A Manual for Recreation Committees of Local Defense Councils,* offers suggestions on how to organize a recreation committee, what a recreation committee does, typical activities that it sponsors, and related subjects. OCD publication No. 3637, *Volunteers for Youth Recreation Programs,* was prepared "with the cooperation of church groups, group work and recreation agencies and Federal agencies concerned with children and youth to encourage and assist communities in the recruitment and training of leaders through united effort."

In *What About Us? A Report of Community Recreation for Young People,* the Office of Community War Services records the story of recreation for youth in wartime America, with examples from the big city, the small town, rural areas, and quiet villages that overnight became war production areas. Experience has shown that every town in the United States needs recreation for its young people and can see to it that they get it. Another publication of the Office of Community War Services, *Community Recreation Comes of Age,* sets down the ten essentials of a public recreation system and then shows how they work out in day-to-day community progress. The essentials are: know your community; pool your resources; check your legislation; establish a legal managing authority; get good leadership; make the most of existing facilities; secure a separate budget; see that your program is community-wide, year-round, and has broad appeal; maintain public partnership; and plan for the future.

The Office of Community War Services has published a study, *Youth Centers—An Appraisal and a Look Ahead,* which is based primarily on a questionnaire survey of over three hundred individual youth centers located in thirty-four states in communities ranging in population from 700 to 900,000. *Planning for Recreation Areas and Facilities in Small Towns and Cities,* prepared for the Office of Community War Services by J. Lee Brown, is directed toward meeting the needs of communities of up to 25,000 population.

The Tennessee Valley area offers unusual recreational opportunities, and the Tennessee Valley Authority has issued publications describing them. Included are: *Recreational Development of the Southern Highlands Region; A Study of the Use and Control of Scenic and Recreational Resources* and *The Scenic Resources of the Tennessee Valley; A Descriptive and Pictorial Inventory.*

STATE AND LOCAL GOVERNMENTAL ACTIVITIES

State governments provide a number of direct recreational services —state parks, forests, wildlife areas, historic sites, parkways, and the like. They also facilitate local recreation programs through the adoption of enabling legislation and through leadership, advisory, and promotional services. Included among the agencies concerned in varying degrees with recreational opportunities for the people of their respective states are planning boards, departments of education, welfare departments, library extension services, and conservation, natural resources, forestry, and park departments, boards, and commissions. As has been mentioned, a number of states have recreation specialists in the extension department of the state agricultural college who train persons for local recreation leadership, assist local groups in planning programs and conducting activities, and prepare and distribute literature on recreational opportunities and programs. One exam-

ple of pamphlets thus produced which has general interest is June
Donahue's *Rural Recreation*. It covers such matters as the place of
recreation in rural life, recreation leadership, goals for a successful
program, and specific activities such as dramatics, parties, camps and
picnics, games, stunts, and family and community fun. Numerous
state Extension Service pamphlets describe specific recreational activities or are aimed to meet the needs of such groups as 4-H Clubs. The
planning boards in a number of states have issued surveys of state recreational resources, recreation plans, compilations of basic recreation
legislation, and other types of publications relating to state recreational resources and activities.

Mention has been made above of the studies of parks, parkways,
and recreational areas made by appropriate state agencies in cooperation with the National Park Service. Studies for a number of states
have been issued by the state agencies. The Park Service also issues
statistics compiled from state sources on acreage and accommodations
of state parks, their activities, and their facilities, expenditures,
sources of funds, personnel, and attendance. In 1941 there were 1,060
state parks with an area of over 4,000,000 acres. The attendance reported for 547 parks was 81,000,000. The National Park Service has
also issued a *Digest of Laws Relating to Local Parks and Recreation
as of January 2, 1940.*

An article "State Agencies and Recreation" in the June, 1946, issue
of *Recreation* provides information on state parks and forests, recreational activities of state Extension Services and state universities,
state conservation programs that have recreational implications, highways and roadside park developments, library extension services, and
the activities of educational authorities.

"State Parks in Wartime," in *The Book of the States, 1945-46,* presents data on attendance, sources of funds, and expenditures in 1944
and acreage and land acquisition, 1941-44.

In comparison with the need, the recreational opportunities provided by local governments in rural areas are slight. George Hjelte,
in a chapter "County and Rural Recreation" in *The Administration
of Public Recreation,* points out that the problem of providing local
recreational services in unincorporated county territory and in rural
areas is as yet unsolved. In many places counties still lack the legal
authority to provide recreational services. Hjelte suggests that such
services for local communities might be provided by special districts
established within counties; by setting up a county recreation department which would render general recreational services for the

county and would furnish specific services to incorporated villages, towns, boroughs, and townships on a contractual basis; or by adapting the structure and program of the public schools to include a wider variety of recreational services.

There are in the United States a number of county parks—areas that as a general rule serve to fill the gap between city park systems on the one hand and the state parks on the other. Data relating to these parks are presented in *Municipal and County Parks in the United States, 1940*. In that year, 152 counties reported 779 properties totaling 197,350 acres. While it is known that some additional counties have parks, the proportion of all counties providing them is small. This volume presents for both municipal and county parks such data as acreage, types and value of properties, facilities and buildings, recreational activities, and income and expenditures.

County-owned forest lands in twenty-three states total almost seven million acres, according to *Forests and Employment; Report of the Chief of the Forest Service, 1945*.

Community forests are another type of public development providing recreational opportunities to both rural and urban residents. According to a pamphlet of the United States Forest Service, *Community Forests*, published in 1939, "incomplete reports . . . show approximately 1,500 community forests in the United States, varying in development from the initial to the more advanced stages. These properties contain an estimated 3 million acres of land. On them more than 146 million trees have been planted." These forests may be known as "town, village, municipal, city, county, city watershed, school, hospital, church, or memorial forests." They have been established for many different reasons—to afford protection to watersheds and the public water supply, to meet needs for various kinds of recreation, to serve as demonstrations of forestry practice—to mention a few. Properly managed, community forests contribute not only recreational opportunities and aesthetic values; they also provide work opportunities and the possibility of profit to the community. *Forests and Employment; Report of the Chief of the Forest Service, 1945*, reports 2,278 community forests in the United States totaling 3 million acres. Two-thirds of this area is in the larger units. Most units are of 100 acres or less.

THE SCHOOLS AND RURAL RECREATION

The role of the schools in rural recreation is discussed in a chapter in *Rural America Today; Its Schools and Community Life*, by George

A. Works and Simon O. Lesser. Recreation has been a traditional interest of rural schools, and there are a number of evidences of increased appreciation of this function of the schools. "In recent years both educators and the general public have tended to broaden their conception of the function of education. Many subjects concerned with the use of leisure time have been added to the curriculum. Teacher-education institutions have begun to provide preservice and in-service instruction in recreational fields." In many places, stronger administrative units are also making it possible for many schools to broaden their curriculums and support more adequate programs. A growing number of rural schools are actively engaged in meeting the leisure-time needs of their communities, to the mutual benefit of school and community. On the debit side, "most small schools have practically no indoor facilities for recreation, and a surprising number are located on small unimproved plots of ground. Furthermore, many rural teachers have neither training nor special aptitude for recreation leadership, and crowded schedules restrict the time teachers have available for work with community groups."

The Educational Policies Commission, in its pamphlet *Educational Policies for Rural America* (described more fully in Chapter 1), states that it is sound educational policy for boards of education to promote community recreation. It suggests an inventory of the local situation to determine the area to be served by a recreation program; the facts about the people, their customs, and traditions; and information as to facilities, leaders, and funds available for recreation. It also suggests that there is ample opportunity in rural places for reviving many of the simple rural activities popular years ago and that it is wise to build part of the program around inexpensive cooperative activities and to promote activities growing out of the natural rural setting.

The Commission makes these same points in a section on rural recreation in *Educational Policies for Community Recreation*. It concludes the section as follows:

Cooperation of existing agencies is needed in the provision of rural recreation as in few other places. In states where boards of education are authorized to establish and conduct programs, some boards undertake the task with enthusiasm, but others, unfortunately, permit this opportunity for rendering educational service to go unheeded. *It is sound educational policy for boards of education to promote community recreation, through such means as are within their power, as part of their educational responsibility.* Where school authorities are slow in realizing this responsibility, some other agency must take steps to initiate a recreational program on either a formal or informal basis and draw the schools into the community program.

VOLUNTARY AGENCIES

Private voluntary agencies bring some recreational opportunities to rural communities, although the programs of some of the best-known national organizations are directed principally to city groups. Programs of the Y.M.C.A., the Y.W.C.A., the Boy Scouts, the Girl Scouts, and the Camp Fire Girls are described in Chapter 9. In many rural communities churches supply such leisure-time activities as suppers, picnics, dramatic productions, and folk singing. Recreation is an increasingly important feature of the programs of church-sponsored organizations for young people. The recreational activities of the Farm Bureau are described in two papers in *Education for Rural America*—"Philosophy and Activities of the Michigan State Farm Bureau in Adult Education," by Eugene A. Smaltz, and "Training Rural Youth for Leadership," by B. F. Hennink. A paper in the same volume, "The Educational Program of the Farmers Union," by Mrs. Jerome Evanson, describes some of the recreational activities of that organization.

In inventorying the recreation facilities of a rural community, those supplied by private enterprise should not be overlooked. While movies, theaters, amusement parks, swimming pools, skating rinks, bowling alleys, and numerous other facilities provided on a commercial basis are more apt to be located in cities than in rural areas, improved transportation is bringing them ever closer to the rural resident. Although some such individual activities may be unwholesome or unduly expensive, many provide excellent opportunities for wholesome diversion at a reasonable cost and thus are a valuable supplement to the recreational opportunities offered by governmental agencies and various voluntary nonprofit organizations.

The National Recreation Association, established in 1906, has been a principal leadership and coordinating agency in the development of leisure-time activities at the community level on a nonprofit basis. It helps communities to obtain or develop more and better facilities or activities and offers special services to communities to further recreational leadership, activities, organization and administration, legislation, and planning. The monthly magazine of the Association, *Recreation,* carries brief articles and reports on current programs and specific sports and other leisure-time activities. It also lists books, periodical articles, and pamphlet materials in recreation and related fields. The Association publishes pamphlets which, while directed principally to the needs and interests of urban communities, offer many suggestions valuable to rural areas. Some recent titles are:

(1) *Securing and Maintaining Standards in Community Recreation Personnel;* (2) *Standards; Playgrounds, Playfields, Recreation Buildings, Indoor Recreation Facilities;* (3) *Standards for Neighborhood Recreation Areas and Facilities;* (4) *Training Volunteers for Recreation Service;* (5) *Recreation and the Church; A Manual for Leaders;* (6) *Teen Age Centers;* and (7) *Know Your Community; Suggestions for Making a Study of Community Recreation Needs.* Publications directed toward meeting rural needs are: (1) *Suggestions for Organization of Recreation Centers in Rural Communities;* (2) *How Rural People Are Using Their Leisure;* and (3) *A Brief Bibliography on Rural Recreation.*

OTHER PUBLICATIONS

Rural Planning; The Social Aspects of Recreation Places, by Wayne C. Nason, "records actual experiences of rural communities and organizations in creating grounds and reserving for local use spots of natural beauty and historic interest . . . . These new recreation places . . . add to the satisfactions of country life and enable larger groups of farm people to assemble, mingle, and learn each others' thoughts and habits." *Rural Buildings for Business and Social Uses,* by the same author, points out that business interest may be the original aim of farmers in establishing buying and selling organizations, but the ultimate object is better living on the farm and a better rural civilization. In recognition of this fact, modern farm business organizations are erecting buildings that closely relate economic and social factors in the conduct of their business.

Four books on specific types of recreational activity of interest to rural people may be mentioned. Marjorie Patten's *The Arts Workshop of Rural America* is a study of the rural arts program of the Agricultural Extension Service in Wisconsin, Iowa, North Dakota, Colorado, Ohio, North Carolina, New York, and West Virginia. Allen H. Eaton's *Handicrafts of the Southern Highlands* was written to help the Highland people in solving their handicraft problem, to acquaint those outside the region with this great reservoir of handwork and enlist their interest in its continuation, and to present findings that may contribute to the development of the handicraft movement. Willem van de Wall, in *The Music of the People,* describes the efforts toward musical expression in the state of Vermont of the State Extension Service, the WPA music project, the public schools, colleges, and women's clubs. The author also describes the rural task of a university music program as conducted in Kentucky and the rural music program sponsored by the state of Delaware. Nature recreation opportunities are described in William G. Vinal's *Nature Recreation; Group Guidance for the Out-of-Doors.*

Persons interested in an interpretation of the significance, functions, objectives, program content, methods of operation, and relationships of community recreation should consult George D. Butler's *Introduction to Community Recreation.* Although major consideration is given to the work of governmental agencies and to problems of community recreation in cities, much of the material applies equally well to the services of private and semipublic agencies, and much will be found useful to rural recreation leaders.

In *Time on Their Hands,* a report prepared for the American Youth Commission, C. Gilbert Wrenn and D. L. Harley consider "the leisure needs of youth against the background of modern social changes and the functions of recreation they imply." They review the recreational situation of young people, discuss how it needs to be altered, and indicate the part various agencies can take in effecting the necessary changes.

In a chapter, "Opportunities for Recreation," in her book *Your Community,* Joanna C. Colcord offers suggestions to persons desirous of securing information on such opportunities in their home communities.

Recreation Bibliography, compiled by the American Association for Health, Physical Education, and Recreation, presents numerous references on general, physical, social, handicraft, drama, music, and nature recreation.

BIBLIOGRAPHY

American Association for Health, Physical Education, and Recreation. *Recreation Bibliography.* Washington: The Association (1201 Sixteenth St. N. W.), 1944, variously paged.

Butler, George D. *Introduction to Community Recreation.* Prepared for the National Recreation Association. New York: McGraw-Hill Book Co., 1940, 547 pp. (Bibliography, pp. 517-30.)

——. "Recreation," in *Social Work Year Book, 1945,* pp. 363-75. (Bibliography, pp. 374-75.)

Colcord, Joanna C. "Opportunities for Recreation," in *Your Community; Its Provision for Health, Education, Safety, and Welfare.* New York: Russell Sage Foundation, 1941, pp. 148-56. (List of references, pp. 241-51.)

Donahue, June. *Rural Recreation.* Extension Circular No. 373. Fayetteville, Arkansas: University of Arkansas, 1940, 27 pp.

Eaton, Allen H. *Handicrafts of the Southern Highlands; With an Account of the Rural Handicraft Movement in the United States and Suggestions for the Wider Use of Handicrafts in Adult Education and in Recreation.* New York: Russell Sage Foundation (130 East 22nd St.), 1937, 370 pp.

Evanson, Mrs. Jerome. "The Educational Program of the Farmers Union," in *Education for Rural America.* Chicago: University of Chicago Press, 1945, pp. 200-7.

Gardner, Ella. *Development of a Leisure-Time Program in Small Cities and Towns.* U. S. Children's Bureau Publication No. 241. Washington: Government Printing Office, 1937, 12 pp. (Suggestions for further reading, pp. 11-12.)

——. *Handbook for Recreation Leaders.* U. S. Children's Bureau Publication No. 231. Washington: Government Printing Office, 1936, 121 pp.

Hennink, B. F. "Training Rural Youth for Leadership," in *Education for Rural America.* Chicago: University of Chicago Press, 1945, pp. 184-99.

Hjelte, George. *The Administration of Public Recreation.* New York: Macmillan Co., 1940, 416 pp.

Lindeman, Eduard C. *Leisure—A National Issue; Planning for the Leisure of a Democratic People.* New York: Association Press (347 Madison Ave.), 1939, 61 pp.

Municipal and County Parks in the United States, 1940. A Report of a Study Conducted by the National Park Service with the Cooperation of the American Institute of Park Executives and the National Recreation Association under the Direction of George D. Butler. New York: National Recreation Association, [1942?], 173 pp.

Nason, Wayne C. *Rural Buildings for Business and Social Uses.* U. S. Department of Agriculture Farmers' Bulletin No. 1622. Washington: Government Printing Office, 1930, 38 pp.

——. *Rural Planning; The Social Aspects of Recreation Places.* U. S. Department of Agriculture Farmers' Bulletin No. 1388. Washington: Government Printing Office, 1932, 30 pp.

National Education Association of the United States. Educational Policies Commission and American Association for Health, Physical Education, and Recreation. *Educational Policies for Community Recreation.* Washington: The Association (1201 Sixteenth St. N. W.), 1940, 31 pp.

National Recreation Association, 315 Fourth Ave., New York.
A Brief Bibliography on Rural Recreation. 1939, 5 pp.
How Rural People Are Using Their Leisure. 1941, 3 pp.
Know Your Community; Suggestions for Making a Study of Community Recreation Needs. 1943, 24 pp.
Recreation and the Church; A Manual for Leaders. 1944, 40 pp.
Securing and Maintaining Standards in Community Recreation Personnel. A Report of the Committee on Standards of Training, Experience and Compensation in Community Recreation Work. 1940, 15 pp.
Standards for Neighborhood Recreation Areas and Facilities. 1943, 16 pp.

Standards; Playgrounds, Playfields, Recreation Buildings, Indoor Recreation Facilities. 13 pp.

Suggestions for Organization of Recreation Centers in Rural Communities. 1943, 2 pp.

Teen Age Centers. 1944, 23 pp.

Training Volunteers for Recreation Service. 1942, 35 pp.

Patten, Marjorie. *The Arts Workshop of Rural America; A Study of the Rural Arts Program of the Agricultural Extension Service.* New York: Columbia University Press, 1937, 202 pp.

Recreation. Monthly publication of the National Recreation Association, 315 Fourth Ave., New York.

Smaltz, Eugene A. "Philosophy and Activities of the Michigan State Farm Bureau in Adult Education," in *Education for Rural America.* Chicago: University of Chicago Press, 1945, pp. 171-83.

"State Agencies and Recreation." *Recreation,* Vol. XL, No. 3, June 1946, pp. 115-37, 162.

"State Parks in Wartime," in *The Book of the States, 1945-46.* Chicago: The Council of State Governments, 1945, pp. 281-92.

U. S. Bureau of Reclamation. *Columbia Basin, Joint Investigations: Problem 25, Rural Recreation Areas.* Washington: Government Printing Office, 1945, 65 pp.

U. S. Civilian Conservation Corps. *The Civilian Conservation Corps and Public Recreation.* Washington: Government Printing Office, 1941, 23 pp.

U. S. Forest Service. *Community Forests.* Washington: Government Printing Office, 1939, 36 pp.

——. *Forests and Employment; Report of the Chief of the Forest Service, 1945.* Washington: Government Printing Office, 1946, 35 pp.

——. *Forest Outings.* By Thirty Foresters. Russell Lord, ed. Washington: Government Printing Office, 1940, 311 pp.

——. *The Work of the U. S. Forest Service.* U. S. Department of Agriculture Miscellaneous Publication No. 290. Rev. ed. Washington: Government Printing Office, 1945, 32 pp.

——. Library. *Forest Recreation; A Bibliography.* Washington: The Service, 1938, 129 pp.

U. S. National Park Service. *Annual Report of the Director . . . Fiscal Year Ended June 30, 1945.* Washington: Government Printing Office, 1946, pp. 207-31. (Reprinted from *Annual Report of the Secretary of the Interior for the Fiscal Year Ended June 30, 1945.*)

——. *Digest of Laws Relating to Local Parks and Recreation as of January 2, 1940,* by Roy A. Vetter. Washington: Federal Security Agency, Civilian Conservation Corps, 1941, 534 pp.

——. *Information Relating to the National Park System.* Washington: Government Printing Office, 1944, 44 pp.

——. *A Study of the Park and Recreation Problem of the United States.* Washington: Government Printing Office, 1941, 279 pp.

——. *Yearbook, Park and Recreation Progress, 1937—.* Washington: Government Printing Office, 1938—. Yearbooks for 1942 and 1943 published by National Conference on State Parks, 901 Union Trust Building, Washington, D. C.

U. S. National Resources Planning Board. "Public Works and Recreational Land," in *Public Works and Rural Land Use.* Washington: Government Printing Office, 1942, pp. 140-55.

U. S. Office of Civilian Defense. *Recreation in War Time; A Manual for Recreation Committees of Local Defense Councils.* OCD Publication No. 3624. Washington: Government Printing Office, 1943, 16 pp.

——. *Volunteers for Youth Recreation Programs; Suggestions for Joint Recruiting and Training.* OCD Publication No. 3637. Washington: Government Printing Office, 1944, 28 pp.

U. S. Office of Community War Services. Division of Recreation. *Community Recreation Comes of Age; The Story of One American Town.* Washington: Government Printing Office, 1944, 30 pp. (Suggested bibliography, p. 30.)

——. ——. *Planning for Recreation Areas and Facilities in Small Towns and Cities.* By J. Lee Brown. Washington: Government Printing Office, 1945, 51 pp. (Bibliography of recreation planning, pp. 50-51.)

——. ——. *What About Us? A Report of Community Recreation for Young People.* Washington: Government Printing Office, 1944, 41 pp.

——. ——. *Youth Centers—An Appraisal and a Look Ahead.* Washington: Government Printing Office, 1945, 34 pp. (Suggested bibliography, p. 34.)

U. S. Office of Education. *Planning Schools for Tomorrow; The Schools and Recreation Services.* U. S. Office of Education Leaflet No. 73. Washington: Government Printing Office, 1944, 21 pp.

U. S. Tennessee Valley Authority. Department of Regional Planning Studies. *Recreational Development of the Southern Highlands Region; A Study of the Use and Control of Scenic and Recreational Resources.* Knoxville, Tennessee: The Authority, 1938, 61 pp.

——. *The Scenic Resources of the Tennessee Valley; A Descriptive and Pictorial Inventory.* Washington: Government Printing Office, 1938, 222 pp.

U. S. Work Projects Administration. *American Recreation Series.* Fifty-two booklets edited by the Federal Writers' Project, WPA. New York: Bacon and Wieck, Inc. (118 East 28th St.).

——. *Community Recreation Programs: A Study of WPA Recreation Projects.* Washington: The Administration, 1940, 54 pp.

——. *Rural Recreation Area.* WPA Technical Series, Recreation Circular No. 6. Washington: The Administration, 1939. Variously paged.

Vinal, William G. *Nature Recreation; Group Guidance for the Out-of-Doors.* New York: McGraw-Hill Book Co., 1940, 322 pp.

van de Wall, Willem. *The Music of the People.* New York: American Association for Adult Education, 1938, 128 pp.

Works, George A. and Simon O. Lesser. "The Schools and Rural Recreation," in *Rural America Today; Its Schools and Community Life.* Chicago: University of Chicago Press, 1942, pp. 215-41. (Authorities for the facts, pp. 239-41.)

Wrenn, C. Gilbert and D. L. Harley. *Time on Their Hands; A Report on Leisure, Recreation, and Young People.* Washington: American Council on Education, 1941, 266 pp.

9 *CHILDREN AND YOUTH*

So MANY PROGRAMS and so large a body of materials relating to special problems of rural children and youth have been developed in recent years that it has seemed desirable to describe them in a separate chapter, although some of these descriptions might well be included in the chapters on welfare services, health services, recreation, or schools. White House Conferences, held at approximately ten-year intervals since 1909, have highlighted the problems of children in the United States. The Children's Bureau, created in 1912, has done yeoman's service in the interest of children in both rural and urban areas. The 4-H Club program of the Agricultural Extension Service and the federally aided program of vocational agriculture of the United States Office of Education are directed to meeting the needs of rural youth. A number of federal agencies, especially the National Youth Administration and the Civilian Conservation Corps, helped to meet the special needs of youth in the depression period. State and local health and welfare agencies have provided a variety of services for children and youth. The American Youth Commission of the American Council on Education, in the period from 1935 to 1942, canvassed the gamut of youth problems and published a series of volumes setting forth findings and recommendations. A number related to the special problems of rural youth. Other private agencies have carried forward programs in furtherance of various phases of child and youth welfare.

WHITE HOUSE CONFERENCES

The first White House Conference (1909) was concerned with the care of dependent children; the second (1919) with child welfare standards; the third (1930) with child health and protection. The fourth conference (January 18-20, 1940) considered the whole range of problems of children. As stated in the introduction to the recommendations made by this fourth conference, which constitute Part IV of the *Final Report*, they are intended to form a program of action for the welfare of children to be undertaken in the succeeding ten years. They cover all phases of child life in all parts of the United States and are based upon a wide variety of factual material concerning the major aspects of national life that directly affect children. They are intended to supplement, strengthen, and improve existing activities carried on for children and to expand and extend programs for social security, education, and health along lines already undertaken. Many call for governmental action. The various publications relating₁ to the Conference were issued by the Children's Bureau in the years 1939 to 1942 and are listed in the bibliography at the end of this chapter. The activities undertaken by a National Citizens Committee to effectuate the recommendations of the Conference are described in the letter transmitting the *Final Report,* which was published in 1942. The *General Report* of the Conference, issued in 1940, served as the basis for a Public Affairs Pamphlet by Maxwell S. Stewart, *America's Children,* which sets forth the principal items contained in the *Report.*

THE CHILDREN'S BUREAU

The federal Children's Bureau promotes the health, educational opportunity, and welfare of children throughout the country. Many of its activities have been of special benefit to rural children. The methods employed by the Bureau to achieve its ends, as stated in the annual report of the Bureau for 1944 (contained in the *Annual Report of the Secretary of Labor*), include "studying the facts surrounding child life; reporting on these facts to parents and to the general public; administering grants to the States for maternal and child-health services, services for crippled children, and child-welfare services under . . . the Social Security Act, and grants to the States for emergency maternity and infant care for families of men in the armed services; and administering the child-labor provisions of the Fair Labor Standards Act." When the Children's Bureau was transferred from the Department of Labor to the Federal Security Agency in 1946, its functions under the Fair Labor Standards Act were kept in the Department of Labor. The functions of the Children's Bureau are described in its publication, *History and Functions of the Children's Bureau.*

The annual appropriation to the states under the Social Security Act for maternal and child health services is $5,820,000; for services for crippled children, $3,870,000; and for child welfare services, $1,510,000. According to the *Thirty-third Annual Report of the Chief of the Children's Bureau, Fiscal Year Ended June 30, 1945,* federal aid payments to the states for the fiscal year 1945 for emergency maternity and infant care of wives and infants of men in the lowest four pay grades of the armed forces amounted to $45,000,000. From the beginning of the program, in March, 1943, to June 30, 1945, care had been authorized by state health agencies for 884,273 mothers and infants.

The accomplishments of the Children's Bureau under provisions of the Social Security Act are described in *Ten Years of Services for Children under the Social Security Program, August 1935–August 1945*. Beneficiaries of the maternal and child health program "are, for the most part, mothers and children who live in the rural areas of the United States." In the ten-year period "a basis has been laid for State-wide health services to mothers and children through the establishment and strengthening of maternal and child health divisions of State health departments, and the strengthening, too, of local health agencies." In 1945, the states budgeted at least $4,800,000 of their own and local money for maternal and child health services in addition to the money they received from the federal government. In a single year (1942) under the program made possible with the use of Social Security funds, more than 160,000 mothers received prenatal care, 185,000 babies and some 300,000 young children were given health check-ups at medical conferences, more than 1,600,000 school-age children were examined by physicians, more than 2,000,-000 children were vaccinated against smallpox, more than 1,600,000 children were immunized against diphtheria, and public health nurses gave care to some 1,500,000 mothers and children. Under the Social Security program of services for crippled children, state services have been materially strengthened. Over a third of a million crippled children are listed on state registers. In a single year more than 100,000 received care under state programs. The Social Security program of child welfare services has made possible the establishment of such services in some states and their extension and strengthening in others. State and local funds "are being used to pay the salaries of more than 1300 workers who give their full-time to children. . . . The greatest stimulus from the use of Federal moneys has been experienced in the rural areas. . . . Federal funds are being used to pay the salaries of 651 child-welfare workers, all except a few of whom were working in rural counties." The ten-year summary also points out the extent of the need for further services and outlines next steps in meeting the need.

In a paper "The Rural Child and the Children's Bureau," presented at the White House Conference on Rural Education, Katharine F. Lenroot, chief of the Children's Bureau, describes the special meaning for children in rural areas of the activities of the Bureau. Of the 36,000,000 children under sixteen years of age in the continental United States, 51 per cent live in rural areas. These children have at their disposal far less than their due share of the resources of the nation for health, education, and home life. Infant and maternal mortality rates have been consistently higher for rural than for urban areas, and while reductions in rates over the years have been impressive, progress in rural areas has been less rapid than in urban. A greater proportion of farm than of nonfarm children are at work and a greater proportion are not attending school. The Children's Bureau has made many studies of child labor and the welfare of children in the families of farm laborers, particularly agricultural migrants. Under the provisions of Title V of the Social Security Act, "prenatal and child-health conferences, public-health-nursing service, diagnostic and other services for crippled children, and child-welfare services have been developed in hundreds of rural counties. Administrative activities under the child-labor provisions of the Fair Labor Standards Act take the Children's Bureau into canneries and packing sheds and into farms where products are raised for interstate commerce, tho the jurisdiction conferred in the act over child labor in agriculture is exceedingly limited."

The Children's Bureau has been especially concerned with the problems of children in wartime and the maintenance of standards and services, and also with the goals to be achieved in the postwar period. Its Commission on Children in Wartime, appointed in 1942, later renamed National Commission on Children in Wartime, gave serious consideration to these matters and issued a number of publications related thereto. *Goals for Children and Youth in the Transition from War to Peace* sets forth the objectives of the Commission under such headings as safeguarding family life; extending health service and medical care; regulating child labor and developing policies to assure education and employment opportunities to youth; developing community recreation and leisure-time services for young people; and assuring social services to every child needing special attention. *Our Concern—Every Child* "is intended to serve as a guide for the study of State and community resources and action needed to safeguard childhood and provide opportunities for youth. The outlines for evaluating resources and planning State and community action are based upon the standards of child health, education, and social welfare which were developed by the 1940 White House Conference on Children in a Democracy. The Conference recognized that the State and the local communities, together with parents, have primary responsibility for making these standards a reality." *Building the Future for Children and Youth* describes the steps the American people can take to achieve the *Goals for Children and Youth*. *State and Community Planning for Children and Youth* suggests "ways in which leadership and joint action in behalf of children and youth may be developed in the States and local communities." Full citations for these and other publications of the Bureau related to the program of the National Commission on Children in Wartime are listed at the end of this chapter.

Following the discontinuance of the National Commission on Children in Wartime, early in 1946, the Children's Bureau took the initiative in establishing a National Commission on Children and Youth "to raise the levels of health, education, and welfare of the children of the Nation so that they may have full opportunity to develop their potentialities and to become responsible and cooperative members of society. . . ."

The Children's Bureau has been concerned with all aspects of child labor and has made a number of studies of the subject and issued publications reporting them. Two such studies relating to agriculture are Elizabeth S. Johnson's *Welfare of Families of Sugar-Beet Laborers; A Study of Child Labor and Its Relation to Family Work, Income, and Living Conditions in 1935* and *The Work and Welfare of Children of Agricultural Laborers in Hidalgo County, Texas,* by Amber Arthun Warburton; Helen Wood; and Marian Crane. During the war the Bureau also issued publications to serve as guides in the employment of nonfarm youth in agriculture. These and other citations appear in Floy Hendricks' *Selected References on Child Labor and Youth Employment.*

OTHER FEDERAL AGENCIES

The National Youth Administration was in operation from June 26, 1935, to June 30, 1943. In that period it made possible the employment for varying lengths of time of approximately 4,800,000 different needy unemployed youth. Some 2,700,000 were given work experience and training on work projects producing useful goods and services. Over 2,000,000 were school, college, and graduate students who had an opportunity to earn money to assist them in remaining in school through work in public and semipublic nonprofit-making institutions. In the eight-year period, NYA expenditures totaled $662,300,000; of this sum, $467,600,000 was used for the payment of wages for the employment of needy, unemployed, out-of-school youth and $169,500,000 for wages to needy persons in order that they might continue their education. An account of the major activities and accomplishments of the NYA is contained in the *Final Report of the National Youth Administration, Fiscal Years 1936-1943.*

Summary data on the work of the Civilian Conservation Corps are contained in Federal Security Agency's *Annual Reports for the Fiscal Years 1941-1942; 1942-1943.* In the period of its operation, April 5, 1933, to June 30, 1943, the CCC provided work training to more than three million men. They planted almost three billion trees on cut-over and burned-over waste lands and on farms threatened or damaged by soil erosion. They constructed over a hundred thousand miles of truck trails and minor roads through timbered areas to improve transportation in forests and parks subject to forest fire hazards. About twelve million man-days were expended fighting forest fires or safeguarding forests from fire danger. Nearly six million check dams were constructed in gullies to prevent soil wastage, and thousands of lakes, ponds, and reservoirs were built in sections where water conservation is a major problem.

A description of the CCC program, with constructive criticism, is contained in *Youth in the CCC,* prepared for the American Youth Commission by Kenneth Holland and Frank Ernest Hill. A description of the organization and program of the NYA and some evaluation of its accomplishments are presented in *The National Youth Administration,* by Palmer O. Johnson and Oswald L. Harvey, prepared for the Advisory Committee on Education. The volume by Ernest K. and Betty Lindley, *A New Deal for Youth; The Story of the National Youth Administration,* originated in the desire of the National Advisory Committee of the NYA for an independent survey. "Youth and Work Opportunities," the *Bulletin of the National Association of Secondary-School Principals* for April, 1940, compiled by Paul B. Jacobson, presents selected practices in inaugurating and supervising NYA student aid in individual secondary schools. The NYA in 1937 issued *Youth; A World Problem: A Study in World Perspective of Youth Conditions, Movements and Programs,* prepared by W. Thacher Winslow. A statement by the Educational Policies Commission of the National Education Association, *The Civilian Conservation Corps, the National Youth Administration, and the Public Schools,* is directed to the problems of federal relations to education arising out of the educational activities included in these programs.

The Work Projects Administration undertook several studies of rural youth—*Rural Youth on Relief* (1937); *Rural Youth; Their Situation and Prospects* (1938); and *Youth in Agricultural Villages* (1940). Bruce L. Melvin was author or co-author of each of these volumes. He has drawn on these studies of rural youth and the extensive literature on urban youth to produce *Youth—Millions Too Many?* In his preface he states:

> Some who have read this book in manuscript have felt that the rural aspect of the youth situation has been disproportionately emphasized. There is some justification for this impression. . . . The genesis of the youth problem in our country today is on the farms, because that is where young people are "piling up" in surplus. My contention is, therefore, that if the problems of youth on farms are solved, the youth in the cities will have much less difficulty solving their problems.

National Resources Development; Report for 1942 of the National Resources Planning Board contains a section "Post-war Planning for Children and Youth."

The Division of Bibliography of the United States Library of Congress has compiled *Children and War; A Selected List of References* which lists books, pamphlets, and periodical articles.

The Interagency Committee on Youth Employment and Education has issued *Your Community and Its Young People; Their Employment and Educational Opportunities.*

Two important federal-state programs for rural youth are described elsewhere in this volume: the 4-H Club program in Chapter 2 and the Future Farmers of America program in Chapter 1.

A number of state agencies have issued studies on various social and economic problems of rural youth. Among such agencies are the agricultural experiment stations, the extension services, departments of agriculture and of education, and planning boards. Some of the studies are general in subject matter; others relate to specific problems. Some are statewide in scope, some regional, and some concerned with a single county.

THE AMERICAN YOUTH COMMISSION

The American Youth Commission was established by the American Council on Education in 1935 to conduct a comprehensive investigation of the problems facing young people in the United States. It employed a research staff and issued a number of studies of various phases of youth problems. In its final report, *Youth and the Future,* issued in 1942, the Commission rounded out the formulation of its recommendations in regard to youth. Three of the publications of the Commission relate especially to the problems of the eleven million rural youth in the United States.

Guideposts for Rural Youth, by E. L. Kirkpatrick, tells the story of efforts initiated by a few rural communities to encourage programs directed toward possible solutions of local youth problems. The programs described suggest practical steps that communities can take to improve the situation of rural youth.

On the basis of the evidence presented in *Guideposts for Rural Youth,* the American Youth Commission "determined to experiment, in selected areas within a few states, with marshaling all available resources—state, county, and local—in an effort to demonstrate possible ways by which such resources could be used to solve some of the problems of rural youth." A report on the objectives and procedures of this experiment, a summary of its lessons and achievements, and an appraisal of its results are presented in Edmund deS. Brunner's *Working with Rural Youth.* As described in the preface, "This volume is a report of an experimental project in social engineering in the area of rural youth . . . on the basis of known facts, it sought to develop and operate programs for meeting the needs of rural youth through existing agencies and organizations, in the hope that significant patterns of action would develop for workers in this area. Though stimulated by the American Youth Commission, the study operated through agencies already existing in states, counties, and communities."

David Cushman Coyle's *Rural Youth in Action* was issued as a sort of supplement to the more formal report *Working with Rural Youth* to encourage rural youth and their leaders to action to improve some of the situations and solve some of the problems with which they are faced.

Because of the special disadvantages under which two and a quarter million Negro youth between sixteen and twenty-four years of age live, the American Youth Commission conducted extensive studies of the problems of this particular group. *In a Minor Key,* by Ira DeA. Reid, issued in 1940, presents in compact form much of the general information available about American Negro youth. It was followed by five volumes on the personality development of Negroes. One of these, *Growing Up in the Black Belt,* by Charles S. Johnson, is concerned with Negro youth in the rural South. *Color, Class, and Personality,* by Robert L. Sutherland, summarizes the chief findings of the entire Negro project conducted by the Commission.

The Commission also made several studies of employment opportunities for youth. Paul T. David's book *Postwar Youth Employment; A Study of Long-Term Trends* contains a chapter on population and employment trends in agriculture and a section on the problem of surplus farm youth.

In the introduction to *Youth and the Future,* the final report of the Commission, it is stated that it is "the purpose of the American Youth Commission in this report to set forth a program in regard to youth —a program based on the experience of the past, adjusted to the harsh realities of the present, and adequate to the foreseeable needs of the future. . . . In this report, the Commission of necessity looks mainly to the future." Topics considered include the basic problems of employment opportunity for youth, education, occupational readjustment, the use of leisure time, marriage and the home, health and fitness, delinquency and youthful crime, and citizenship.

Dorothy Canfield Fisher served as a member of the American Youth Commission during its entire existence. In *Our Young Folks* she sets down her impressions of youth needs, problems, and solutions. The book is based as to fact on the findings of the Commission; as to opinion it represents the author's "quite unofficial impression of the situation of young folks as revealed in the research undertaken by the professional experts in the Commission's employ."

Following completion of the work of the American Youth Commission, the parent organization, the American Council on Education, set up a Committee on Youth Problems to implement the Commission's findings. The Committee issues a small bulletin, which may be had free upon request.

THE AMERICAN COUNTRY LIFE ASSOCIATION

The Youth Section of the American Country Life Association has held national conferences annually since 1930. In cooperation with various agencies concerned with the improvement of rural living, it has also issued a series of bulletins designed "to encourage and assist young people in improving their local community life through discussion as a means of discovering the needs and figuring out ways of meeting them." All have been intended for use in connection with national or regional youth conferences; one of the most recent, *Youth in the Rural Community,* is pointed more especially, however, toward effective meetings in the rural community. It covers such topics as "Is There a Place for Me after the War?" "What Kind of a Home Shall We Have?" "How Can I Contribute Most to My Com-

munity?" "What Kind of a World Can We Have?" It is stated early
in the pamphlet, under the heading "Where to Start":

> In searching for more light on solving important world-wide problems we
> must look first at the home community. It is there that we earn our living,
> get our education, have most of our recreation, find our religion, live as
> citizens of the world. It is in our communities that we, using the available
> facilities, develop as human beings.
>
> . . . .
>
> In trying to get at the basic issues for discussion and study we considered
> first the different groups or interests that characterize any community—the
> farm organizations, the service clubs, the church, the school. Through these
> we find our opportunities for service and enjoy some of the things whereby
> we live. But few of us get into all the various interest groups—some of us in
> none. Let us look, then, for the principal things which people in the com-
> munity do have in common—a place to work, a home in which to live, group
> aims to achieve, and a new world to build.

Another recent publication of the Youth Section of the ACLA is
Needs of Rural Youth; Digest of Viewpoints from Selected Leaders.
Earlier titles include *The Rural Community; A Study Guide* and
Youth and Democracy in the Rural Community. The Section also
issues a quarterly publication, *Rural Youth News.*

OTHER NATIONAL ORGANIZATIONS

Over a long period the National Child Labor Committee has carried on an active campaign against child labor. In *The Long Road;
Fortieth Anniversary Report* (1944) the Committee reviews lessons
of the past and considers present trends, in the belief that such action
"will help to secure postwar action on child labor that will be wisely
planned and strongly supported." The *Report* contains a bibliography of major field studies and other publications of the Committee. A number of field studies have related to child labor in rural
areas. Some recent titles are (1) James E. Sidel's *Pick for Your Supper;
A Study of Child Labor among Migrants on the Pacific Coast;* (2)
A Summer in the Country (a study of seasonal workers in agriculture
in New Jersey); (3) Raymond G. Fuller's *Children in Strawberries*
(a study of children of migratory families working in the strawberry
fields of Arkansas and Kentucky) ; (4) Gertrude Folks Zimand's
Children Who Work on the Nation's Crops; and (5) Kate Clugston's
Cotton or School (a study of five Missouri cotton counties).

Numerous other organizations and agencies are devoting their
efforts to solving special problems of children and youth. The activities of a number of these agencies are described in articles contained

in the *Social Work Year Book, 1945,* which summarize existing conditions and carry bibliographies. The Associated Youth Serving Organizations, Inc. has issued a pamphlet, *11,000,000 Boys and Girls,* intended for the guidance of any national youth-serving agency in its approach to a rural community. Activities of the YMCA, YWCA, Boy Scouts, Girl Scouts, and Camp Fire Girls as they relate to rural areas are described in the paragraphs that follow.

The Young Men's Christian Association carries on fairly extensive work in a number of towns and small cities, and some of this work reaches into rural areas. Some of the small-city units are affiliated with larger metropolitan organizations, some are organized on a county or district basis, and some are independently organized. A number of YMCA activities are directed especially to meeting the needs of high-school and grade-school boys. YMCA activities, described in a folder *Communities Serve Their Young People,* issued by the National Council of the organization, 347 Madison Ave., New York, include dramatic and music groups, informal short courses on a variety of subjects, social-educational programs, club work of various kinds for different age groups, youth centers, conferences, and camping.

The Young Women's Christian Association has organizations in some 1,500 rural communities and small towns. Most of these organizations, in turn, are included in district organizations that employ professional leadership. The characteristic set-up in the smaller rural communities consists of two cooperating groups—an adult organization of women and girls over eighteen years of age and a school girl or Girl Reserve group usually centered in the high school. Rural membership, adult and junior, totals about 95,000 persons, approximately 44 per cent of whom are from farms and 56 per cent from villages and towns. In addition, there is some extension work in rural areas around cities. YWCA groups engage in a variety of educational, vocational, and recreational activities. *From Faith to Action in the YWCA,* by Kathleen W. MacArthur, describes the social and religious purposes of the organization. *Types of Rural YWCA Work in the United States of America,* by Elizabeth B. Herring, is devoted largely to describing the organization for rural work. The National Board of the Young Women's Christian Associations, 600 Lexington Ave., New York, maintains a rural secretary and issues programs and other materials of aid to local leaders and groups.

The program of the Boy Scouts of America is well adapted to the needs of rural youth. Scouting includes three distinct programs—Cub

Scouting for the age group nine through eleven; Boy Scouting for the group twelve and over; and Senior Scouting for those fifteen and over. Several organization plans have been set up to bring the program to rural boys. The rural troop organized in town or village may be sponsored by a church, Grange, or community group. Boys living outside of town may form a rural patrol within the town troop. A neighborhood patrol is organized as a separate unit in a small community and the Lone Scout plan serves isolated boys who find it impossible to join any group of Scouts. At the close of 1945 there were 17,482 strictly rural Scouting units over the country. Scouting offers such activities as first aid, rope work, nature lore, community service, signaling, use of tools, tracking, fire building, hiking, mapping, and camping. It gives merit badges for qualification in 111 subjects, 27 of which deal with farm interests. *Fundamentals of the Boy Scout Movement* describes the history of the movement, its essentials, and how the community uses the program. *It's Fun to Be a Scout* tells some of the items the individual Scout needs to know. *Scouting Is for Country Boys* is a folder describing programs and organization. A manual for rural leaders bears the title *Scouting for Rural Boys*. The National Council of the Boy Scouts of America, 2 Park Ave., New York, maintains a rural Scouting service.

The program of the Girl Scouts is also adapted to rural needs, and efforts are being made to bring a larger proportion of rural girls into the program. Statistics in the pamphlet *Girl Scouting for Rural Girls* indicate that 49 per cent of all girls seven to eighteen years of age in the United States live in rural areas but that only two out of a hundred are Girl Scouts, whereas ten out of a hundred in urban areas are members. There are three types of Girl Scout troups—Brownie Scouts for girls seven through nine years of age; Girl Scouts for girls ten through fourteen; and Senior Girl Scouts for high-school girls. Each troop consists of a group of girls, their leaders, and a troop committee. There are projects and badges for various arts and crafts, literature and dramatics, homemaking, health and safety, nature and agriculture, music and dancing, sports and games, out-of-doors, community life, and international friendship. *How to Start a Girl Scout Troop* is a pamphlet designed to answer questions of prospective leaders. *Girl Scouting in the Small Community* also tells how to start a troop and keep it going. *Girl Scout Troops in Country Schools* offers a plan to take care of small groups of girls of Scout age in country schools. Girl Scouts, Inc. also issues publications on leadership, on girls, and on special fields of activity. The national headquarters of the Girl Scouts, 155 East 44th St., New York, employs a rural adviser.

The Camp Fire Girls program is planned for both urban and rural girls ten years of age or older. A junior Blue Bird program is designed for girls seven to nine years of age. A Camp Fire group may be organized wherever girls request it and a volunteer leader agrees to accept responsibility. Each group must be sponsored by three responsible adults. "Lone" groups have direct contact with the national headquarters. Local councils have been formed in approximately two hundred cities for the purpose of promoting work in the community. They take responsibility for engaging an executive and staff, operate a camp, recruit and train leaders, and supervise the groups. The trend is toward area or county-wide councils serving the surrounding small towns and rural areas as well as the city. *A Part for You in Shaping Tomorrow* describes the organization and objectives of the Camp Fire Girls. National headquarters are located at 88 Lexington Ave., New York.

OTHER MATERIALS

A few pertinent titles in addition to those already mentioned are here listed. They are believed to provide basic or suggestive materials. In no sense do they constitute an exhaustive bibliography. Grace Abbott is the editor of a two-volume work, *The Child and the State . . . Select Documents, with Introductory Notes.* Volume I is concerned with legal status of the family and apprenticeship and child labor; Volume II is devoted to the dependent and the delinquent child and the child of unmarried parents. Henry W. Thurston's *Concerning Juvenile Delinquency; Progressive Changes in Our Perspectives* inquires into the causes and treatment of delinquency. The entire issue of the *Survey Midmonthly* of March, 1944, is devoted to "Juvenile Delinquency; A Challenge to Concerted Action Now and after the War." Thacher Winslow and Frank P. Davidson are editors of *American Youth; An Enforced Reconnaissance,* which contains a review of youth's relation to society in the broadest sense by authorities from academic, professional, and public life. *Youth and Jobs,* prepared by Douglas S. Ward and Edith M. Selberg for the Committee on Experimental Units of the North Central Association of Colleges and Secondary Schools, is designed to inform secondary school youth on what youth surveys show about jobs for young Americans, why many youths have been unable to find desirable work, what is being done to help youth, how youth can find jobs, and how they can grow in their jobs. Three recent volumes of *The Annals of the American Academy of Political and Social Science* have been devoted to matters relating to children and youth: "Children in a Depression Decade" (November, 1940, James H. S. Bossard, ed.); "The American Family in World War II" (September, 1943, Ray H. Abrams, ed.); and "Adolescents in Wartime" (November, 1944, James H. S. Bossard and Eleanor S. Boll, eds.). The March, 1945, issue of the *Journal of Educational Sociology,* edited by Frederic M. Thrasher, is entitled "Coordination for Youth Service." The Public Affairs Committee has issued a pamphlet, *Youth and Your Community,* by Alice C. Weitz. Louis Wirth and Ray Lussenhop are authors of *Urban and Rural Living; Planning Post-war Ways of Life for American Youth.* M. M. Chambers is the author of *Guidance for Rural Youth; A Report of the Institute for Rural Youth Guidance Held in Washington, D. C., February 27-28, 1941.* Charlotte Leeper Hanson is the author of an article "Child Welfare," appearing in *Social Work Year Book, 1945,* which covers in brief compass the whole range of child welfare needs and activities.

A number of periodicals are devoted to the interests of children—*The Child,* monthly publication of the Children's Bureau; *Child Welfare League of America, Inc., Bulletin,* monthly except July and August; *The Crippled Child,* bimonthly publication of the National Society for Crippled Children of the United States of America, Inc.; *The Crippled Child Bulletin,* bimonthly publication of the National Society for Crippled Children and Adults, Inc.; *The American Child,* publication of the National Child Labor Committee, monthly October to May inclusive; and *The Family; Journal of Social Case Work,* publication of the Family Welfare Association of America, monthly except August and September.

BIBLIOGRAPHY

Abbott, Grace, ed. *The Child and the State . . . Select Documents, with Introductory Notes.* Chicago: University of Chicago Press, 1938, 2 vols. (Selected bibliography, Vol. I, pp. 657-67; Vol. II, pp. 669-83.)

Abrams, Ray H., ed. "The American Family in World War II." *The Annals of the American Academy of Political and Social Science,* Vol. CCXXIX, September 1943, entire issue.

The American Child. Published by the National Child Labor Committee, 419 Fourth Ave., New York, monthly October to May, inclusive.

American Country Life Association. Youth Section (734 Jackson Place, N. W., Washington, D. C.).
Needs of Rural Youth; Digest of Viewpoints from Selected Leaders. 1945, 9 pp.
The Rural Community; A Study Guide, Looking toward the Improvement of Rural Life in the Community. 1940, 30 pp.
Rural Youth News. Quarterly.
Youth and Democracy in the Rural Community. 1941, 35 pp.
Youth in the Rural Community. 1945, 30 pp. (References, pp. 26-27.)

American Youth Commission of the American Council on Education (744 Jackson Place, N. W., Washington, D. C.).
Brunner, Edmund deS. *Working with Rural Youth.* 1942, 113 pp.
Coyle, David Cushman. *Rural Youth in Action.* 1943, 43 pp.
David, Paul T. *Postwar Youth Employment; A Study of Long-Term Trends.* 1943, 172 pp.
Holland, Kenneth and Frank Ernest Hill. *Youth in the CCC.* 1942, 263 pp.
Johnson, Charles S. *Growing Up in the Black Belt; Negro Youth in the Rural South.* 1941, 360 pp.
Kirkpatrick, E. L. *Guideposts for Rural Youth.* 1940, 167 pp. (Selected bibliography on youth activities, pp. 165-67.)
Reid, Ira DeA. *In a Minor Key; Negro Youth in Story and Fact.* 1940, 134 pp.
Sutherland, Robert L. *Color, Class, and Personality.* 1942, 135 pp.
Youth and the Future; General Report of the Commission. 1942, 296 pp.

Associated Youth Serving Organizations, Inc. *11,000,000 Boys and Girls.* New York: The Author (134 East 56th St.), 15 pp.

Bossard, James H. S., ed. "Children in a Depression Decade." *The Annals of the American Academy of Political and Social Science,* Vol. CCXII, November 1940, entire issue.

—— and Eleanor S. Boll, eds. "Adolescents in Wartime." *The Annals of the American Academy of Political and Social Science,* Vol. CCXXXVI, November 1944, entire issue.

Boy Scouts of America. *Fundamentals of the Boy Scout Movement.* New York: The Author (2 Park Ave.), 1945, 40 pp.

——. *It's Fun to Be a Scout.* New York: The Author, 1946, unpaged.

——. *Scouting for Rural Boys; A Manual for Leaders.* New York: The Author, 1938, 453 pp.

——. *Scouting Is for Country Boys.* New York: The Author, leaflet.

Camp Fire Girls, Inc. *A Part for You in Shaping Tomorrow.* New York: The Author (88 Lexington Ave.), 31 pp.

Chambers, M. M. *Guidance for Rural Youth; A Report of the Institute for Rural Youth Guidance Held in Washington, D. C., February 27-28, 1941.* 22 pp. Reprinted from *The Educational Record,* April 1941, pp. 187-204.

The Child. Monthly publication of the U. S. Children's Bureau, Washington, D. C.

Child Welfare League of America, Inc., Bulletin. Published by the League, 130 East 22nd St., New York, monthly September to June, inclusive.

The Crippled Child. Bimonthly publication of the National Society for Crippled Children of the United States of America, Inc., Elyria, Ohio.

The Crippled Child Bulletin. Bimonthly publication of the National Society for Crippled Children and Adults, Inc., Elyria, Ohio.

The Family; Journal of Social Case Work. Published by the Family Welfare Association of America, 122 East 22nd St., New York, monthly October to July, inclusive.

Fisher, Dorothy Canfield. *Our Young Folks.* New York: Harcourt Brace & Co., 1943, 329 pp.

Girl Scouts, Inc. *Girl Scouting in the Small Community.* New York: The Author (155 East 44th St.), 32 pp.

——. *Girl Scouting for Rural Girls.* New York: The Author, 15 pp.

——. *Girl Scout Troops in Country Schools.* New York: The Author, leaflet.

——. *How to Start a Girl Scout Troop.* New York: The Author, 1942, 88 pp.

Hanson, Charlotte Leeper. "Child Welfare," in *Social Work Year Book, 1945,* pp. 73-84. (Bibliography, p. 84.)

Hendricks, Floy. *Selected References on Child Labor and Youth Employment.* Washington: U. S. Children's Bureau, 1944, 18 pp.

Herring, Elizabeth B. *Types of Rural YWCA Work in the United States of America.* New York: National Board of the YWCA's of the U.S.A. (600 Lexington Ave.), 10 pp.

Jacobson, Paul B., comp. and ed. "Youth and Work Opportunities." *Bulletin of the National Association of Secondary-School Principals,* No. 90, April 1940, 164 pp.

Johnson, Elizabeth S. *Welfare of Families of Sugar-Beet Laborers; A Study of Child Labor and Its Relation to Family Work, Income, and Living Conditions in 1935.* U. S. Children's Bureau Publication No. 247. Washington: Government Printing Office, 1939, 100 pp.

Johnson, Palmer O. and Oswald L. Harvey. *The National Youth Administration.* Washington: Government Printing Office, 1938, 121 pp.

"Juvenile Delinquency; A Challenge to Concerted Action Now and after the War." *Survey Midmonthly,* Vol. LXXX, No. 3, March 1944, entire issue.

Lenroot, Katharine F. "The Rural Child and the Children's Bureau," in *The White House Conference on Rural Education, October 3, 4, and 5, 1944.* Washington: National Education Association of the United States (1201 Sixteenth St. N. W.), (1945?), pp. 86-97.

Lindley, Ernest K. and Betty Lindley. *A New Deal for Youth; The Story of the National Youth Administration.* New York: Viking Press, 1938, 315 pp.

MacArthur, Kathleen W. *From Faith to Action in the YWCA.* New York: The Woman's Press (600 Lexington Ave.), 1946, 48 pp.

Melvin, Bruce L. *Rural Youth on Relief.* Washington: Government Printing Office, 1937, 112 pp.

——. *Youth—Millions Too Many? A Search for Youth's Place in America.* New York: Association Press, 1940, 220 pp.

—— and Elna N. Smith. *Rural Youth; Their Situation and Prospects.* Washington: Government Printing Office, 1938, 167 pp.

——. ——. *Youth in Agricultural Villages.* Washington: Government Printing Office, 1940, 143 pp.

National Child Labor Committee (419 Fourth Ave., New York).
Clugston, Kate. *Cotton or School.* Publication No. 387. 1943, 31 pp.
Fuller, Raymond G. *Children in Strawberries.* 1940, 22 pp.
The Long Road; Fortieth Anniversary Report. Publication No. 390. 1944, 56 pp.
Sidel, James E. *Pick for Your Supper; A Study of Child Labor among Migrants on the Pacific Coast.* Publication No. 378. 1939, 67 pp. (References, pp. 66-67.)
A Summer in the Country. Publication No. 377, 1939, 39 pp.
Zimand, Gertrude Folks. *Children Who Work on the Nation's Crops.* Publication No. 384. 1942, 19 pp. (References, p. 17.)

National Council of Young Men's Christian Associations. *Communities Serve Their Young People.* New York: The Author (347 Madison Ave.), folder.

National Education Association of the United States. Educational Policies Commission. *The Civilian Conservation Corps, the National Youth Administration, and the Public Schools.* Washington: The Commission (1201 Sixteenth St. N. W.), 1941, 79 pp.

Social Work Year Book, 1945; A Description of Organized Activities in Social Work and in Related Fields, Russell H. Kurtz, ed. New York: Russell Sage Foundation (130 East 22nd St.), 1945, 620 pp.

Stewart, Maxwell S. *America's Children.* Public Affairs Pamphlet No. 47. New York: Public Affairs Committee (30 Rockefeller Plaza), 1940, 31 pp.

Thrasher, Frederic M., ed. "Coordination for Youth Service." *Journal of Educational Sociology,* March 1945, entire issue.

Thurston, Henry W. *Concerning Juvenile Delinquency; Progressive Changes in Our Perspectives.* New York: Columbia University Press, 1942, 236 pp.

U. S. Children's Bureau.
History and Functions of the Children's Bureau. 1944, 23 pp.
Ten Years of Services for Children under the Social Security Program, August 1935–August 1945. Part 1, Maternal and Child Health, 1946, 8 pp.; Part 2, Services for Crippled Children, 1946, 5 pp.; Part 3, Child-Welfare Services, 1946, 7 pp.

Thirty-third Annual Report of the Chief of the Children's Bureau, Fiscal Year Ended June 30, 1945. Washington: The Bureau, 1946, 34 pp.

Publications related to the programs of the National Commission on Children in Wartime, U. S. Children's Bureau, as listed in recent publications of the Commission:

A Children's Charter in Wartime. Children in Wartime No. 2. Publication No. 283. 1942.

For Our Children in Wartime—A Program of State Action. Reprint from *The Child,* 1942.

Community Action for Children in Wartime. Publication No. 295. 1943, 10 pp.

Controlling Juvenile Delinquency. Publication No. 301. 1943, 28 pp.

To Mothers and Fathers of the Nation's Wartime Children; A Letter from the Chief of the Children's Bureau. 1943, 4 pp.

Legislation for the Protection of Children in Wartime. 1943, 36 pp.

Children in a Democracy; General Report Adopted by the White House Conference on Children in a Democracy, January 19, 1940. 86 pp.

White House Conference on Children in a Democracy—Final Report. Publication No. 272. 1943, 392 pp.

Standards of Child Health, Education and Social Welfare, Based on Recommendations of the White House Conference on Children in a Democracy and Conclusions of Discussion Groups. Publication No. 287. 1942, 21 pp.

Our Concern—Every Child; State and Community Planning for Wartime and Post-war Security of Children, by Emma O. Lundberg. Publication No. 303. 1944, 84 pp.

Goals for Children and Youth in the Transition from War to Peace. Publication No. 306. 1944, 12 pp.

Building the Future for Children and Youth. Publication No. 310. 1945, 59 pp.

State and Community Planning for Children and Youth. Publication No. 312. 21 pp.

U. S. Department of Labor. *Annual Report of the Secretary of Labor, Fiscal Year Ended June 30, 1944.* Washington: Government Printing Office, 1945, 77 pp.

U. S. Federal Security Agency. *Annual Reports for the Fiscal Years 1941-1942; 1942-1943.* Washington: Government Printing Office, 1943, 65 pp.

U. S. Interagency Committee on Youth Employment and Education. *Your Community and Its Young People; Their Employment and Educational Opportunities.* U. S. Children's Bureau Publication No. 316. Washington: Government Printing Office, 1946, 31 pp. (What to Read, pp. 30, 31.)

U. S. Library of Congress. Division of Bibliography. *Children and War; A Selected List of References.* Rev. ed. Washington: The Library, 1943, 56 pp.

U. S. National Resources Planning Board. "Post-war Planning for Children and Youth," in *National Resources Development; Report for 1942.* Washington: Government Printing Office, 1942, pp. 113-30.

U. S. National Youth Administration. *Final Report of the National Youth Administration, Fiscal Years 1936-1943.* Washington: Government Printing Office, 1944, 269 pp.

Warburton, Amber Arthun; Helen Wood; and Marian Crane. *The Work and Welfare of Children of Agricultural Laborers in Hidalgo County, Texas.* U. S. Children's Bureau Publication No. 298. Washington: Government Printing Office, 1943, 74 pp.

Ward, Douglas S. and Edith M. Selberg. *Youth and Jobs; Young America Rolls Up Its Sleeves.* Boston: Ginn & Co., 1942, 102 pp. (Bibliography at end of each chapter. Pamphlets about vocations, pp. 94-97. A bibliography of youth studies, pp. 101-2.)

Weitz, Alice C. *Youth and Your Community.* Public Affairs Pamphlet No. 108. New York: Public Affairs Committee (30 Rockefeller Plaza), 1945, 31 pp.

White House Conference on Children in a Democracy. Publications issued by the U. S. Children's Bureau, as listed in *White House Conference on Children in a Democracy; Final Report.*
Conference on Children in a Democracy; Papers and Discussions at Initial Session, April 26, 1939. Publication No. 265. 117 pp.
Proceedings of the White House Conference on Children in a Democracy, January 18-20, 1940; Including the General Report Adopted by the Conference. Publication No. 266. 125 pp.
Preliminary Statements Submitted to the White House Conference on Children in a Democracy, January 18-20, 1940. 257 pp.
Separates from *Preliminary Statements:*
Child Labor and Youth Employment. 13 pp.
Health and Medical Care for Children. 45 pp.
Social Services for Children. 33 pp.
Children in a Democracy; General Report Adopted by the White House Conference on Children in a Democracy, January 19, 1940. 86 pp.
The Follow-Up Program of the White House Conference on Children in a Democracy. Supplement to "The Child." July 1940, 16 pp.
White House Conference on Children in a Democracy: Final Report. Publication No. 272. 1942, 392 pp.

Winslow, W. Thacher. *Youth; A World Problem: A Study in World Perspective of Youth Conditions, Movements and Programs.* Washington: Government Printing Office, 1937, 138 pp.

—— and Frank P. Davidson, eds. *American Youth; An Enforced Reconnaissance.* Cambridge: Harvard University Press, 1940, 216 pp.

Wirth, Louis and Ray Lussenhop. *Urban and Rural Living; Planning Postwar Ways of Life for American Youth.* Problems in American Life Unit No. 21. Washington: National Association of Secondary-School Principals (1201 Sixteenth St. N. W.), 1944, 56 pp.

10 *COOPERATIVES AND GENERAL FARM ORGANIZATIONS*

COOPERATIVE organizations provide a variety of business and social services for rural people. Although the cooperative movement has developed rapidly in cities in recent years, the great majority of cooperative organizations in the United States are in rural areas. This chapter is largely devoted to describing the nature of cooperative organizations and the services they render. It also includes brief descriptions of three major general farm organizations. The promotion of farmer cooperatives is one of the principal activities of each of these organizations.

COOPERATIVES

There are in the United States at the present time more than 19,000 farmer-owned and farmer-controlled cooperative associations and mutual companies with a combined membership of approximately 3,000,000. Included are more than 10,000 cooperatives engaged in marketing farm products and purchasing farm supplies, 4,400 mutual irrigation companies, 1,900 mutual insurance companies, 2,000 mutual telephone companies, 800 rural electric cooperatives, and 600 cooperative frozen food locker plants. In 1943 the volume of business of marketing and purchasing associations totaled more than $5,000,-000,000. Mutual fire insurance companies have in force more than $12,000,000,000 of insurance; mutual irrigation companies supply water to millions of acres of land in the Far West; electric cooperatives supply power and light to almost a million farm families.

These are but a few of the facts presented in *Agricultural Cooperatives in the Postwar Period,* a publication of the Inter-Bureau Committee on Postwar Programs of the United States Department of Agriculture which describes the status and possibilities of cooperative activity in specific fields, suggests procedures to determine the cooperative possibilities of communities, and indicates sources of information and assistance in planning and establishing cooperative undertakings.

The cooperatives in which farmers participate perform many kinds of services. Grain and livestock farmers, producers of dairy and poultry products, fruit growers, and cotton planters are among those who have formed cooperative associations to market their products. Feed, petroleum, fertilizer, and seed are the principal supplies that farmers purchase cooperatively. Forest cooperatives offer possibilities of improved management of farm woodlands and other small forest properties. Electric cooperatives and frozen food locker plants bring large benefits to rural families and communities. Farmers secure credit through national farm loan associations, production credit associations, and credit unions. These are but a few examples of the many types of cooperative associations of farmers.

A cooperative is a business organization owned and controlled by the people it serves. Its primary objective is to provide services at cost rather than for profit. Certain organizational and operating principles are fundamental. Membership is open to all interested persons, and procedures are democratic. In determining the policies of the organization, each member has one vote regardless of the number of shares he owns. The interest paid on capital is not greater than the legal or current rate. After provision is made for interest on capital, reserves, and educational activities, surplus earnings are returned to members in proportion to their patronage.

A number of advantages are claimed for cooperatives. They save money for their members—the profits derived from marketing and retailing belong to the members. Marketing cooperatives have achieved a better standardization of grades of agricultural products. Consumer cooperatives can provide for the testing of products and have sufficient bargaining power to secure quality products. Cooperatives have extended their activities to processing and many products now bear the "co-op" label. Cooperatives also offer educational benefits and spiritual satisfactions. Through experience in cooperatives people come to appreciate the close interrelations of producer and consumer. They gain an understanding of rural-urban interdependence. Farmers appreciate more keenly how world markets affect their products. They learn democracy through participation in the democratic management of their own enterprises. Cooperatives also provide social, recreational, and educational activities for their members.

The vitality of cooperatives depends to a high degree upon local or grass-roots support. Cooperation is not imposed from above; it must grow out of the needs, desires, interests, and active participation of the persons served.

The relationships of individual cooperative societies with other community agencies and with the general cooperative movement are important. A cooperative organization is only one of a number of community institutions. It will make its best contribution to the community through working closely with libraries, schools, churches, and other educational and social agencies. Cooperative societies of various types have established regional and national organizations. The Cooperative League of the United States of America is made up of cooperative distributive and purchasing associations, credit unions, mutual insurance companies, and the like. It assists and advises local cooperative groups, organizes cooperative societies, maintains a book and pamphlet service, and conducts a variety of educational activities. The League maintains offices at 167 West 12th St., New York; 726 Jackson Place, Washington, D. C.; and 343 South Dearborn St., Chicago. The National Council of Farmer Cooperatives, 1731 Eye St. N. W., Washington, D. C., is made up of federations of farmers' cooperative business organizations. It conducts a general service program for member organizations, which includes a biweekly bulletin service describing Washington developments of general agricultural and cooperative interest. It issues pamphlets and an annual *Blue Book*.

Both the federal and state governments encourage cooperatives. Legislation has been passed to facilitate their establishment and various governmental agencies provide counsel and aid. The interest of the federal government in the development of cooperatives in rural areas is evidenced in the activities of the Farm Credit Administration, the Rural Electrification Administration, and the Farm Security Administration. Mention may also be made of the special six-member commission of inquiry to study European cooperatives, appointed by President Roosevelt in 1936. Its *Report of the Inquiry on Cooperative Enterprise in Europe 1937,* based on firsthand observation and an extensive examination of printed materials, contains a wealth of information. The Tennessee Valley Authority has furthered the development of farmer cooperatives in the Tennessee Valley area. The state agricultural colleges distribute bulletins and circulars relating to cooperatives and have staff members equipped to advise with groups interested in exploring the possibilities of cooperatives.

The Farm Credit Administration organization has been established with the general purpose of providing a complete and coordinated system of credit for agriculture through making long- and short-term credit available to farmers. It also provides credit facilities for farmers' cooperative marketing, purchasing, and business service organizations. The United States is divided into twelve farm credit districts and in one city in each district there are a federal land bank, a federal intermediate credit bank, a production credit corporation, and a bank for cooperatives. Applications for loans are made to local production credit associations, which are cooperative organizations of farmers and stockmen. The Central Bank for Cooperatives and the twelve district banks have been organized to provide a permanent source of credit on a sound basis to farmers' cooperative associations. The Central Bank serves national and large regional cooperative organizations and the district banks serve associations in their areas. To be eligible to borrow, a cooperative must be an association in which farmers act together in marketing farm products, purchasing farm supplies, or furnishing farm business services.

The FCA maintains in Washington a cooperative research and service division which engages in research, service, and educational activities. It explores problems of organization, management, policy, merchandising, sales, costs, competition, and membership arising in connection with the cooperative marketing of agricultural products and the cooperative purchasing of farm supplies and services. It has issued a number of pamphlets describing farm cooperative activities in various states and regions. It also issues bulletins, handbooks, reports, and statements summarizing activities or special problems of farm cooperative enterprises for the country as a whole, such as *Handbook on Major Regional Farm Supply Purchasing Cooperatives, 1941 and 1942* and *Producer-Marketing Cooperatives in the United States,* both under the authorship of Joseph G. Knapp, and *Legal Phases of Cooperative Associations,* by L. S. Hulbert. Circulars such as *Three Principles of Agricultural Cooperation,* by Ward W. Fetrow; *Managing Farmers' Cooperatives,* by Kelsey B. Gardner; *Sizing Up Your Cooperative,* by J. E. Wells, Jr.; and *The Story of Farmers' Cooperatives,* by R. H. Elsworth, provide practical suggestions for cooperative organizations and groups contemplating the establishment of such organizations. Information on current developments is contained in the monthly publication *News for Farmer Cooperatives.* A bibliography of publications of the FCA, titled *Publications on Agricultural Cooperation,* was issued in November, 1941.

The Rural Electrification Administration, Boatmen's Bank Building, St. Louis, Missouri, created in 1935, has been a part of the United States Department of Agriculture since July 1, 1939. It provides full financing for the construction and operation of electric distribution lines determined to be sound financial risks to bring electricity to rural people who do not have central station electric service. It also makes loans for operating plants and transmission lines when necessary to provide REA-financed distribution systems with adequate power at reasonable rates. A very high proportion of the borrowers in the REA program are cooperatives organized and controlled by farmers for the purpose of supplying themselves with electricity on a nonprofit basis. More than 800 such cooperatives have been established. The REA also makes loans for the wiring of property of rural consumers and the financing of the purchase and installation of electrical appliances and plumbing to any of the borrowers for line construction and to persons or firms supplying or installing wiring, plumbing, or electrical appliances. The funds available to the REA are determined annually by Congress. Up to June 30, 1946, authorizations had amounted to approximately $825,628,000, of which $817,087,000 had been allotted for loans to qualified borrowers. Loan funds totaling $250,000,000 were made available for the fiscal year 1947. Cooperatives and other borrowers have established an excellent record of financial responsibility. Virtually all systems have met their interest and principal payments and many borrowers have made advance payments.

As of June 30, 1944, REA-financed power systems served 1,152,000 consumers of whom about 900,000 were farmers. Others included schools, rural industries, rural nonfarm residences, Army camps, and Navy bases. It is estimated that as of January 1, 1944, there were 2,557,000 electrified and 3,540,000 unelectrified farms in the United States. The estimate of rural dwellings (farm and nonfarm) electrified was 9,365,000; of dwellings unelectrified, 6,344,000. These figures appear in a pamphlet of the Interbureau Committee on Post-War Programs, *Rural Electrification after the War,* which sets the goals of electric service to all rural people and full use of electricity for farm production, farm-family living, rural-community welfare, and rural industrial use. The pamphlet includes a five-year program to be accomplished with private and government financing and a proposed three-year REA program.

A readable, small book on the evolution of rural electrification in the United States in relation to economic security and the well-being of American agricultural life, which contains chapters on electric cooperatives, is Harry Slattery's *Rural America Lights Up.* Mr. Slattery was administrator of REA at the time this book was published. Frederick William Muller, in *Public Rural Electrification,* describes the development of rural electrification, the activities of the REA (the rural electric cooperative, the control of allotment and construction, the control of operations, program planning), and possible future developments. The REA has issued *A Guide for Members of Cooperatives,* set up in question-and-answer form, which presents information about electric cooperatives—the principles upon which they are based, how they are organized, uses and costs of electricity, and the like. Another pamphlet put out by the REA is *Profits from Farm Power,* which describes many of the uses to which electricity may be put on the farm. The REA also issues numerous statistical bulletins as well as pamphlets showing how to build various types of equipment which use electric power. *Rural Electrification News,* issued monthly by the REA, reports current developments in the field.

The Farm Security Administration, United States Department of Agriculture, is engaged in rural rehabilitation activities and the making of a limited number of loans to farm tenants, sharecroppers, and laborers to enable them to buy family-type farms. These activities are described in Chapters 5 and 6. The FSA has issued two leaflets on cooperatives that should be helpful to groups interested in establishing cooperative organizations—*Co-ops for the Small Farmer,* which describes the advantages of cooperatives and how they are organized and financed, and *Managing the Small Farmers' Co-op,* which sets forth some of the rules for managing such cooperatives successfully.

As of November 1, 1946, the credit facilities and services of the Farm Security Administration and the emergency crop and feed loan division of the Farm Credit Administration were merged into a new agency, the Farmers Home Administration.

The Tennessee Valley Authority, working through the state extension services, aids in the development and operation of cooperative associations that further the long-term agricultural objectives of the Valley program. County associations of farmers distribute test-demonstration fertilizers and in many cases purchase supplies and market produce on a service basis. The test-demonstration program has provided the nucleus for development of a number of cooperatives. The TVA has also encouraged the development of farm electricity cooperatives and some forty-six cooperative systems distribute power in the Valley area at TVA rates. Further information relative to cooperatives and the TVA program may be found in David E. Lilienthal's *TVA—Democracy on the March.*

Additional information relating to these federal agencies interested in cooperatives may be found in the *United States Government Manual—1947,* or in the annual reports of the agencies.

Background information on the cooperative movement may be gleaned from a number of sources in addition to those already mentioned. Public Affairs Pamphlet No. 32, *Cooperatives in the U. S.— A Balance Sheet,* by Maxwell S. Stewart, provides a good introduction to the subject. *The Journal of Educational Sociology* for April, 1943, is devoted to a series of articles on consumer cooperatives under the over-all title "Consumer Cooperatives in the American Pattern." The issue was developed with the collaboration of the Cooperative League of the U. S. A. A committee report of the American Country Life Conference, "Cooperative Activities of Farm People," appears in *Farm and Rural Life after the War; Proceedings of the Twenty-Fourth American Country Life Conference.*

A number of longer treatises that have been issued in recent years may also be mentioned. James Peter Warbasse's *Cooperative Democracy through Voluntary Association of the People as Consumers* provides a statement of the philosophy, methods, and accomplishments of the cooperative movement. *A Cooperative Economy; A Study of Democratic Economic Movements,* by Benson Y. Landis, aims to orient citizen readers in "certain of the most potent influences in the economic world." Another good background volume is *Sweden; The Middle Way,* by Marquis W. Childs. A reference work for consumers and producers who wish to organize cooperatively is Gerald Richardson's *A B C of Cooperatives.* Donald F. Blankertz' *Marketing Cooperatives* places emphasis on agricultural cooperatives—their origins, development, principles, practices, problems, achievements, failures, and future possibilities. Two additional volumes on consumer cooperatives are Joshua K. Bolles' *The People's Business; The Progress of Consumer Cooperatives in America* and Orin E. Burley's *The Consumers' Cooperative as a Distributive Agency.*

E. R. Bowen in "Economic Co-operation and Adult Education," a chapter in *Education for Rural America,* describes the educational methods and activities of cooperatives as well as their principles, growth, and problems.

Joseph W. Eaton's *Exploring Tomorrow's Agriculture* is "a study of the co-operative group farm—an association of a number of farm families who operate jointly a large-scale farming enterprise and who equitably share the returns of their group effort." Projects included cooperative corporation farms of the Farm Security Administration and private enterprises.

The Library of Congress has issued *Cooperation in the United States and Foreign Countries; A List of Bibliographies,* compiled by Anne L. Baden, which contains a section on agriculture.

GENERAL FARM ORGANIZATIONS

The American Farm Bureau Federation is a general farm organization established with the purpose of representing the interests of all types of farmers and promoting the welfare of agriculture throughout the nation. It is made up of 45 state federations which, in turn, consist of approximately 2,000 county farm bureaus and 16,000 community units. In a number of states county bureaus are the legally recognized agencies through which the extension work of the United States Department of Agriculture and the land-grant colleges is carried on. The national office maintains information and service bureaus for members. It also maintains a legislative bureau in Washington. State and county organizations plan and carry out their own programs which cover a wide range of educational, legislative, promotional, and cooperative activities. The Federation issues a variety of pamphlet material providing information about the agency and promoting its objectives. *Of, By, and For Farmers; The Farm Bureau* is a general descriptive pamphlet. *Voice of a Million Farmers* is devoted primarily to legislative accomplishments of the American Farm Bureau Federation in the period from 1919 to 1946. The *Official News Letter* is a biweekly publication. *The Nation's Agriculture* is issued monthly.

The Farmers Educational and Cooperative Union of America has a membership of 450,000 farm men, women, and youth organized in 31 state unions, which in turn are affiliated with the national organization. The Farmers Union promotes cooperative business associations among farmers to sell their products and to buy farm necessities. It encourages scientific farming and marketing and advocates and supports agricultural legislation. It carries on an educational program to meet the needs of working farm families and a program for junior members that includes classes, camps, institutes, and projects. The most important activities of the organization are local, county, or state projects. The development of the Union and its current activities are described in some detail in *The Farmers Union Triangle*, by Gladys Talbott Edwards. *The ABC's of the Farmers Union* is a brief folder setting forth the objectives and programs of the organization. *United We Stand*, by Gladys Talbott Edwards, is designed for use by junior discussion groups to acquaint them with farm problems and the relationship of the Farmers Union thereto. *Living by the Way*, by Frances Walther Butts, is a study and discussion manual relating to the development of creative recreation. Current activities of the Union may be followed in the *National Union Farmer*, published semimonthly.

The National Grange, Patrons of Husbandry, has a membership of 800,000 farmers and agriculturalists organized in 8,000 local Granges and 37 state organizations. It also maintains a national secretariat. State and local Granges organize cooperative undertakings and other community projects. The organization represents the interests of agriculture at state and national capitals, sponsors a program of agricultural legislation, and supports economic, social, and educational activities beneficial to farmers. The Grange has pioneered in the good roads movement and conducts an annual highway essay contest. *The Grange Blue Book* describes the organization and activities of the Grange. Current activities of the organization may be followed in *The National Grange Monthly.*

BIBLIOGRAPHY

The ABC's of the Farmers Union. Denver, Colorado: The Union (3501 East 46th Ave.) 1944, 8 pp.

American Farm Bureau Federation. *Official News Letter.* 58 East Washington St., Chicago, Illinois. Biweekly.

Baden, Anne L., compiler. *Cooperation in the United States and Foreign Countries; A List of Bibliographies.* Washington: Library of Congress, Division of Bibliography, 1943, 35 pp.

Blankertz, Donald F. *Marketing Cooperatives.* New York: Ronald Press Co., 1940, 488 pp. (Bibliographies, p. 475.)

Bolles, Joshua K. *The People's Business; The Progress of Consumer Cooperatives in America.* New York: Harper & Bros., 1942, 170 pp. (Annotated bibliography, pp. 161-65.)

Bowen, E. R. "Economic Co-operation and Adult Education," in *Education for Rural America.* Chicago: University of Chicago Press, 1945, pp. 160-70.

Burley, Orin E. *The Consumers' Cooperative as a Distributive Agency.* New York: McGraw-Hill Book Co., 1939, 388 pp. (Selected references, pp. 297-300.)

Butts, Frances Walther. *Living by the Way.* Denver, Colorado: National Farmers Union Education Service (3501 East 46th Ave.), 1944, 60 pp.

Childs, Marquis W. *Sweden; The Middle Way.* Rev. ed. New Haven, Connecticut: Yale University Press, 1938, 184 pp.

"Consumer Cooperatives in the American Pattern." *The Journal of Educational Sociology,* Vol. XVI, No. 8, April 1943, entire issue. (Bibliography, pp. 529-32.)

"Cooperative Activities of Farm People," in *Farm and Rural Life after the War; Proceedings of the Twenty-Fourth American Country Life Conference.* Champaign, Illinois: The Garrard Press, 1944, pp. 88-94. (Materials used, p. 93.)

Eaton, Joseph W. *Exploring Tomorrow's Agriculture; Co-operative Group Farming—A Practical Program of Rural Rehabilitation.* New York: Harper & Bros., 1943, 255 pp.

Edwards, Gladys Talbott. *The Farmers Union Triangle.* Jamestown, North Dakota: Farmers Union Education Service, 1941, 165 pp.

——. *United We Stand.* Denver, Colorado: National Farmers Union, Department of Education, 1945, 97 pp.

Elsworth, R. H. *The Story of Farmers' Cooperatives.* U. S. Farm Credit Administration Circular E-23. Washington: Government Printing Office, 1939, 28 pp.

Fetrow, Ward W. *Three Principles of Agricultural Cooperation.* U. S. Farm Credit Administration Circular E-24. Washington: Government Printing Office, 1940, 9 pp. (Suggested publications for additional reading, p. 9.)

Gardner, Kelsey B. *Managing Farmers' Cooperatives.* U. S. Farm Credit Administration Circular E-21. Washington: Government Printing Office, 1939, 13 pp. (Suggested material for further reading, p. 13.)

The Grange Blue Book. Springfield, Massachusetts: National Grange Publicity Bureau, 20 pp.

Hulbert, L. S. *Legal Phases of Cooperative Associations.* U. S. Farm Credit Administration Bulletin No. 50. Washington: Government Printing Office, 1942, 456 pp.

Knapp, Joseph G. *Handbook on Major Regional Farm Supply Purchasing Cooperatives, 1941 and 1942.* Farm Credit Administration, Miscellaneous Report No. 67, 1943, 61 pp.

——. *Producer-Marketing Cooperatives in the United States.* Farm Credit Administration, 1944, 12 pp.

Landis, Benson Y. *A Cooperative Economy; A Study of Democratic Economic Movements.* New York: Harper & Bros., 1943, 197 pp. (Bibliography pp. 185-93.)

Lilienthal, David E. *TVA—Democracy on the March.* New York: Harper & Bros., 1944, 248 pp. (Some references for technicians, pp. 227-41.)

Muller, Frederick William. *Public Rural Electrification.* Washington: American Council on Public Affairs, 1944, 183 pp.

National Council of Farmer Cooperatives. *Blue Book.* Annual.

The National Grange Monthly. Official publication of the National Grange, Myrick Building, Springfield, Massachusetts.

National Union Farmer. Official publication of the Farmers Educational and Cooperative Union of America, 3501 East 46th Ave., Denver, Colorado. Semimonthly.

The Nation's Agriculture. Official publication of the American Farm Bureau Federation, 58 East Washington St., Chicago, Illinois. Monthly except bimonthly in July and August.

News for Farmer Cooperatives. Published monthly by the Farm Credit Administration, United States Department of Agriculture, Kansas City, Missouri.

Of, By, and For Farmers; The Farm Bureau. Chicago: The American Farm Bureau Federation, 12 pp.

Report of the Inquiry on Cooperative Enterprise in Europe 1937. Washington: Government Printing Office, 1937, 321 pp.

Richardson, Gerald. *A B C of Cooperatives: A Handbook for Consumers and Producers.* New York: Longmans, Green & Co., 1940, 263 pp.

Rural Electrification News. Published monthly by the Rural Electrification Administration, United States Department of Agriculture, St. Louis, Missouri.

Slattery, Harry. *Rural America Lights Up.* Washington: National Home Library Foundation, 1940, 142 pp.

Stewart, Maxwell S. *Cooperatives in the U. S.—A Balance Sheet.* Public Affairs Pamphlet No. 32 (revised). New York: Public Affairs Committee, 1941, 32 pp. (For further reading, pp. 31-32.)

U. S. Department of Agriculture. Inter-Bureau Committee on Postwar Programs. *Agricultural Cooperatives in the Postwar Period.* Washington: The Department, 1945, 41 pp.

——. ——. *Rural Electrification after the War.* Washington: Government Printing Office, 1945, 18 pp.

U. S. Division of Public Inquiries. Government Information Service. Bureau of the Budget. *United States Government Manual—1947.* 1st ed. Washington: Government Printing Office, 1946, 718 pp.

U. S. Farm Credit Administration. *Publications on Agricultural Cooperation.* Circular A-23. Washington: Government Printing Office, 1941, 30 pp.

U. S. Farm Security Administration. *Co-ops for the Small Farmer.* Washington: Government Printing Office, 1940, 8 pp.

——. *Managing the Small Farmers' Co-op.* Washington: Government Printing Office, 1940, 8 pp.

U. S. Rural Electrification Administration. *A Guide for Members of Cooperatives.* Washington: Government Printing Office, 1940, 48 pp.

——. *Profits from Farm Power.* Washington: Government Printing Office, 1940, 47 pp.

Voice of a Million Farmers. Chicago: American Farm Bureau Federation, 1946, folder.

Warbasse, James Peter. *Cooperative Democracy through Voluntary Association of the People as Consumers: A Discussion of the Cooperative Movement, Its Philosophy, Methods, Accomplishments, and Possibilities, and Its Relation to the State, to Science, Art, and Commerce, and to Other Systems of Economic Organization.* 4th ed. New York: Harper & Bros., 1942, 285 pp. (Bibliography pp. 271-73.)

Wells, J. E., Jr. *Sizing Up Your Cooperative.* U. S. Farm Credit Administration Circular E-18. Washington: Government Printing Office, 1939, 13 pp.

11 *LOCAL GOVERNMENT*

THE IMPORTANCE of governmental action and services has been indicated in many of the preceding chapters. There has been a steady increase in the functions that citizens wish their governments to perform. The activities of governments during the depression and war periods, especially, have served to give the individual citizen a feeling of being close to his government, whether local, state, or national. Relationships between the three levels of government have also quickened and deepened through programs of federal and state aid for various activities that have been administered largely by local governments.

Some of the problems and weaknesses of local government have already been suggested. Local governmental units are created by the states. Their powers are set out in state constitutions and state enabling legislation. Large cities, generally, have won a large measure of home rule. In many states, however, counties and other comparable local units lack the powers necessary to provide one or another badly needed service. In considering whether it is desirable for their local government to undertake a new function, citizens must first determine whether this government is permitted to do so. They may have to put their first efforts into securing necessary constitutional changes or enabling legislation to permit the local unit to embark upon the desired program. A comparative analysis of the provisions of state constitutions regarding counties is contained in *County Government Manual for the Missouri Constitutional Convention of 1943,* by William L. Bradshaw.

Another set of problems results from the large number and small size of local governmental units. Many small units lack the necessary tax base and financial resources to provide adequate services. The number of persons served is frequently too small to warrant the specialized professional staffs needed for such services as health, welfare, and education. Again, overhead costs in small units are apt to be unduly large.

In preceding chapters it has been pointed out that large amounts of federal and state aid are currently provided for many programs locally administered. Such aid has done much to reduce inequalities among areas in ability to provide services. It has supplied outside leadership and stimulation and programs of education relating to the functions aided and has improved standards of service. Grants-in-aid may have the unfortunate result, however, of insuring the continuance of uneconomic local units. There is also a danger of possible outside control and the destruction of local initiative. Local initiative is needed to secure modifications of programs to fit local needs, to secure desirable innovations and experimentation, and to preserve the American tradition of solving problems at the grass roots through local democratic action.

Some of these problems are discussed in William Anderson's *The Units of Government in the United States; An Enumeration and Analysis.* A unit of government is defined "as a resident population occupying a defined area that has a legally authorized organization and governing body, a separate legal identity, the power to provide certain public or governmental services, and a substantial degree of autonomy including legal and actual power to raise at least a part of its own revenue." As of January, 1941, there was in the United States a total of 165,000 units of local government distributed as follows: counties, 3,050; incorporated places, 16,262; townships, 18,998; school districts, 118,308; and other special districts, 8,382. In addition to an extensive analysis of the units of American government as they existed in 1941, this publication also presents a discussion of the adequacy of the system of local units.

COUNTIES, TOWNSHIPS, AND SCHOOL DISTRICTS

The government and administration of the rural county, township, and school district in the United States, as well as the government of the New England town, are described in *Government in Rural America,* by Lane W. Lancaster.[1] The author indicates throughout his discussion how economic and psychological factors peculiar to the rural setting affect the conduct of government. The following description of the organization and activities of counties, townships, and school districts is based largely on this book.

The more than 3,000 counties carry on a wide variety of functions. Among their major responsibilities are education, health and welfare services, highways, protection, and judicial functions. In county government "powers and duties are divided between a more or less extensive list of individual administrative officers and the general supervisory authority known as the county commissioners, the board

---

[1] Copyrighted by D. Van Nostrand Company, Inc.

of supervisors or simply as the county board." In a majority of states the county board "is a small body of three or five members chosen at large from the county or from districts into which the county is divided for this purpose." In some states, however, the townships are the units for the choice of members of the board, which is known as a board of supervisors. County boards in these states vary in size from 16 to 141 members. Terms of office of county board members are two or four years. County boards exercise no effective supervision over elective officers, who may include the county judge, attorney, sheriff, clerk, treasurer, auditor, assessor, register of deeds, surveyor, coroner, superintendent of schools, and others. The board has full power over its own appointees, however, the number of whom continues to grow. The board "determines what undertakings shall be launched, what buildings and institutions shall be built, what permissive statutes shall be adopted for the county, what and how much equipment shall be bought, and what roads and bridges shall be built." It awards contracts, within the detailed provisions of statutes; has "a growing power to appoint minor officials and to make rules and regulations for various county institutions"; controls welfare policy; is responsible in large part for the purchase of supplies of various sorts for the county offices; passes upon claims and allows bills against the county; has a number of duties in connection with finances—making and adopting the budget, fixing the tax rate, and equalizing assessments; approves official bonds; and supervises the machinery of state and local elections.

Townships exist in sixteen states and number approximately 19,000. Although they are declining in significance and have little justification for continuance, rural townships carry on a number of functions in many states, among the principal of which are maintaining country roads and administering poor relief. In some instances they are also the unit for school administration. Township affairs, generally, are administered by one or more elected trustees or supervisors, with whom may be associated other elective officers.

Except in New England where the town is the unit and in a number of southern states where the county is the unit, education in rural areas is provided generally by small districts that do not correspond with any other governmental unit. The weaknesses of these small units are pointed out in Chapter 1. Responsibility for the schools is vested in elected boards which have "almost complete authority over the routine conduct of the schools, including the power to levy taxes, borrow money, employ and dismiss teachers, erect and maintain buildings and buy supplies, and, in some degree, to control the curriculum." The small size of school districts and the board form of organization result in the election of almost as many board members to supervise the work of the schools as there are teachers to carry it on.

In addition to county, township, and school units, there are in rural America a great number of villages incorporated to carry on governmental functions and numerous districts set up to provide special services, such as drainage, irrigation, highway and road, and health and sanitation services—to mention a few that are common.

RURAL GOVERNMENT AND LAND USE

The results of this situation are described as follows in a section on the structure and functions of rural local government in *State Legislation for Better Land Use,* a special report of an interbureau committee of the United States Department of Agriculture:

> In this multiplicity of small units lie many of the weaknesses of rural local governments as now constituted: Diffusion of taxing and borrowing power; duplication of functions, officers and equipment; wastes in purchasing; heavy overhead costs; wide variations in tax resources, tax burdens, and quality of services; lack of unity in planning and location and quality of public facilities and appraising and supervising the administration of local services.

This report indicates the close interrelationships of rural government and land-use policy. It discusses such problems as rural zoning, state water laws, soil conservation districts, farm tenancy law, procedure for rural tax-delinquent lands, state land purchase for land-use adjustment, and the management and development of state and county lands.

Studies of land-grant colleges and other agencies have also pointed to the close relationship between the quality of rural government and land use. One such study is Fred A. Clarenbach's *Needed Local Government Reorganization in Ozark Land Use Adjustment Areas.* The development of land-use committees and soil conservation districts is discussed in Chapter 13.

COUNTY AND FUNCTIONAL CONSOLIDATION

County consolidation is frequently suggested as a method of overcoming weaknesses resulting from small size, limited financial resources, and limited populations, and in a number of states there are statutes under which consolidations may be effected. Several difficulties or obstacles in connection with consolidation may be suggested. First, there is no assurance that consolidation will produce desired areas, populations, or resources. Second, although reduction in overhead costs may follow consolidation, this result does not necessarily follow. Consolidation requires the consent of the voters of the units consolidating. There may be powerful interests lined up against consolidation—officeholders, business interests, social groups, and so forth. Units in good financial condition will object to uniting with units in a less satisfactory financial position. There is also fear on the part of local residents that they will lose control over their government. Although there is facilitating legislation in many states, there have been only two instances of consolidation—two Tennessee counties consolidated in 1919, and three Georgia counties in 1932.

Short of actual consolidation, units may join forces for the performance of individual functions such as health, welfare, school, or library services, tax administration, and the purchase of supplies. Counties may work out agreements for the joint performance of functions or services, or cities or towns and counties may effect such arrangements. This type of action involves no merging of units but merely cooperation among them. One unit may contract with another to provide it service, or the units may agree on joint performance and support. Functional consolidation permits solution of immediate problems and provides an administrative area that may be altered to meet changing conditions; however, it serves to complicate the administrative map and does not effect a thoroughgoing reassignment of functions among units. There are numerous examples of such cooperative arrangements in various parts of the country.

Another suggested solution of problems of rural local government is the reallocation of functions among units and levels of government. One such reallocation might be the assignment of school functions to units of general government. Many functions performed by townships might be better administered by counties or states, and some county functions might become state functions. There is, at present, a trend toward a reallocation of functions upward—transfers of township road, health, and other functions to the county or the state, and transfers of such county functions as education, health, relief and welfare, law enforcement, and highway administration to the state.

INTERGOVERNMENTAL RELATIONS

A study of local government that stresses problems of intergovernmental relationships is *American Local Government,* by Roger Hewes Wells. Following a discussion of such matters as the citizen and local government, areas and structures, the states and local government, and the role of the federal government, the author suggests that the nation, the states, and local governments are becoming partners in the common task of solving current governmental problems.

Despite many discouraging factors, it is possible to speak of "the rise of a new local government" in our country—a local government which provides a more effective nucleus for the citizen and for citizen groups; which is proceeding toward a better adjustment of areas, governmental structures, and functions; and which is increasingly conscious of the value of state-local and federal-state-local cooperation. At a time when to many democracy seems on the defensive, it is well to reexamine and strengthen the local foundations of popular rule.[2]

Another study intended "to aid in the critical discussion of . . . American intergovernmental relationships" is George C. S. Benson's *The New Centralization.* A few of the author's conclusions may be cited. "A good many of the present local difficulties can most satisfactorily be solved . . . by changes in other governmental levels. . . . Probably the most critically defective part of our present system is the state government. . . . In many cases the solution of local, interstate, federal-state, federal-local, and even federal problems depends upon the improvement of state legislation and administration. . . . It cannot be said that the increase in direct federal activity during recent years has been alarming." It seems probable, however,

. . . that the fields of education, welfare, and—to a great extent—police protection, should be reserved to state and local governments, and that where federal aid is necessary it should be limited to unconditional—or largely unconditional—grants. These are activities in which administrative decentralization, adaptation to local needs, education of citizens, and the diffusion of political power are so important that they outweigh completely any slight gains in efficiency from centralized control.[3]

The Council on Intergovernmental Relations, with the assistance of the Spelman Fund, has initiated several local experiments aimed at finding a formula for "blending more harmoniously the powers and interests of federal, state and local governments in the execution of their common purposes." A report on one of these experiments is *Democracy Trains Its Microscope on Government in Blue Earth County, Minnesota.* In that county the county Council on Intergovernmental Relations spent a year and a half "photograph-

[2] Reprinted by permission from *American Local Government* by Roger H. Wells, copyrighted, 1939, by the McGraw-Hill Book Co., Inc.

[3] Reprinted by permission from *The New Centralization* by George C. S. Benson, copyrighted, 1941, by Rinehart & Company, Inc.

ing" the nearly two hundred governmental organizations whose actions directly or indirectly affect citizens of the county. At the end of its study it proposed the adoption of a "community budget," not as an instrument to control member units in the preparation of their individual budgets but to assist them by providing a complete and usable report on all governmental activities being carried on within the community. It is believed that this budget will provide a means for reporting all governmental activities in the community on a uniform basis; will furnish local, state, and federal governments with a guide to more intelligent planning and administration of work programs; will serve as a basis for budget analysis by all levels of government; will bring about more frequent contacts among personnel of separate units and agencies; and will strengthen local controls.

Adventure in Governmental Gearing is a progress report issued by the Henry County [Indiana] Council on Intergovernmental Relations. It is stated in the foreword:

Now, after approximately two years of study, this Council has proposed a teamwork plan which it is felt will result in better meshing of governmental gears and in the process enable local government to regain and maintain a major role in solving the problems of our complex economy and government. State and federal committees on intergovernmental relations have expressed their willingness to aid in every way possible to give the idea a fair trial. Now it's up to the officials and the people of Henry County.

Recommendations include more federal-state counsel and technical assistance with less centralized control; furthering citizen participation; self-help by enabling legislation and more local activity; more central-local shared revenue plans; the elimination of duplication and greater coordination; and property assessment revisions.

Greene County, Georgia, is another county in which an experimental program sponsored by the Council on Intergovernmental Relations is being conducted. T. Hamp McGibony has prepared a report which describes cooperative action in that county resulting from efforts to improve agriculture, under the title *Governmental Cooperation in Greene County, Georgia.*

Such matters as deorganization of rural units, transfer of functions, use of special districts, modernization of local government structure, flexibility in governmental forms, financial relations, expansion of local functions, and physical and functional consolidation are discussed in an article, "State-Rural Relations," in *The Book of the States, 1945-46.* It is concluded that townships of the midwestern type will ultimately be abolished or further emasculated; the number of rural school districts will be drastically reduced; the New England town, the Louisiana parish, and the county in other states will be strengthened; there will be little consolidation of counties; and special purpose districts will continue to be used.

In *State-Local Relations* the Committee on State-Local Relations of the Council of State Governments describes existing relations and makes suggestions for improved practices relating to some of the most pressing problems, especially financial problems.

Two other publications concerned with problems of intergovernmental relations may be mentioned. W. Brooke Graves is the editor of "Intergovernmental Relations in the United States," the January, 1940, issue of *The Annals of the American Academy of Political and Social Science*. There is a section on the interrelations of local units. *Metropolitan Government,* by Victor Jones, contains a discussion of the reorganization of the urban county.

A number of studies have also been made of intergovernmental fiscal relations. The most comprehensive is *Federal, State, and Local Government Fiscal Relations,* a study of the Committee on Intergovernmental Fiscal Relations of the United States Treasury Department. A 45-page summary of major conclusions and recommendations is presented at the beginning of the report. It concludes with recommendations in terms of an action program for each level of government. To assist the Treasury Committee in its work and make available for its consideration the viewpoint and attitude of local government on this problem, the Committee on Local Government Activities and Revenues of the Municipal Finance Officers Association issued a report prepared by Thomas H. Reed entitled *Federal State Local Fiscal Relations.*

IMPROVEMENT OF ADMINISTRATIVE PRACTICES

In addition to suggesting changes in basic governmental units and reassignments of functions among them, persons interested in improving local government have made a number of recommendations relating to governmental organization and administration. Some of the more common of these are: reduction in the number of elected officials; the separation of policy-making and administrative functions; adoption of the merit system and improved personnel practices; improvement in taxing, budgeting, accounting, and auditing practices; centralized purchasing of equipment and supplies; more adequate planning services; and an improved system of public relations.

It is frequently suggested that the manager form of government, which has proved so effective in many cities, be applied to counties. The National Municipal League has issued a pamphlet, *The County Manager Plan,* which indicates the merits of the plan and describes its operation in eleven counties that have the closest approach to the pure county manager form of government. In this pamphlet it is stated that county government generally "is distinguished from the best practice in other governmental units by four characteristics: lack of any central executive, popular election of numerous administrative officers, dispersion of the appointment power in many different hands and among several levels of government, and limited discretion of the board over allocation of funds and over policy generally." Under the county manager plan, voters would elect at large a small county board (five, seven, nine, or eleven members), which board would appoint a county manager—a professional public administrator—who would be responsible for carrying out the policies adopted by the board. He would serve as the central executive "with power to direct, to appoint, to remove and to discipline." In a small county one person may be treasurer, county clerk, register of deeds, and court stenographer; the road commissioner may also do the work of the surveyor and be helpful at the court.

Indeed, administratively, the manager himself may be almost "the whole works." In a larger county he may act as sheriff and supervise all the rest of the county administration without being overworked.

In a still larger county, with fifty or a hundred employees, he can save his salary many times a year by expressing in daily contact with the staff the demand of the public for efficiency and economy and exercising practical controls to those ends.

Under this plan all fees should go into revenue and pay should be according to work done regardless of whether one office shows a profit and the next a loss. Employees should be shifted from one department to another as work varies and should be kept at work full time.

Although many units of local government in rural areas have too few employees to justify the adoption of many of the procedures of a formal personnel program, certain parts of such a program would seem to be applicable in most jurisdictions. Many suggestions may be gleaned from *Personnel Programs for Smaller Cities as Exemplified by Installations in Various Cities in Michigan,* a publication of Public Administration Service, which describes the need for the merit system, its adaptation to local needs, the problem of technical assistance at low cost, the organization for personnel administration, the position-classification plan, the pay plan, the recruitment program, and the in-service personnel program.

Another useful publication is *Merit System Installation: Problems and Procedures in Establishing a Public Personnel Agency,* also published by Public Administration Service, which describes the various steps in setting up a merit system in a jurisdiction that has decided to operate under the merit plan of recruiting and managing administrative personnel.

A report of the Committee on County Accounting of the Municipal Finance Officers Association, *County Finance and Accounting Standards,* has the joint aims of helping county officials to determine whether their present procedures meet accepted standards and helping state officials charged with the supervision of county accounts. It covers financial organization; the preparation and adoption of the budget and the system of budgetary control; the accounting system—records, accounts, funds, and accounting procedure; financial reports; and post-auditing. The report concludes:

> When one considers that some of the more significant services rendered by the county are those relating to relief, hospitals, jails, and the administration of justice, the importance of the proper execution of duties becomes evident. It is not only a question of performing these activities at the lowest possible cost but also of rendering effective service. County officials have a right to demand that they be furnished with proper management tools to carry out these important tasks.
>
> It is realized that the essentials of practice enumerated above will not be fully applicable in all cases. Some minor adjustments to suit local conditions will have to be made; but in the main a county should encounter little difficulty in following standard practice.

Another pamphlet that may prove helpful is *Purchasing for Small Cities,* by Russell Forbes and Others. It describes the establishment of a centralized purchasing system and the various purchasing procedures involved.

County Fiscal Procedures in New York, by C. A. Bratton, describes these procedures and analyzes some of the problems. "For each of the financial transactions discussed, the legal basis for the procedures, the actual practices that have developed, and an analysis of some of the essential features of an adequate system are presented."

Planning for the Small American City, by Russell Van Nest Black and Mary Hedges Black, "tells operating officials and interested citizens of the average small city, in simple and nontechnical language, how to make a plan and how to carry it out."

STUDIES OF SPECIFIC SITUATIONS

The discussion thus far has aimed to cover some of the principal problems of governmental organization and administration in rural areas, citing general works relating thereto and some material on specific management practices. It may be useful also to cite a few of the many studies of specific local governments as examples of different types of studies made under various auspices.

A study that "undertakes to describe some of the more important developments and trends in county government in the seven Tennessee Valley States" is *County Government and Administration in the Tennessee Valley States,* issued by the Tennessee Valley Authority.

Local government in a single state is described by William Anderson in *Local Government and Finance in Minnesota.* In his concluding chapter he presents a brief sketch giving recommendations for an improved system of local government for Minnesota.

Another study of local government in a single state is *Indiana State and Local Government,* by Pressly S. Sikes.

Rural Government in New York, by M. P. Catherwood and Others, is an Extension Bulletin of Cornell University, which describes town, county, and school administration and finance.

The *Montgomery County Survey* is a detailed report on local governmental services in the City of Dayton and Montgomery County, Ohio, resulting from a survey made by Public Administration Service for the Montgomery County Survey Board. It covers the public schools and the government of the county, the Miami Conservancy District, and cities, villages, and townships.

Four other recent studies of county government may be mentioned. Claude R. Tharp's *A Manual of County Administrative Organization in Michigan* was prepared to make available in a single reference work "a concise and comprehensive description of all county offices, boards, commissions, and committees." Melvin Clyde Hughes in *County Government in Georgia* covers county governmental organization, the relation of counties to the state, and the administration of county services. The book concludes with a chapter on county consolidation. It is the opinion of the author that "the greatest obstacle to effective and efficient operation of county government in Georgia is the existence of an unusually large number of small poor counties in the state." Karl A. Bosworth has made two intensive studies of Alabama counties. *Black Belt County; Rural Government in the Cotton Country of Alabama* describes a county typical of perhaps ten counties in the Alabama black belt. *Tennessee Valley County;*

Rural Government in the Hill Country of Alabama discusses a county representative of eight or ten counties in northern Alabama. In these two studies "an attempt has been made . . . to catch the spirit of democratic government at the grass roots."

For a number of years the December issue of *The American Political Science Review* has carried a survey of developments in county and township government during the preceding year.

The *National Municipal Review* frequently has articles and news notes on developments in county government.

BIBLIOGRAPHY

The American Political Science Review. Published by the American Political Science Association, 1822 Sheridan Road, Northwestern University, Evanston, Illinois, bimonthly.

Anderson, William. *Local Government and Finance in Minnesota.* Minneapolis: University of Minnesota Press, 1935, 355 pp.

———. *The Units of Government in the United States; An Enumeration and Analysis.* Publication No. 83. Rev. ed. Chicago: Public Administration Service (1313 East 60th St.), 1945, 49 pp.

Benson, George C. S. *The New Centralization; A Study of Intergovernmental Relationships in the United States.* New York: Rinehart & Company, Inc., 1941, 181 pp. (Selected bibliography, pp. 170-75.)

Black, Russell Van Nest and Mary Hedges Black. *Planning for the Small American City; An Outline of Principles and Procedure Especially Applicable to the City of Fifty Thousand or Less.* Publication No. 87. Rev. ed. Chicago: Public Administration Service, 1944, 86 pp. (Bibliography, pp. 84-86.)

Bosworth, Karl A. *Black Belt County; Rural Government in the Cotton Country of Alabama.* University, Alabama: Bureau of Public Administration, University of Alabama, 1941, 114 pp.

———. *Tennessee Valley County; Rural Government in the Hill Country of Alabama.* University, Alabama: Bureau of Public Administration, University of Alabama, 1941, 115 pp.

Bradshaw, William L. *County Government Manual for the Missouri Constitutional Convention of 1943.* Columbia, Missouri: University of Missouri, 1943, 58 pp.

Bratton, C. A. *County Fiscal Procedures in New York.* Bulletin No. 805. Ithaca, New York: Cornell University, Agricultural Experiment Station, 1944, 32 pp.

Catherwood, M. P. and Others. *Rural Government In New York.* Extension Bulletin No. 331. Ithaca, New York: Cornell University, New York State College of Agriculture, 1942, 28 pp.

Clarenbach, Fred A. *Needed Local Government Reorganization in Ozark Land Use Adjustment Areas.* Agricultural Experiment Station Research Bulletin No. 331. Columbia, Missouri: University of Missouri, 1941, 132 pp. (Literature cited, pp. 130-32.)

The Committee on State-Local Relations. The Council of State Governments. *State-Local Relations.* Chicago: The Council (1313 East 60th St.), 1946, 228 pp.

Council on Intergovernmental Relations. *Democracy Trains Its Microscope on Government in Blue Earth County, Minnesota.* Mankato: The Council (202 First National Bank Building), 1945, 35 pp.

Forbes, Russell and Others. *Purchasing for Small Cities.* Publication No. 66. Chicago: Public Administration Service, 1939, 22 pp.

Graves, W. Brooke, ed. "Intergovernmental Relations in the United States." *The Annals of the American Academy of Political and Social Science,* Vol. CCVII, January 1940, entire issue.

Henry County [Indiana] Council on Intergovernmental Relations. *Adventure in Governmental Gearing.* New Castle, Indiana: The Council (214½ South 14th St.), 1946, 48 pp.

Hughes, Melvin Clyde. *County Government in Georgia.* Athens: University of Georgia Press, 1944, 197 pp. (Bibliography, pp. 187-93.)

Jones, Victor. *Metropolitan Government.* Chicago: University of Chicago Press, 1942, 364 pp. (List of bibliographies, pp. 343-44.)

Lancaster, Lane W. *Government in Rural America.* New York: D. Van Nostrand Co., 1937, 416 pp. (References at end of each chapter.)

McGibony, T. Hamp. *Governmental Cooperation in Greene County, Georgia.* Washington: Council on Intergovernmental Relations (Transportation Building), 1945, 33 pp.

Montgomery County [Ohio] Survey Board. *Montgomery County Survey: Report on Local Governmental Services in Dayton and Montgomery County, Ohio; Conclusions and Recommendations of the Survey Board; Survey Staff Report.* Chicago: Public Administration Service, 1940, 529 pp.

Municipal Finance Officers Association of the United States and Canada. Committee on County Accounting. Accounting Publication No. 4. *County Finance and Accounting Standards.* Chicago: The Association (1313 East 60th St.), 1937, 35 pp.

National Municipal League. *The County Manager Plan.* New York: The League (299 Broadway), 1945, 22 pp.

National Municipal Review. Published by the National Municipal League, 299 Broadway, New York, monthly except August.

Public Administration Service. *Merit System Installation: Problems and Procedures in Establishing a Public Personnel Agency.* Publication No. 77. Chicago: The Service, 1941, 58 pp. (A selected bibliography on public personnel administration, pp. 32-34.)

——. *Personnel Programs for Smaller Cities as Exemplified by Installations in Various Cities in Michigan.* Publication No. 73. Chicago: The Service, 1940, 46 pp.

Reed, Thomas H. *Federal State Local Fiscal Relations.* Chicago: Municipal Finance Officers Association, 1942, 60 pp.

Sikes, Pressly S. *Indiana State and Local Government.* Bloomington: Principia Press, Inc., 1940, 242 pp. (Selected bibliography, pp. 234-37.)

"State-Rural Relations," in *The Book of the States, 1945-46.* Chicago: The Council of State Governments, 1945, pp. 54-60.

Tharp, Claude R. *A Manual of County Administrative Organization in Michigan.* Michigan Governmental Studies, No. 15. Ann Arbor: University of Michigan Press, 1944, 291 pp.

U. S. Department of Agriculture. Interbureau Committee on State Legislation for Better Land Use. *State Legislation for Better Land Use; A Special Report.* Washington: Government Printing Office, 1941, 122 pp. (Selected bibliography, pp. 118-22.)

U. S. Tennessee Valley Authority. Department of Regional Studies. Government Research Division. *County Government and Administration in the Tennessee Valley States.* Knoxville, Tennessee: The Authority, 1940, 144 pp. (Selected bibliography on county government in the seven Valley states, pp. 135-37.)

U. S. Treasury Department. Committee on Intergovernmental Fiscal Relations. *Federal, State, and Local Government Fiscal Relations.* 78th Cong., 1st sess., Senate Document No. 69. Washington: Government Printing Office, 1943, 595 pp.

Wells, Roger Hewes. *American Local Government.* New York: McGraw-Hill Book Co., 1939, 200 pp.

12 COMMUNITY ORGANIZATION

THE IMPORTANCE of the community as a unit for the accomplishment of various social, economic, and cultural objectives has been indicated at a number of points in earlier chapters. In the chapter on schools, for example, are cited a number of references to the school as a community institution. There are references in the chapters on library service, welfare services, recreation, and others that indicate the vitality of the community as an agency of social action.

THE DEVELOPING RURAL COMMUNITY

It is pointed out by Dwight Sanderson, in a bulletin entitled *Locating the Rural Community,* that little was heard of the rural community prior to World War I. That war gave rise to activities and conditions that brought rural people together as never before and gave them a new appreciation of the values and satisfactions of community life. The automobile and surfaced roads have contributed to community development, and in the last twenty years the community has come to be recognized as the functional unit for the social organization of rural life. The community consists of a group or company of people who live fairly close together in a more or less compact contiguous territory and who tend to act together in the chief concerns of life. People must associate in several of their more common interests if there is to be a true community. The rural community usually has two distinct but interdependent parts—the village center, where are located the organizations and business agencies serving the community, and the tributary open-country area. The community, in recent years, has tended to supersede the neighborhood as the primary rural unit. The term "neighborhood" is coming to mean only a group of houses fairly near to each other. In many cases the neighborhood provides a unit for certain purposes of social organization such as school district or church parish, but it cannot function in the same way as the community, which unites people in several of their chief interests. Rural school consolidation has been the most notable influence in making people aware of the importance of the rural community as a unit of social organization. Community life usually disregards political boundaries.

In the preface to *Rural Community Organization,* by Dwight Sanderson and Robert A. Polson, it is pointed out that planning units, state and county, are aware that all planning is ultimately directed to human welfare and that this involves planning for and by communities. The county land committees of the United States Department of Agriculture have emphasized the importance of developing local community units. These committees are described in Chapter 13. Other forces in rural life have brought out the need for better integration of the rural community. The integration of the older neighborhood and smaller community groups into the life of the larger emerging rural community is a real problem in many parts of the country. A rational, realistic approach to the social problems that affect its people is the essential idea of community organization, whatever its methods or mechanisms.

T. Lynn Smith, in an article entitled "Trends in Community Organization and Life," *American Sociological Review,* June, 1940, notes the following changes in the role of the community unit: (1) it is expanding in size; (2) it is supplanting the neighborhood as the basic locality grouping; (3) there is a tendency for the internal structure of the community to become more differentiated; (4) the boundaries between communities are becoming less distinct; and (5) local functions, especially governmental functions, are being taken over by other governmental units—county, state, and federal. The author concludes that both the neighborhood and the community are losing their exclusive claims to the loyalty and patronage of the individual family; that neighborhoods are not doomed to extinction but will find their principal role as a complementary part of the enlarged community; that communities, in turn, are developing complementary and supplementary relationships among themselves, are allowing the neighborhood to play a definite role, and are seeing individual families participate in the greater society.

According to Edmund deS. Brunner and T. Lynn Smith, in "Village Growth and Decline, 1930-1940," *Rural Sociology,* June, 1944, recent data on village population behavior suggest that two distinct types of service centers for the rural population may be emerging: (1) the traditional type of service station village and (2) the "market town" of 2,500 to 10,000 or even larger population which extends the number and enlarges the scope of services to the farming population.

Rural Trends in Depression Years; A Survey of Village-Centered Agricultural Communities, 1930-1936, by Edmund deS. Brunner and

Irving Lorge, presents the results of a study of changes in rural social life in the United States from 1930 to 1936. It also traces the life story of 140 village-centered agricultural communities through a third phase of their development and history. The initial investigation, made in 1923-24, was the first national study of farmers' towns of less than 2,500 population. It showed rural America increasingly centered in villages and towns rather than crossroads hamlets. This study was reported in five volumes, plus a summary volume, *Village Communities,* by Mr. Brunner. The second study, begun in the summer of 1929, became the rural section of the study of President Hoover's Research Committee on Social Trends. It was published in 1933 as *Rural Social Trends,* under the authorship of Edmund deS. Brunner and J. H. Kolb. The third study of these same villages, referred to above, indicates that the village or town center has become the capital of rural America. The crossroads neighborhood is no longer the chief integrating social factor in rural life. Farmers are steadily increasing their use of the village or town center for education, especially at the high-school level, for church activities, for social life, for professional services, and for purchasing the daily necessities. The trend is clear even though it was slowed by the depression. Village and country relations have reached a considerable degree of harmonious interaction.

A study by David Ross Jenkins, *Growth and Decline of Agricultural Villages,* is based largely on the materials relating to the 140 village-centered agricultural communities described in the preceding paragraph. The conclusions of the study should help in formulating criteria to be used in selecting village centers for consolidated rural school districts as well as village centers for other agencies and services.

Both neighborhood and community groups in Dane County (Madison), Wisconsin, have been studied over a period of twenty-three years by systematic field surveys at ten-year intervals, by numerous intensive studies of sample cases, and by personal contacts and observation throughout the period. *Neighborhood-Community Relationships in Rural Society,* by John H. Kolb and Douglas G. Marshall, is a report setting forth important findings and some of their implications. The bibliography gives digests of a number of studies of communities in various parts of the United States selected because of their bearing on the problems and purposes of the Dane County study and because of their recent date.

CASE STUDIES OF COMMUNITIES

The Bureau of Agricultural Economics of the United States Department of Agriculture has issued a series of six studies of rural communities, each bearing the over-all title *Culture of a Contemporary Rural Community*. The communities were selected as samples of, or points on, a continuum from high community stability to great instability. They were studied contemporaneously by six different field workers during 1939. Each study covers the same general subject matter—identification and characterization of the community, the history and background of the settlement, the people on the land, the community, the farmer's expanding world, and integration and disintegration in community and individual life. Full titles of the studies are given in the bibliography. A related study is Walter M. Kollmorgen's *The German-Swiss in Franklin County, Tennessee; A Study of the Significance of Cultural Considerations in Farming Enterprises*. The author reports upon "an examination of the farming practices of a German-Swiss community . . . and . . . of several groups of native, or traditional, farmers in the same county on physically comparable soil. . . ."

The Bureau of Agricultural Economics in 1943-44 made studies of the effect of the war on twelve communities in twelve counties in twelve different states to determine what changes had occurred in the community pattern of organization and in the function of each organization and institution, what new organizations had come into being, and their effect. The communities are all village centered and each is believed to be fairly typical of communities in the broad area which each county represents. The analysis includes the entire community area, farm and village. Citations to seven of these studies are given in the bibliography.

It has been mentioned that action on a community basis is important in developing land-use plans and in carrying such plans into effect. Several studies of communities in relation to land-use planning may be listed. John B. Holt, in *Rural Neighborhoods and Communities of Lee County, Alabama, and Their Significance for Land Use Planning*, reports a reconnaissance survey of natural neighborhood and community groupings of the rural farm population living in the county in an effort to help solve the problem of enlisting the cooperation of farm families in adopting the recommendations of the county land-use planning committee. A study, *Rural Community Organization in Washington and Frederick Counties, Maryland*, by Linden S. Dodson, Douglas Ensminger, and Robert N. Woodworth, was undertaken to determine and map natural communities as a basis for land-use planning, to determine the cohesive forces operative in communities, to experiment with a simple method of determining natural community areas, and to make available information on the several communities as an aid in planning activities. *Kansas Rural Communities; A Study of Nemaha County,* by the United States Bureau of Agricultural Economics in cooperation with the Kansas Agricultural Experiment Station, also indicates the importance of community organization in effective land-use planning.

Numerous other studies of community organization and of individual communities have been issued by the United States Department of Agriculture and the agricultural experiment stations and extension services of the various states. A few such studies are here listed: Douglas Ensminger, *Measuring the Effectiveness of Your Community;* Harold Hoffsommer and Herbert Pryor, *Neighborhoods and Communities in Covington County, Mississippi;* Ralph R. Nichols and John S. Page, *Community and Neighborhood Areas; Lincoln County, Oklahoma;* Irwin T. Sanders and Douglas Ensminger, *Alabama Rural Communities; A Study of Chilton County;* Dwight Sanderson, *School Centralization and the Rural Community;* Leland B. Tate, *Lebanon; A Virginia Community;* and Frank Winchester, *Rural Neighborhoods and Communities in Thirteen Kentucky Counties, 1941: Size, Population, and Social Structure.*

BUILDING THE RURAL COMMUNITY

A pamphlet of the United States Department of Agriculture, *Rural Communities; What Do They Need Most?,* has been prepared especially for use by discussion groups. It presents in brief form some of the more important trends affecting rural communities and some of the current suggestions for rural organization suitable to meet current trends.

Leadership is an important element in community organization and action. *Leadership for Rural Life,* by Dwight Sanderson, is a volume for the use of teachers of college classes and for ministers, schoolmen, extension workers, and executives of rural organizations concerned with enlisting and developing rural leadership. A pamphlet by A. H. Anderson, *Rural Community Leadership; A Vital Part of the Home Front,* describes specific problems in the development of rural community leadership.

H. C. Brearley and Marian Tippit are the editors of *The Rural South; A Reading Guide for Community Leaders,* a publication prompted by "the need for selected reading materials on the rural South readily available." It presents summaries of books on a variety of topics, including the land, the community, farming and the farmer, the church, and health.

The Southeastern Workshop in Community Development, sponsored by Furman University Summer School and the Greenville [South Carolina] County Council for Community Development, has produced *A Handbook in Community Development,* which covers such items as how to begin a community development program; the place of fact finding in community development; and the relationship of government, the health program, recreation, social agencies, the schools, and the church to community development.

Clarence B. Loomis' *An Experience in Community Development and the Principles of Community Organization* presents an account of the five-year experience of the Greenville Council for Community Development under a grant from the General Education Board, with related discussion of the principles of community organization as recorded in selected literature of the past thirty years. The county is almost half rural and the Council's activities were centered more in the rural than in the urban areas.

Edmund deS. Brunner, in *Community Organization and Adult Education,* also describes the five-year experimental program developed in Greenville County, discusses its methods of operation and accomplishments, and draws some conclusions from the experience relative to general problems of community organization.

The Twenty-third American Country Life Conference, held in 1940, was devoted to the problems of rural communities, and the conference proceedings are titled *Building Rural Communities.* They include numerous short articles on such subjects as the rural community and the schools, youth in the rural community, and program planning in the rural community.

Your Community; Its Provision for Health, Education, Safety, and Welfare, by Joanna C. Colcord, contains suggestions for persons desirous of securing a rounded picture of their own community, especially as to the provision it makes to conserve the health and safety and to promote the education and general welfare of its inhabitants. It suggests "the type of information that might be assembled and studied by intelligent citizens and citizens-to-be, in order to have a background from which to attack the problem of supplying community lacks and improving existing services."

A chapter, "Local Planning: What Rural Communities Are Doing to Improve Their Own Situation," in *Rural America Today; Its Schools and Community Life,* by George A. Works and Simon O. Lesser, discusses various phases of cooperative agricultural planning, cites some outstanding examples of such planning, and discusses the relationship of the schools thereto.

ADDITIONAL REFERENCES

The Small Community, Foundation of Democratic Life, by Arthur E. Morgan, advances the thesis that the small primary group or community is being greatly neglected in America and is tending to disappear, although the need for it continues. The preservation and perfecting of small communities is one of the greatest present issues in this country.

A study by Carle C. Zimmerman, *The Changing Community,* focuses attention on the small community. It supplies a series of case descriptions of specific communities in various parts of the world. These studies reveal the individuality of the towns and suggest that local communities, like people, possess personalities that are an expression both of internal structure and of the surrounding and larger environment.

Two publications relating to postwar community planning are *Rural Communities of Wisconsin; Getting Ready for Tomorrow* and *Postwar Guide for Iowa Communities.*

Agencies Concerned with the Quality of Rural Life in the South; A Directory 1944 lists national, regional, and state agencies contributing to the improvement of rural living in the South. It was prepared to guide local community leaders and agencies interested in southern community development to sources of useful information.

General texts in rural sociology also are useful in studying the community in relationship to general social organization and functioning. Several may be mentioned: J. H. Kolb and Edmund deS. Brunner, *A Study of Rural Society; Its Organization and Changes;* Paul H. Landis, *Rural Life in Process;* Dwight Sanderson, *Rural Sociology and Rural Social Organization;* and T. Lynn Smith, *The Sociology of Rural Life.*

Numerous community studies are reviewed, as they appear, in the quarterly journal *Rural Sociology.*

BIBLIOGRAPHY

Agencies Concerned with the Quality of Rural Life in the South; A Directory 1944. Nashville, Tennessee: Southern Rural Life Council, 1944, 99 pp.

Anderson, A. H. *Rural Community Leadership; A Vital Part of the Home Front.* Lincoln, Nebraska: U. S. Department of Agriculture, Bureau of Agricultural Economics, 1944, 5 pp.

Brearley, H. C. and Marian Tippit, eds. *The Rural South; A Reading Guide for Community Leaders.* Nashville, Tennessee: Southern Rural Life Council, George Peabody College for Teachers, 1946, 86 pp.

Brunner, Edmund deS. *Community Organization and Adult Education.* Chapel Hill: University of North Carolina Press, 1942, 124 pp.

———. *Village Communities.* New York: George H. Doran Co., 1927, 244 pp.

—— and J. H. Kolb. *Rural Social Trends.* New York: McGraw-Hill Book Co., 1933, 386 pp.

—— and Irving Lorge. *Rural Trends in Depression Years; A Survey of Village-Centered Agricultural Communities, 1930-1936.* New York: Columbia University Press, 1937, 387 pp.

—— and T. Lynn Smith. "Village Growth and Decline, 1930-1940." *Rural Sociology,* Vol. IX, No. 2, June 1944, pp. 103-15.

Building Rural Communities; Proceedings of the Twenty-third American Country Life Conference, 1940. Chicago: University of Chicago Press, 1941, 171 pp.

Colcord, Joanna C. *Your Community; Its Provision for Health, Education, Safety, and Welfare.* 2nd ed. New York: Russell Sage Foundation, 1941, 261 pp.

Dodson, Linden S.; Douglas Ensminger; and Robert N. Woodworth. *Rural Community Organization in Washington and Frederick Counties, Maryland.* Agricultural Experiment Station Bulletin No. 437. College Park, Maryland: The University of Maryland, 1940, pp. 105-64.

Ensminger, Douglas. *Measuring the Effectiveness of Your Community.* Agricultural Extension Service Bulletin No. 444. Ithaca, New York: Cornell University, 1940, 43 pp.

Hoffsommer, Harold and Herbert Pryor. *Neighborhoods and Communities in Covington County, Mississippi.* Washington: U. S. Department of Agriculture, Bureau of Agricultural Economics, 1941, 31 pp.

Holt, John B. *Rural Neighborhoods and Communities of Lee County, Alabama, and Their Significance for Land Use Planning.* Washington: U. S. Department of Agriculture, Bureau of Agricultural Economics, 1941, 21 pp.

Jenkins, David Ross. *Growth and Decline of Agricultural Villages.* New York: Bureau of Publications, Teachers College, Columbia University, 1940, 95 pp. (Bibliography, pp. 91-95.)

Kolb, J. H. and Edmund deS. Brunner. *A Study of Rural Society; Its Organization and Changes.* Rev. ed. Boston: Houghton Mifflin Co., 1940, 694 pp. (Reference reading at ends of chapters. General bibliography, pp. 663-69.)

—— and Douglas G. Marshall. *Neighborhood-Community Relationships in Rural Society*. Agricultural Experiment Station Research Bulletin No. 154. Madison, Wisconsin: University of Wisconsin, 1944, 55 pp. (Selected bibliography, pp. 49-51.)

Kollmorgen, Walter M. *The German-Swiss in Franklin County, Tennessee; A Study of the Significance of Cultural Considerations in Farming Enterprises*. Washington: U. S. Department of Agriculture, Bureau of Agricultural Economics, 1940, 113 pp. (References, pp. 109-13.)

Landis, Paul H. *Rural Life in Process*. New York: McGraw-Hill Book Co., 1940, 599 pp. (Collateral reading at ends of chapters.)

Loomis, Clarence B. *An Experience in Community Development and the Principles of Community Organization.* Clayton, Georgia: The Rabun Press, 1944, 190 pp. (Bibliography, pp. 189-90.)

Morgan, Arthur E. *The Small Community, Foundation of Democratic Life; What It Is and How to Achieve It*. New York: Harper & Bros., 1942, 312 pp. (Suggested readings, pp. 283-303.)

Nichols, Ralph R. and John S. Page. *Community and Neighborhood Areas; Lincoln County, Oklahoma*. Washington: U. S. Department of Agriculture, Bureau of Agricultural Economics, in Cooperation with Oklahoma Joint Land-Grant College B. A. E. Committee, 1941, 20 pp.

Postwar Guide for Iowa Communities. Agricultural Extension Service Pamphlet No. 91. Ames, Iowa: Iowa State College, 1944, 24 pp.

Rural Communities of Wisconsin; Getting Ready for Tomorrow. Agricultural Extension Service Circular No. 353. Madison, Wisconsin: University of Wisconsin, 1945, 24 pp.

Rural Sociology. East University, Louisiana: Louisiana State University Press. Quarterly.

Sanders, Irwin T. and Douglas Ensminger. *Alabama Rural Communities; A Study of Chilton County*. Montevallo, Alabama: Alabama College Bulletin, Vol. XXXIII, No. 1A, 1940, 80 pp.

Sanderson, Dwight. *Leadership for Rural Life*. New York: Association Press, 1940, 127 pp. (Bibliography, pp. 121-24.)

——. *Locating the Rural Community*. Extension Bulletin No. 413. Ithaca, New York: New York State College of Agriculture at Cornell University, 1939, 18 pp.

——. *Rural Sociology and Rural Social Organization*. New York: John Wiley & Sons, 1942, 806 pp. (References at ends of chapters.)

——. *School Centralization and the Rural Community*. Extension Bulletin No. 445. Ithaca, New York: New York State College of Agriculture at Cornell University, 1940, 16 pp.

—— and Robert A. Polson. *Rural Community Organization*. New York: John Wiley & Sons, 1939, 448 pp. (Readings at ends of chapters. Bibliography, pp. 421-25.)

Smith, T. Lynn. *The Sociology of Rural Life.* New York: Harper & Bros., 1940, 595 pp. (Bibliography, pp. 548-80.)

——. "Trends in Community Organization and Life." *American Sociological Review,* Vol. V, No. 3, June 1940, pp. 325-34.

Southeastern Workshop in Community Development, Greenville, South Carolina. *A Handbook in Community Development.* Greenville, South Carolina: Furman University Press, 1941, 114 pp.

Tate, Leland B. *Lebanon; A Virginia Community.* Virginia Agricultural Experiment Station Bulletin No. 352. Blacksburg, Virginia: Polytechnic Institute, 1943, 55 pp.

U. S. Department of Agriculture. Bureau of Agricultural Economics. Rural Life Studies 1-6. General title of each: *Culture of a Contemporary Rural Community.*
  1. Leonard, Olen and C. P. Loomis. *El Cerrito, New Mexico.* 1941, 72 pp.
  2. Bell, Earl H. *Sublette, Kansas.* 1942, 113 pp.
  3. Mac Leish, Kenneth and Kimball Young. *Landaff, New Hampshire.* 1942, 117 pp.
  4. Kollmorgen, Walter M. *The Older Order Amish of Lancaster County, Pennsylvania.* 1942, 105 pp.
  5. Moe, Edward O. and Carl C. Taylor. *Irwin, Iowa.* 1942, 93 pp.
  6. Wynne, Waller. *Harmony, Georgia.* 1943.

——. ——. Studies of the effect of the war on rural communities.
  Alexander, Frank D. *A Rural Community in Time of War; The Valley Community in Rabun County, Georgia.* 1945, 40 pp.
  Anderson, A. H. *The Rural Community and the War; A Study of Ryder, North Dakota.* 1945, 28 pp.
  Frame, Nat T. *Rushmore; Village Centered Community in the Cornbelt in Wartime.* [1945?], 25 pp.
  Longmore, T. Wilson. *Watson, Arkansas; Effect of War on a Mississippi Delta Community.* 1945, 27 pp.
  Lyall, Lawrence B. *The Rural Community and the War; A Study of Beaver Crossing, Nebraska.* 1945, 19 pp.
  Niederfrank, E. J. *The Massachusetts Hill Towns in Wartime.* 1945, 26 pp.
  Pryor, Herbert and Theo L. Vaughan. *A Rural Community in Wartime; Roby, Texas.* 1945, 33 pp.

——. Bureau of Agricultural Economics in Cooperation with the Extension Service. *Rural Communities; What Do They Need Most?* Washington: Government Printing Office, 1940, 14 pp.

——. Bureau of Agricultural Economics in Cooperation with the Kansas Agricultural Experiment Station. *Kansas Rural Communities; A Study of Nemaha County,* 1940, 30 pp.

Winchester, Frank. *Rural Neighborhoods and Communities in Thirteen Kentucky Counties, 1941: Size, Population, and Social Structure.* Agricultural Experiment Station Bulletin No. 450. Lexington, Kentucky: University of Kentucky, 1943, 20 pp.

Works, George A. and Simon O. Lesser. "Local Planning: What Rural Communities Are Doing to Improve Their Own Situation," in *Rural America Today; Its Schools and Community Life*. Chicago: University of Chicago Press, 1942, pp. 371-405.

Zimmerman, Carle C. *The Changing Community*. New York: Harper & Bros., 1938, 661 pp.

13 *LAND USE*

LAND is a basic resource of rural areas and of the nation. The quality of the land in the community and the way the land is used affect all phases of the life of the community. It has therefore seemed advisable to add to this volume, which is concerned primarily with social organization and activities in rural communities, a chapter describing some of the principal agencies concerned with land-use practices and the programs they are sponsoring to promote the wise use of land.

SOIL CONSERVATION SERVICE

The Soil Conservation Service in the United States Department of Agriculture was organized in 1935 with the purpose of bringing about desirable adjustments in land use and farming methods. Its efforts are directed to controlling erosion on farm and range lands and to introducing soil and water conservation methods into farming and ranching throughout the nation. These objectives are achieved chiefly through local soil conservation districts organized in the forty-eight states and Puerto Rico. Each of the states also has a state soil conservation committee, or similar agency, established by law. A state conservationist is responsible for general administration of the work of the Service in the state. The Service, which maintains seven regional offices, makes assistance available to the conservation districts, but has no voice in the administration of these local units of government.

In most states whenever a sufficient number of farmers in a locality desire to form a district, they submit a petition to the state committee which then conducts public hearings in the community to determine whether a district will be feasible. If the findings are favorable, the state committee will call for a referendum of all farmers and other land operators within the boundaries of the proposed district to determine whether a majority of them favor formation of a district. If they do, the state committee grants the district a certificate of organization, and a governing board of five supervisors is formed—three elected by farmers and two appointed by the state committee from among people of the district. This board is the governing body of the conservation district; it conducts the affairs of the district which may include dealing with other agencies and levels of government.

The district prepares a program of work and a plan for carrying it out. Most districts have entered into a working agreement with the Department of Agriculture for assistance in achieving their programs. The Department makes available to the district the services of a staff member of the Soil Conservation Service, known as a district conservationist, as well as staff members to make surveys within the district, to help farmers in making individual farm plans and in applying them to the land, and to serve in an advisory capacity. The district determines priorities for work, maintains any field equipment made available by the Service, and keeps records on services, materials, and equipment lent by the Service. Individual farmers who obtain assistance from the district enter into cooperative agreements with their local districts covering the farm conservation plans they will put into effect. These plans are designed to adjust farming operations to a conservation basis. The farmer agrees to follow a long-range plan of conservation operations, to furnish certain equipment and materials, and to do certain conservation farming operations. As of September 15, 1946, there had been organized almost 1,700 soil conservation districts covering an area of more than 900,000,000 acres; most of these districts had their programs actively under way. Included in the program were approximately 4,000,000 farms or two-thirds of all the farms in the country.

The Soil Conservation Service carries on a number of additional and directly related activities. It surveys the conservation needs of the agricultural land of areas, watersheds, farms, and ranges. In cooperation with state agricultural experiment stations, federal research agencies, and others, it conducts a practical research program designed to develop, refine, and improve soil and water conservation practices. It acquires and manages agricultural lands that are submarginal or not primarily suitable for cultivation for grazing and forestry use. Such purchases aggregate over 11,000,000 acres, of which the Soil Conservation Service manages approximately 7,000,000. The Service also carries on educational and informational programs, largely in cooperation with state agricultural extension services, to disseminate conservation and land-use knowledge.

Several publications may be consulted for information about the activities and methods of the Soil Conservation Service. General references include the *Report of the Chief of the Soil Conservation Service, 1945;* an article by H. H. Bennett, Chief of the Service, "The Soil

Conservation Service: Organization and Operations," which appeared in *The Book of the States, 1945-46;* and the description of the Service appearing in the *United States Government Manual—1947*. A popular description of the work of the agency is given in *The Work of the Soil Conservation Service*. The pamphlet *Soil Conservation Districts for Erosion Control* describes how these districts operate. These last two publications are under the authorship of the Service. *Soil Conservation Districts; In Action on the Land,* by Glenn K. Rule, describes in detail two examples of how the district idea works as it moves from theory to practice. *Soils and Security,* by H. H. Bennett, is a pamphlet that discusses such matters as the value of the soil, soil waste in the United States, the effects and cost of erosion, and the accomplishments and objectives of conservation work. *Teamwork to Save Soil and Increase Production,* by P. A.Waring, is the story of soil conservation in the Honey Hollow Creek watershed, told by one of the farmers participating in the program. Kenneth Davis, in *Farms the Rains Can't Take,* describes the results of a long study of run-off on a farm near La Crosse, Wisconsin. *Classifying Land for Conservation Farming,* by R. D. Hockensmith and J. G. Steele, is a popular presentation of the land capability survey methods used by the Soil Conservation Service.

Two bulletins may be cited to illustrate more technical publications relating to soil conservation: *Strip Cropping for Soil Conservation,* by Walter V. Kell and Grover F. Brown, and C. L. Hamilton's *Terracing for Soil and Water Conservation.*

The Soil Conservation Service has issued a number of publications on soil conservation problems in particular regions. Three such publications, all by Glenn K. Rule, are *Conserving Corn Belt Soil, Toward Soil Security on the Northern Great Plains,* and *Crops against the Wind on the Southern Great Plains.* E. M. Rowalt's *Soil Defense in the South* describes farming practices that conserve soil and how such practices may be applied to farms in a large part of the South. A similar study for another part of the United States by the same author is *Soil Defense of Range and Farm Lands in the Southwest.* Three studies that deal with the conditions and problems that must be met in effecting soil and water conservation on a distinctive kind of land are: Tom Dale's *Conservation Farming for the Hard Lands of the Southern Great Plains; Conservation Farming on the Sandy Lands of the Southern Great Plains,* by the same author; and *Conservation Practices for the Range Lands of the Southern Great Plains,* by J. S. McCorkle and Tom Dale.

The Soil Conservation Service has also issued a series of survey bulletins under the over-all title "Erosion and Related Land Use Conditions" which may cover a county, a watershed, a demonstration project, or other unit.

The state soil conservation committees also issue reports of various kinds. Most, for instance, have issued bulletins describing the provisions of their state laws, how to set up soil conservation districts, and the like.

Bibliographies of publications on soil conservation and information about motion pictures available may be secured from the division of information of the Soil Conservation Service. Current information and publications may be followed in the official monthly publication of the Service, *Soil Conservation*.

FOREST SERVICE

The Forest Service in the United States Department of Agriculture carries on a variety of activities designed to protect and improve the forests of the country and promote conservation practices. It administers 154 national forests comprising over 179,000,000 acres in the interests of growing and harvesting timber, protecting watersheds, providing popular outdoor recreation, maintaining wildlife resources, and regulating livestock grazing. In the fiscal year 1945 more than three billion board feet of timber were cut in national forests. Grazing permits were issued in 1944 to over 23,000 owners in and near the national forests to graze 1,225,000 cattle and horses and 4,280,000 sheep and goats. The Service conducts research in twelve forest and range experiment stations and in its Forest Products Laboratory. It cooperates with states and private owners in the application of sound forest management and fire protection practices and in the distribution of planting stock to farmers for windbreaks, shelterbelts, and farm woodlands and with states, counties, communities, and organizations in the development and management of their forests.

Farm woodlands are an important national resource. More than one-third of the 341,000,000 acres of commercial forest land in private ownership is in some 3,500,000 farm woodlands. The few thousand owners with more than 5,000 acres account for about one-third, and hundreds of thousands of small nonfarm owners for the balance. Farm woodlands have a greater acreage of commercial forest land than the national forests. Their present productivity is only one-third to one-half what it might be, yet commercial farm woodlands supply about one-third of the national cut.

For more than twenty years the Department of Agriculture has recognized farm forestry in the cooperative work of the Agricultural Extension Service. County agricultural agents have interested farm people in forestry and, under the guidance of state extension foresters and in connection with other farm programs, have promoted improved management of farm woodlands and have advised on tree plantings for windbreaks, shelterbelts, erosion control, Christmas tree crops, and the like. The Department cooperates through the Forest Service in employing 100 resident foresters to aid farmers in 403 counties in marketing forest products and in the proper management of their woodlands. Farm forestry is also encouraged in other departmental programs. The Soil Conservation Service includes forest planting and woodland management in the farm plans of farms in soil conservation districts. Federal Land Banks consider the productiveness of farm woodlands in making farm loans. The Agricultural Adjustment Agency made payments to farmers in some states for protecting farm woodlands.

Additional general information as to the activities of the United States Forest Service may be found in *Forests and Employment; Report of the Chief of the Forest Service, 1945;* in the *United States Government Manual—1947;* and in *The Work of the U. S. Forest Service,* a publication of the Service.

The Department of Agriculture, and particularly its Forest Service, has issued a number of pamphlets on farm woodlands and other matters related to the interest of rural people in forestry. *Woodlands in the Farm Plan,* by John F. Preston, is for farmers interested in developing a good woods and an income therefrom, or in saving through management the woodlands they now have. C. R. Tillotson's *Care and Improvement of the Farm Woods* is concerned with such matters as essentials of good farm woods, improvement cuttings, pasturing in farm woods, care in logging, and perpetuating the stand. *Forest Farming* is a general pamphlet of the Forest Service which points out some of the advantages of this occupation. *Forestry and Farm Income,* by Wilbur R. Mattoon, indicates the value and uses of woodland products and some desirable woodland practices. Two publications on forest cooperatives are *Cooperative Management and Marketing for the Woodland Owner,* a bulletin of the division of state forestry of the Forest Service, and *Farm Forest Cooperatives Help to Solve Timber Growing and Marketing Problems,* by F. S. Fuller and Others. A more technical publication is *Measuring and Marketing Farm Timber,* by Wilbur R. Mattoon and William B. Barrows. *Farm Forestry in the Lake States; An Economic Problem,* by Raphael Zon and William A. Duerr, describes, among other things, the farm forest resources in these states and outstanding needs. The several values of windbreaks are described in *The Windbreak as a Farm Asset,* by Carlos G. Bates. *Community Forests for Rural People,* prepared by the Forest Service and the Extension Service, describes several community forests and outlines how a county 4-H Club forest may be established. It points out that a community forest and recreation center is an ideal place for either adult or youth groups to get together for mutual benefit and collaboration. *New Forest Frontiers for: Jobs, Permanent Communities, A Stronger Nation,* another publication of the Forest Service, calls attention to the fact that "much of our rural poverty is within forest regions with large areas of poor soils. Here, vanishing forest resources and forest industries leave farm people and rural communities stranded, minus the employment in the forest and the income from the forest so much needed to supplement the meager returns from their cultivated crops."

A few additional publications of the Forest Service or the Department of Agriculture less directly related to the interests of rural people are here listed. Martha Bensley Bruère's *What Forests Give* lists a wide variety of forest contributions. R. F. Hammatt's *Forestry and Permanent Prosperity* indicates how forestry may be an aid to economic recovery and describes how various forestry practices may contribute. *Living and Forest Lands* was prepared by the Forest Service as a guide for study groups especially interested in the social and economic aspects of forests and forestry. *State Forests for Public Use* points out the possibilities of state forests as administrative centers in a broad conservation program on private lands. Much remains to be done to improve present methods and to extend operations to cover areas as yet unprotected. *Community Forests,* by Nelson C. Brown, describes the characteristics and merits of such forests.

The Forest Service issues bibliographies of publications relating to forestry and of films available on loan for educational purposes.

OTHER ACTIVITIES OF THE DEPARTMENT OF AGRICULTURE

Many of the other programs—planning and research, educational, and action—of the United States Department of Agriculture have had direct relationship to proper land-use practices. The work of the Extension Service has been mentioned. It is described further in Chapter 2. The program of the Agricultural Adjustment Agency (consolidated into the Production and Marketing Administration of the Department in August, 1945) was designed to check erosion and restore soil fertility through proper farm practices while keeping production at levels necessary to meet national needs. It functioned through elected county and community farmer committeemen and a system of agricultural conservation program payments. During 1943-44, 6,500,000 individuals received AAA assistance. Expenditures of the AAA for agricultural conservation program payments totaled approximately $397,000,000 for the fiscal year ended June 30, 1944. Additional information will be found in the *Report of the Chief of the Agricultural Adjustment Agency, 1944.*

The land-use planning program grew largely out of the need for coordinating the many land-use programs sponsored by the Department of Agriculture and the land-grant colleges. Begun in 1938, as the result of an agreement between the Department and the colleges, it operated through an organization of state, county, and community land-use planning committees that endeavored to unite all of the state and federal agricultural programs in a unified attack on the problems of each community. State committees were made up of representatives of state and federal agencies concerned with land use and of farmers from various types of farming areas in the state. Farmer members were in a majority on many state committees and were usually more numerous than representatives of any other single group. Farmer members outnumbered all others on county committees and usually constituted the only type of members on community committees. Many additional farmers took part in open community meetings. Thus, through committee and group activities it was possible to pool the wisdom of farmers, technicians, and administrators interested in improving land-use practices. County committees made area analyses and classification studies of their counties in order to show land resources, the use being made of these resources, the problems of land use, and the adjustments or changes needed to deal with them. Various types and degrees of action grew out of these studies, and although the formal program has been discontinued its effects are still evident in many states.

The land-use planning program is described in *Land Use Planning under Way,* a publication of the Bureau of Agricultural Economics and other Department agencies. As there stated, "land use planning is a national attempt to make democracy work throughout the whole field of agriculture, to make the voice of the people more effective in their government." The program is also described in a series of pamphlets issued by the Bureau of Agricultural Economics and other agencies of the Department as a County Planning Series. Titles are listed in the bibliography at the end of this chapter.

For a number of years the Bureau of Agricultural Economics has issued an annual *Summary of Outstanding Federal and State Legislation Affecting Rural Land Use.*

In 1941 a departmental Interbureau Committee on State Legislation for Better Land Use published *State Legislation for Better Land Use; A Special Report,* which discusses certain outstanding items of state land use essential for promoting wise practices in the United States: rural zoning; state water laws; soil conservation districts; farm tenancy law; the structure and function of rural local government; procedure for rural tax-delinquent lands; state land purchase for land-use adjustment; management and development of state and county lands; and interrelation of measures affecting land use.

Tennessee Valley Authority

A principal objective of the Tennessee Valley Authority is the building of a stronger, more fertile valley through the development of basic soil and forest resources. As pointed out in its *Annual Report* for 1945, "the strength of the economy of the Tennessee Valley area will depend upon the strength—the fertility of the land." And "fertility . . . is the combination of biological, physical, chemical, and economic factors which, brought together in a variety of patterns to fit particular circumstances, add up to the most efficient use of natural resources." A farm test-demonstration program, "conducted cooperatively with the State extension services, county agents, farm communities and associations, and individual farmers, provides the vehicle for carrying out TVA's responsibilities under the Act with respect to the testing and demonstration of improved fertilizers or plant nutrients and the objectives of watershed protection and the development of sound farming practices as part of a comprehensive regional development."

In cooperation with the land-grant colleges, the TVA conducts a research and developmental program that includes chemical research in fertilizers, soil inventory and mapping, research into the relationships between soil conditions and human nutrition, and the development of farm equipment. The Authority, working through the state extension services, aids in the development and operation of cooperative associations. Woodland demonstrations, set up through the cooperation of the TVA with state forestry services and county agents, are being conducted in 78 Valley counties; 360 of the

375 demonstrations have been established on farms. TVA forest nurseries produce millions of seedlings that are planted by private landowners and on TVA lands for reforestation and erosion control. TVA is also actively interested in research in forestry, forest products, and wood utilization.

Among the publications of the TVA directly related to land use are *Soil; The Nation's Basic Heritage,* which pictures what is happening to the farm lands of the Tennessee Valley through the joint activities of the land-grant colleges and universities of the Valley states, the Department of Agriculture, and the TVA in encouraging the conservation of soil and the restoration of its fertility. *Forests and Human Welfare* describes the influence of forests upon some fundamental relations of land, water, and people. Two publications relating to erosion control are *Manual for Soil Erosion Control in the Tennessee Valley—Engineering Phase,* by J. H. Nicholson and J. E. Snyder, and *Manual for Soil Erosion Control in the Tennessee Valley—Reforestation Phase,* by Richard Kilbourne and G. H. Lentz.

TVA; Democracy on the March, by David E. Lilienthal, chairman of the Board of Directors of the Authority, is a book "about real things and real people; rivers and how to develop them; new factories and new jobs and how they were created; farms and farmers and how they came to prosper and stand on their own." *The Valley and Its People; A Portrait of TVA,* by R. L. Duffus, is a popular presentation of the work of the TVA with numerous illustrations provided by the graphics department of the Authority. C. Herman Pritchett's *The Tennessee Valley Authority; A Study in Public Administration* is primarily a study of administrative problems and contributions of the Authority, but a number of chapters are devoted to a description of the TVA program.

OTHER FEDERAL ACTIVITIES

The Bureau of Reclamation in the United States Department of the Interior has in operation, under construction, or authorized numerous irrigation or multiple-purpose projects in seventeen western states. These projects provide flood control and river regulation, aid in preserving fish and wildlife, provide recreational opportunities, make land available for farming, produce electric energy, and furnish municipal and industrial water. In 1945, crops valued at $434,000,000 were produced on lands watered by reclamation systems. This information is from the *United States Government Manual—1947.*

In the period from 1934 to 1943, the National Resources Planning

Board and its predecessor agencies served as the over-all planning organization of the federal government. Its functions, among others, were to collect and make available plans and information helpful to the planned development and use of material resources, to record all federal projects involving the acquisition of land and land research projects, and to provide the agencies concerned with pertinent information. A number of reports of the Board, long-range in nature, relate to land use. Some of the principal studies bearing on land use are: (1) *A Report on National Planning and Public Works in Relation to Natural Resources and Including Land Use and Water Resources with Findings and Recommendations, December 1, 1934* (with eleven supporting volumes); (2) *Land Classification in the United States; Report of the Land Committee to the National Resources Planning Board;* (3) *Tax Delinquency and Rural Land-Use Adjustment, by the Subcommittee on Tax Delinquency of the Land Committee;* and (4) *Public Works and Rural Land Use, September 1942; Report of the Land Committee.* This last publication has major sections on public works and forest lands and on soil conservation, erosion prevention, and run-off retardation which include much valuable information and many pertinent data. A report of the President's Special Committee on Farm Tenancy, *Farm Tenancy,* was prepared under the auspices of the National Resources Committee. The *National Resources Development Reports* of the Board for 1942 and 1943 cover major aspects of human and natural resources development, including land and water resources.

STATE GOVERNMENTAL ACTIVITIES

State governments, too, are concerned with improving land-use practices in the interest of conserving their natural wealth and promoting the welfare of their citizens. Some activities at the state level have already been described in the discussion of federal soil conservation, forestry, and land-use planning work. Forty-three states have administrative organizations for forestry; these organizations vary widely in type and manner of functioning. A principal duty is to protect state and privately owned forest lands from fire. Almost all states carry on a program of furnishing advice and assistance to timberland owners. Many states offer materially lower tax rates or tax exemption on cut-over lands devoted to new forest crops. Forty-two states produce young trees to reforest state lands and to sell at low prices to landowners. Some of the work of state planning boards relates to natural resources, although their emphasis currently is on economic development. The extension services and experiment stations of the land-grant colleges and universities issue many general and technical bulletins relating to soil conservation, woodland management, and other land-use problems, some dealing with the state as a whole, others with particular counties and regions. State departments of education and conservation issue materials for use in conservation education. Three articles in *The Book of the States, 1945–46* relate to land-use activities: "State Planning—1943-45"; "Characteristics of Legislation Creating State Planning and Resources Development Organizations"; and "State Forestry Administration." This last article is by Lyle F. Watts, chief of the United States Forest Service. A *Tentative and Preliminary Report of the Forestry Committee of the Council of State Governments* sets out a program for the encouragement of forestry by the states.

ACTIVITIES OF PRIVATE ORGANIZATIONS

A number of private groups, industries, and business concerns are active in promoting soil conservation and forestry activities. For example, a number of pulp and paper companies and several railroad systems provide direct assistance or educational programs for farm woodland owners and some provide tree seedlings and foresters to mark timber for cutting. Some manufacturers of farm machinery are much interested in soil conservation and improvement and issue and distribute literature on the subject. A few publications of such organizations are listed below.

The Charles Lathrop Pack Forestry Foundation has issued a number of publications, several of which deal with farm forestry. *Centralized Management and Utilization Adapted to Farm Woodlands in the Northeast,* by C. Edward Behre and C. R. Lockard, describes the basic plan of the Cooperstown Forest Unit, which serves as an example of the possibilities in many farm woodland sections. Here, under a plan worked out by the Northeastern Experiment Station of the United States Forest Service, a group of farm woodland owners have formed a capital stock cooperative association whose members voluntarily have agreed to practice sustained-yield forestry on their holdings. *Woodland Opportunities on Dairy Farms in New York,* by Hugh A. Johnson and Others, presents in abbreviated form, with special emphasis on the woodland enterprise, the results of a farm management study conducted by the Bureau of Agricultural Economics in cooperation with the Forest Service in Otsego County, New York.

Joshua A. Cope's *Farm Forestry in the Eastern United States* is a study of educational methods evolved to reach the farmer in order to achieve planned cutting in the woods. *Trends in Land Use in Northern Michigan; A Study of Alpena, Antrim, Ogemaw, and Roscommon Counties,* by Horace J. Andrews and Willard S. Bromley, reports a study undertaken with the financial support of the Pack Foundation to determine trends in land utilization in this region in the hope the analysis would help in directing future use along sounder lines.

The Society of American Foresters and the Pack Foundation have cooperated in *A Survey of State Forestry Administration in North Carolina*. The study was made at the request of the governor of the state "for the purpose of defining and establishing standards for the efficient administration of the forest resources within the state, and to make recommendations as to how these standards may be met."

Progress in American Forest Management, a publication of the American Forest Products Industries, presents descriptions of sixteen examples of progress in forest management supplied by operators who produce lumber, plywood, pulpwood, paper, fiber board, and chemicals. The American Forestry Association's *Progress Report; The Forest Resource Appraisal* describes a project to gather by counties and states information on forest area, standing timber volumes, estimates of probable yields, extent of fire protection, forest management trends, and other matters.

Man and the Soil; A Brief Introduction to the Study of Soil Conservation, by Karl B. Mickey, a publication of the International Harvester Company, was written "to provide a brief and simple introduction to the subject of soil conservation for readers who have no technical knowledge of it and think they have no interest at stake in it, including city-dwellers. . . . in approaching the subject, we have made special effort to give sharp reality to the literal, primary fact that the dirt under man's feet is the source of his physical being and soil conservation is nothing more nor less than conservation of human life wherever it is lived, in the city as well as in the country." *Health from the Ground Up* is another publication of the International Harvester Company prepared by the same author. It is, "in a way, a sequel to *Man and the Soil*. . . ." It "deals with the qualitative conservation of the soil, whereas its predecessor deals with the quantitative. This book deals primarily with the influence of soil characteristics on the individual. . . ." and is "characterized by a medical and nutritional emphasis. . . ."

ADDITIONAL REFERENCES

There are a number of additional books and monographs dealing with soil conservation, forestry, and related problems. Only a few can be mentioned here. Ward Shepard's *Food or Famine; The Challenge of Erosion* sees the need not only of ecological engineering but also of social engineering to save the soil. Hugh Hammond Bennett and William Clayton Pryor, in *This Land We Defend,* give a brief historical account of land use in the United States—from exploitation and waste to conservation through democracy on the land. Hugh Hammond Bennett's *Soil Conservation* is an extensive and authoritative volume on the subject. *Our Use of the Land,* by Ayers Brinser and Ward Shepard, was written to help the citizen to make wise decisions in regard to the growing program of land-use management. Stuart Chase's *Rich Land, Poor Land; A Study of Waste in the Natural Resources of America* points out that this continent "has given us much and will give us more, if we work with her. But if we continue our neglect and contempt for her land and waters, she will exact a calamitous penalty, and all the laboratories, all the machines, all the banks, will not offset it."

Three works relating to farm woodlands are: (1) Cedric H. Guise's *The Management of Farm Woodlands,* designed primarily to meet the needs of students in agricultural colleges and other institutions where instruction in farm forestry is offered; (2) *Forestry in Farm Management,* by R. H. Westveld and Ralph H. Peck, written to give students, county agricultural agents, teachers of vocational agriculture, and farmers "a practical knowledge of the value and usefulness of farm forests, the methods of handling them, and the means of making them real farm assets"; and (3) R. B. Goodman's *A Wisconsin Forest-Farm Working Circle,* in which are described the mills and forest industries at Goodman, Wisconsin, the surrounding forests, and the farms, all of which go to make up a working circle.

General forestry publications are *An Introduction to American Forestry,* by Shirley Walter Allen; *Your Forests,* by Martha Bensley Bruère; *Our Forests,* by David Cushman Coyle; *The Nation's Forests,* by William Atherton DuPuy; *Men and Trees; The Problem of Forest Conservation and the Story of the United States Forest Service,* by Joseph Gaer; and *An Outline of General Forestry,* by Joseph S. Illick.

Current happenings and publications may be followed in a number of periodical publications. *American Forests* is the monthly publication of the American Forestry Association, a citizen's organization. The *Journal of Forestry* is published monthly by the Society of

American Foresters. *The Journal of Land & Public Utility Economics* is published quarterly by the University of Wisconsin. *The Land; A Quarterly Magazine* is published by the Friends of the Land. *Land Policy Review* is published quarterly by the United States Bureau of Agricultural Economics. *Soil Conservation* is the monthly periodical of the United States Soil Conservation Service. The American Society of Planning Officials publishes a monthly *News Letter* which has a section that reviews planning (including zoning) law and legislation.

BIBLIOGRAPHY

Allen, Shirley Walter. *An Introduction to American Forestry.* New York: McGraw-Hill Book Co., 1938, 402 pp.

American Forest Products Industries. *Progress in American Forest Management.* Washington: The Author (1319 18th St. N. W.), 32 pp.

American Forestry Association. *Progress Report; The Forest Resource Appraisal.* Washington: The Association (919 17th St. N. W.), 1945, unpaged.

American Forests; Magazine of the American Forestry Association. Monthly. 919 17th St. N. W., Washington, D. C.

American Society of Planning Officials. *News Letter.* Monthly. 1313 East 60th St., Chicago, Illinois.

Andrews, Horace J. and Willard S. Bromley. *Trends in Land Use in Northern Michigan; A Study of Alpena, Antrim, Ogemaw, and Roscommon Counties.* Washington: The Charles Lathrop Pack Forestry Foundation (1214 16th St., N. W.), 1941, 45 pp. (Literature cited, p. 45.)

Bates, Carlos G. *The Windbreak as a Farm Asset.* U. S. Department of Agriculture Farmers' Bulletin No. 1405. Washington: Government Printing Office, 1944, 22 pp.

Behre, C. Edward and C. R. Lockard. *Centralized Management and Utilization Adapted to Farm Woodlands in the Northeast.* Charles Lathrop Pack Forestry Foundation and New York State College of Forestry, Syracuse University, Syracuse, New York, 1937, 67 pp. (Reference list, p. 67.)

Bennett, Hugh Hammond. *Soil Conservation.* New York: McGraw-Hill Book Co., 1939, 993 pp.

——. "The Soil Conservation Service: Organization and Operations," in *The Book of the States, 1945-46.* Chicago: The Council of State Governments (1313 East 60th St.), 1945, pp. 259-70.

——. *Soils and Security.* Washington: Government Printing Office, 1941, 25 pp.

——and William Clayton Pryor. *This Land We Defend.* New York: Longmans, Green & Co., 1942, 107 pp.

Brinser, Ayers and Ward Shepard. *Our Use of the Land.* New York: Harper & Bros., 1939, 303 pp. (Bibliography, pp. 291-97.)

Brown, Nelson C. *Community Forests.* Washington: Government Printing Office, 1939, 36 pp.

Bruère, Martha Bensley. *What Forests Give.* Washington: Government Printing Office, 1940, 79 pp.

——. *Your Forests.* New York: J. B. Lippincott Co., 1945, 159 pp.

"Characteristics of Legislation Creating State Planning and Resources Development Organizations," in *The Book of the States, 1945-46.* Chicago: The Council of State Governments, 1945, pp. 230-41.

Chase, Stuart. *Rich Land, Poor Land; A Study of Waste in the Natural Resources of America.* New York: McGraw-Hill Book Co., 1936, 361 pp. (Selected bibliography, pp. 351-52.)

Cope, Joshua A. *Farm Forestry in the Eastern United States.* Washington: The Charles Lathrop Pack Forestry Foundation, 1943, 40 pp.

Council of State Governments. *Tentative and Preliminary Report of the Forestry Committee of the Council of State Governments.* Chicago: The Council, 1945, 6 pp.

Coyle, David Cushman. *Our Forests.* Washington: National Home Library Foundation, 1940, 150 pp.

Dale, Tom. *Conservation Farming for the Hard Lands of the Southern Great Plains.* Washington: Government Printing Office, 1941, 27 pp.

——. *Conservation Farming on the Sandy Lands of the Southern Great Plains.* Washington: Government Printing Office, 1941, 25 pp.

Davis, Kenneth. *Farms the Rains Can't Take.* U. S. Department of Agriculture Miscellaneous Publication No. 394. Washington: Government Printing Office, 1940, 14 pp.

Duffus, R. L. *The Valley and Its People; A Portrait of TVA.* New York: Alfred A. Knopf, Inc., 1944, 167 pp.

DuPuy, William Atherton. *The Nation's Forests.* New York: Macmillan Co., 1938, 264 pp.

Fuller, F. S. and Others. *Farm Forest Cooperatives Help to Solve Timber Growing and Marketing Problems.* Washington: U. S. Forest Service and U. S. Extension Service, 1939, 48 pp.

Gaer, Joseph. *Men and Trees; The Problem of Forest Conservation and the Story of the United States Forest Service.* New York: Harcourt Brace & Co., 1939, 118 pp.

Goodman, R. B. *A Wisconsin Forest-Farm Working Circle.* Goodman, Wisconsin: 1944, 24 pp.

Guise, Cedric H. *The Management of Farm Woodlands.* New York: McGraw-Hill Book Co., 1939, 352 pp. (Selected references, pp. 339-41.)

Hamilton, C. L. *Terracing for Soil and Water Conservation.* U. S. Department of Agriculture Farmers' Bulletin No. 1789. Washington: Government Printing Office, 1938, 60 pp.

Hammatt, R. F. *Forestry and Permanent Prosperity.* U. S. Department of Agriculture Miscellaneous Publication No. 247. Washington: Government Printing Office, 1940, 21 pp.

Hockensmith, R. D. and J. G. Steele. *Classifying Land for Conservation Farming.* U. S. Department of Agriculture Farmers' Bulletin No. 1853. Washington: Government Printing Office, 1943.

Illick, Joseph S. *An Outline of General Forestry.* 3rd ed. New York: Barnes & Noble, Inc., 1939, 297 pp.

Johnson, Hugh A.; Irving F. Fellows; Donald Rush; C. R. Lockard; and C. Edward Behre. *Woodland Opportunities on Dairy Farms in New York.* Washington: The Charles Lathrop Pack Forestry Foundation, 1944, 35 pp.

Journal of Forestry; Official Organ of the Society of American Foresters. Monthly. Mills Building, 17th and Pennslyvania Ave. N. W., Washington, D. C.

The Journal of Land & Public Utility Economics. Quarterly. Sterling Hall, University of Wisconsin, Madison, Wisconsin.

Kell, Walter V. and Grover F. Brown. *Strip Cropping for Soil Conservation.* U. S. Department of Agriculture Farmers' Bulletin No. 1776. Washington: Government Printing Office, 1938, 40 pp.

Kilbourne, Richard and G. H. Lentz. *Manual for Soil Erosion Control in the Tennessee Valley—Reforestation Phase.* Knoxville, Tennessee: Tennessee Valley Authority, 1936, 57 pp.

The Land; A Quarterly Magazine. Bel Air, Maryland.

Land Policy Review. Quarterly. Government Printing Office, Washington, D. C.

Lilienthal, David E. *TVA; Democracy on the March.* New York: Harper & Bros., 1944, 248 pp. (Some references for technicians, pp. 227-41.)

Mattoon, Wilbur R. *Forestry and Farm Income.* U. S. Department of Agriculture Farmers' Bulletin No. 1117. Rev. ed. Washington: Government Printing Office, 1937, 33 pp.

—— and William B. Barrows. *Measuring and Marketing Farm Timber.* U. S. Department of Agriculture Farmers' Bulletin No. 1210. Washington: Government Printing Office, 1941, 56 pp.

McCorkle, J. S. and Tom Dale. *Conservation Practices for the Range Lands of the Southern Great Plains.* Washington: Government Printing Office, 1941, 32 pp.

Mickey, Karl B. *Health from the Ground Up.* Chicago: International Harvester Co. (180 North Michigan Ave.), 1946, 125 pp. (Literature cited, pp. 123-25.)

——. *Man and the Soil; A Brief Introduction to the Study of Soil Conservation.* Chicago: International Harvester Co., 1945, 110 pp. (Literature cited, pp. 109-10.)

Nicholson, J. H. and J. E. Snyder. *Manual for Soil Erosion Control in the Tennessee Valley—Engineering Phase.* Knoxville, Tennessee: Tennessee Valley Authority, 1939, 128 pp.

Preston, John F. *Woodlands in the Farm Plan.* U. S. Department of Agriculture Farmers' Bulletin No. 1940. Washington: Government Printing Office, 1943, 22 pp.

Pritchett, C. Herman. *The Tennessee Valley Authority; A Study in Public Administration.* Chapel Hill: University of North Carolina Press, 1943, 333 pp.

Rowalt, E. M. *Soil Defense of Range and Farm Lands in the Southwest.* U. S. Department of Agriculture Miscellaneous Publication No. 338. Washington: Government Printing Office, 1939, 51 pp.

——. *Soil Defense in the South.* U. S. Department of Agriculture Farmers' Bulletin No. 1809. Washington: Government Printing Office, 1938, 64 pp.

Rule, Glenn K. *Conserving Corn Belt Soil.* U. S. Department of Agriculture Farmers' Bulletin No. 1795. Washington: Government Printing Office, 1937, 49 pp.

——. *Crops against the Wind on the Southern Great Plains.* U. S. Department of Agriculture Farmers' Bulletin No. 1833. Washington: Government Printing Office, 1939, 74 pp.

——. *Soil Conservation Districts; In Action on the Land.* U. S. Department of Agriculture Miscellaneous Publication No. 448. Washington: Government Printing Office, 1941, 25 pp.

——. *Toward Soil Security on the Northern Great Plains.* U. S. Department of Agriculture Farmers' Bulletin No. 1864. Washington: Government Printing Office, 1941.

Shepard, Ward. *Food or Famine: The Challenge of Erosion.* New York: Macmillan Co., 1945, 225 pp.

Society of American Foresters and the Charles Lathrop Pack Forestry Foundation. *A Survey of State Forestry Administration in North Carolina.* Washington: The Society, 1946, 38 pp.

Soil Conservation; Official Organ of the Soil Conservation Service. Monthly. Government Printing Office, Washington, D. C.

"State Planning—1943-45," in *The Book of the States, 1945-46.* Chicago: The Council of State Governments, 1945, pp. 227-30.

Tillotson, C. R. *Care and Improvement of the Farm Woods.* U. S. Department of Agriculture Farmers' Bulletin No. 1177. Washington: Government Printing Office, 1939, 26 pp.

U. S. Agricultural Adjustment Agency. *Report of the Chief of the . . . 1944.* Washington: Government Printing Office, 1944, 45 pp.

U. S. Bureau of Agricultural Economics. *Summary of Outstanding Federal and State Legislation Affecting Rural Land Use.* Annual.

—— and Others. County Planning Series. Washington: Government Printing Office, 1940.

    1. *County Land Use Planning.* 12 pp.

    2. *Membership of Land Use Planning Committees.* 8 pp.

    3. *The Land Use Planning Organization.* 8 pp.

    4. *The Scope of Land Use Planning.* 7 pp.

    5. *Pooling Ideas in Land Use Planning.* 8 pp.

    6. *Communities and Neighborhoods in Land Use Planning.* 7 pp.

    7. *Rural Zoning and Land Use Planning.*

    8. *Planning Committees Cooperate with Local Governments.* 11 pp.

——. ——. *Land Use Planning under Way.* Washington: Government Printing Office, 1940, 48 pp.

U. S. Department of Agriculture. *Living and Forest Lands.* Miscellaneous Publication No. 388. Washington: Government Printing Office, 1940, 48 pp.

——. Interbureau Committee on State Legislation for Better Land Use. *State Legislation for Better Land Use; A Special Report.* Washington: Government Printing Office, 1941, 122 pp. (Selected bibliography, pp. 118-22.)

U. S. Division of Public Inquiries. Government Information Service. Bureau of the Budget. *United States Government Manual—1947.* 1st ed. Washington: Government Printing Office, 1946, 718 pp.

U. S. Forest Service. *Cooperative Management and Marketing for the Woodland Owner.* U. S. Department of Agriculture Farmers' Bulletin No. 1927. Washington: Government Printing Office, 1943, 16 pp.

——. *Forest Farming.* U. S. Department of Agriculture Farmers' Bulletin No. 1794. Washington: Government Printing Office, 1938, 18 pp.

——. *Forests and Employment; Report of the Chief of the Forest Service, 1945.* Washington: Government Printing Office, 1946, 35 pp.

——. *New Forest Frontiers for: Jobs, Permanent Communities, A Stronger Nation.* U. S. Department of Agriculture Miscellaneous Publication No. 414. Washington: Government Printing Office, 1941, 76 pp.

——. *State Forests for Public Use.* U. S. Department of Agriculture Miscellaneous Publication No. 373. Washington: Government Printing Office, 1940, 36 pp.

——. *The Work of the U. S. Forest Service.* U. S. Department of Agriculture Miscellaneous Publication No. 290. Rev. ed. Washington: Government Printing Office, 1945, 32 pp.

—— and U. S. Extension Service. *Community Forests for Rural People.* U. S. Department of Agriculture Leaflet No. 244. Washington: Government Printing Office, 1945, 8 pp.

U. S. National Resources Planning Board. *Land Classification in the United States; Report of the Land Committee to the National Resources Planning Board.* Washington: Government Printing Office, 1941, 151 pp. (References, p. 131.)

——. *National Resources Development; Report for 1942.* Washington: Government Printing Office, 1942, 227 pp.

——. *National Resources Development; Report for 1943.* Washington: Government Printing Office, 1943, 3 parts.

——.*Public Works and Rural Land Use, September 1942; Report of the Land Committee.* Washington: Government Printing Office, 1942, 167 pp.

——. *A Report on National Planning and Public Works in Relation to Natural Resources and Including Land Use and Water Resources with Findings and Recommendations, December 1, 1934.* Washington: Government Printing Office, 1934, 455 pp.

——. *Tax Delinquency and Rural Land-Use Adjustment, by the Subcommittee on Tax Delinquency of the Land Committee.* Washington: Government Printing Office, 1942, 190 pp.

U. S. President. Special Committee on Farm Tenancy. *Farm Tenancy.* Washington: Government Printing Office, 1937, 108 pp.

U. S. Soil Conservation Service. *Report of the Chief of the Soil Conservation Service, 1945.* Washington: Government Printing Office, 1946, 55 pp.

——. *Soil Conservation Districts for Erosion Control.* U. S. Department of Agriculture Miscellaneous Publication No. 293. Washington: Government Printing Office, 1937, 19 pp.

——.*The Work of the Soil Conservation Service.* Washington: Government Printing Office, 1941, 12 pp.

U. S. Tennessee Valley Authority. *Annual Report of the Tennessee Valley Authority for the Fiscal Year Ended June 30, 1945.* Washington: Government Printing Office, 1945, 235 pp.

——. *Forests and Human Welfare; A Story of the Use of Forests by Man and of Their Influence upon Control of Water on the Land, with Special Reference to the Tennessee Valley Region.* Knoxville, Tennessee: The Authority, 1940, 46 pp.

——.*Soil; The Nation's Basic Heritage.* Washington: 1936, 58 pp.

Waring, P. A. *Teamwork to Save Soil and Increase Production.* U. S. Department of Agriculture Miscellaneous Publication No. 486. Washington: Government Printing Office, 1944, 64 pp.

Watts, Lyle F. "State Forestry Administration," in *The Book of the States, 1945-46.* Chicago: The Council of State Governments, 1945, pp. 277-80.

Westveld, R. H. and Ralph H. Peck. *Forestry in Farm Management.* New York: John Wiley & Sons, 1941, 339 pp.

Zon, Raphael and William A. Duerr. *Farm Forestry in the Lake States; An Economic Problem.* U. S. Department of Agriculture Circular No. 661. Washington: Government Printing Office, 1942, 34 pp.

GENERAL PUBLICATIONS
ON RURAL AFFAIRS

The Agricultural Index. Subject Index to a Selected List of Agricultural Periodicals and Bulletins, 1916—. New York: H. W. Wilson Co., 1917—. Annual.

American Country Life Association. *Proceedings,* 1919—. Annual.

Association of Land-Grant Colleges Committee on Postwar Agricultural Policy. *Postwar Agricultural Policy; Report of the Committee.* . . . 1944, 61 pp. (Distributed by the Michigan Agricultural Experiment Station and the Michigan Agricultural Extension Service.)

Baker, O. E.; Ralph Borsodi; and M. L. Wilson. *Agriculture in Modern Life.* New York: Harper & Bros., 1939, 303 pp.

Blaisdell, Donald C. *Government and Agriculture; The Growth of Federal Farm Aid.* New York: Farrar and Rinehart, 1940, 217 pp. (Selected bibliography, pp. 203-7.)

Brandt, Karl. *The Reconstruction of World Agriculture.* New York: W. W. Norton & Co., 1945, 416 pp.

Cole, William E. and Hugh Price Crowe. *Recent Trends in Rural Planning.* New York: Prentice-Hall, 1937, 579 pp. (Selected bibliography at end of each chapter.)

Council of State Governments. *Postwar Problems of Agriculture.* Chicago: The Council (1313 East 6oth St.), 1944, 67 pp.

Deering, Ferdie. *USDA: Manager of American Agriculture.* Norman, Oklahoma: University of Oklahoma Press, 1945, 213 pp.

Eaton, Joseph W. *Exploring Tomorrow's Agriculture; Co-operative Group Farming—A Practical Program of Rural Rehabilitation.* New York: Harper & Bros., 1943, 255 pp.

Gaus, John M. and Leon O. Wolcott. *Public Administration and the United States Department of Agriculture.* Chicago: Public Administration Service (1313 East 6oth St.), 1940, 354 pp.

Landis, Benson Y., compiler. *A Guide to the Literature of Rural Life.* 4th ed. New York: Federal Council of the Churches of Christ in America (297 Fourth Ave.), 1939, 15 pp.

McWilliams, Carey. *Small Farm and Big Farm.* Public Affairs Committee Pamphlet No. 100. New York: Public Affairs Committee, Inc. (30 Rockefeller Plaza), 1945, 31 pp. (For further reading, p. 31.)

Moore, Arthur. *The Farmer and the Rest of Us.* Boston: Little, Brown and Co., 1945, 226 pp.

National Planning Association, 800 21st St. N.W., Washington, D. C. Planning Pamphlet Series.
>No. 11. *For a Better Post-War Agriculture.* 1942, 47 pp.
>No. 25-26. *World Needs for U. S. Food and Fiber.* By John D. Black. 1943, 71 pp.
>No. 28. *Farm People and the Land after the War.* By Murray R. Benedict. 1943, 26 pp.
>No. 29. *Food for Europe after Victory.* 1944, 42 pp.
>No. 42. *Fertilizers in the Postwar National Economy.* 1945, 48 pp.
>No. 46. *A Food and Nutrition Program for the Nation.* 1945, 35 pp.
>No. 47. *Farms for Veterans.* By Lowry Nelson. 1945, 22 pp.
>No. 48. *A Farmer Looks at Fiscal Policy.* By Thad Snow. 1945, 22 pp.
>No. 49. *A Retirement System for Farmers.* By Murray R. Benedict. 1946, 44 pp.

National Policy Committee. *Long Term Farm Policy; Soil Management; World Commodity Agreements.* National Policy Report No. 39. Washington: The Committee (1202 National Press Bldg.), 1946, 33 pp.

"A Price Policy for Agriculture, Consistent with Economic Progress, That Will Promote Adequate and More Stable Income from Farming." *Journal of Farm Economics,* Vol. XXVII, No. 4, November 1945, pp. 743-902.

Schmidt, Carl T. *American Farmers in the World Crisis.* New York: Oxford University Press, 1941, 345 pp. (Selected bibliography, pp. 333-34.)

Schultz, Theodore W. *Agriculture in an Unstable Economy.* New York: McGraw-Hill Book Co., 1945, 299 pp.

——. *Redirecting Farm Policy.* New York: Macmillan Co., 1943, 75 pp.

——, ed. *Food for the World.* Chicago: University of Chicago Press, 1945, 352 pp.

Smart, Charles Allen. *R.F.D.* New York: W. W. Norton & Co., 1938, 314 pp.

Taylor, Henry C. and Anne Dewees Taylor. *World Trade in Agricultural Products.* New York: Macmillan Co., 1943, 286 pp.

Tolley, Howard R. *The Farmer Citizen at War.* New York: Macmillan Co., 1943, 318 pp. (Some sources, pp. 309-14.)

U. S. Department of Agriculture. *Agricultural Statistics.* Washington: Government Printing Office. Annual.

——. *Farmers in a Changing World; Yearbook of Agriculture, 1940.* Washington: Government Printing Office, 1940, 1215 pp.

——. Interbureau Committee on Post-War Programs. *Farm Opportunities in the United States; Outlook, Problems, Policies.* Washington: The Committee, 1945, 129 pp.

——. Library. *Bibliography of Agriculture.* Washington: Government Printing Office. Monthly.

——. Office of Experiment Stations. *Experiment Station Record.* Monthly abstracts of station publications. Washington: Government Printing Office.

U. S. Library of Congress. *Monthly Checklist of State Publications.* Washington: Government Printing Office.

U. S. Superintendent of Documents. *United States Government Publications Monthly Catalog.* Washington: Government Printing Office.

West, James. *Plainville, U.S.A.* New York: Columbia University Press, 1945, 238 pp.